ADVENTURES IN MEDICINE

Discovering Your Path to Success

THE RESIDENT'S GUIDE TO LIFE AND PRACTICE

Contents

Introduction: A Great Adventure

MEDICINE IS A GREAT ADVENTURE! And perhaps the most satisfying, rewarding and lucrative of careers! Healing the sick, bringing life and hope. And along the way, you have the opportunity to earn millions of dollars. What great prospects lie ahead!

Yet, the trail through this adventure is **LITTERED WITH VICTIMS** — too many physicians whose lives, for many reasons, have turned to tragedy, loss, bankruptcy, divorce, drug abuse and for some, death. Recent surveys and published articles tell the toll.

For example, studies show:

- Every year 300 to 400 doctors take their own lives, **HIGHER THAN ANY OTHER PROFESSION**.[1]
- 15 % of all physicians will be **IMPAIRED** — unable to perform their professional responsibilities — at some point in their career, due to mental illness, alcoholism, or drug dependency.[2]
- Male physicians are **TWO TO THREE TIMES** more likely to commit suicide than other professionals.[2]
- Female physicians are at even greater risk, with suicide rates nearly 400 % greater than that of other professionals, and 19.5 % experiencing **CLINICALLY SIGNIFICANT DEPRESSION** during their lifetime.[2]
- Only **44 %** of male physicians and a paltry **26 %** of female physicians report being very satisfied with their medical practices.[3]
- While 73 % of physicians say daily interaction with patients is the most rewarding aspect of their practice, 40 % of physicians say they're **BURNED OUT**.[3]
- In an unscientific survey conducted by MomMD.com, 92 % of respondents said they were concerned or very concerned about **BALANCING A MEDICAL CAREER WITH RAISING A FAMILY**, and one third said they had fewer children than they wanted (or none at all) because of their career.[4]

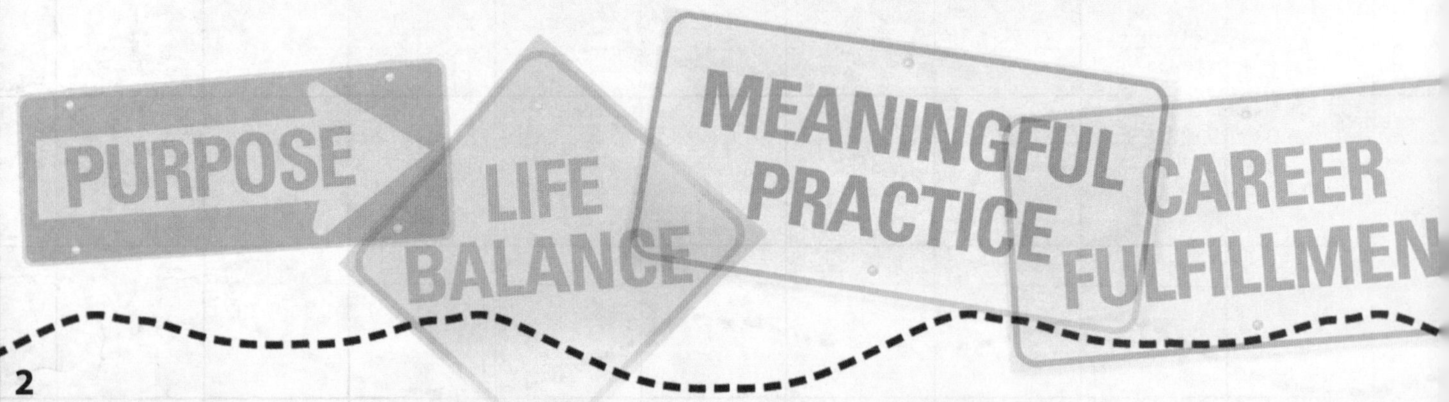

Can This Be Avoided?

How could well-trained, intelligent, well-meaning physicians fall into these pits, slam into brick walls or live in such desperation? Is it avoidable? Can you be a committed physician **AND** have a life and family and pursue other interests as well? The answer is **YES!** But achieving success in medicine and in life doesn't just happen.

THE LANDSCAPE IS CHANGING

Like any adventure, you need to prepare before the journey begins. You need facts about the landscape, pits and snares ahead. You need information. You need to plan carefully and avoid the dangers. As you enter the world of healthcare, your world is changing — **MASSIVELY**. Government legislation, managed care, hospital consolidation, and physician compensation models are changing daily, impacting the industry and rocking your world.

MONEY AND TAR PITS

What does a physician earn today? You need to know! And while earning money is important, many a physician has been **MIRED** in the pursuit of it, destroying valuable relationships. So what kind of employment best suits you, your family and your lifestyle, and where might it be located? How is compensation for a physician structured? What are the telltale signs of a great organization and a stimulating workplace for decades to come?

WHAT JOB FITS YOU BEST?

You will want to seek wise guidance, and determine the best path to the summit. Finally, when all is prepared, you'll be decisive and take that first step with confidence and begin the adventure.

What If...

What if you had one place where pertinent market and compensation information could be found? What if you could talk to other physicians who have walked this road before and have learned these lessons — sometimes the hard way? What if you could hear from experts like hospital CEOs, job coaches, financial counselors, recruiters and legal advisors who could help you map your career, plan your life, manage your debt and give you the wisdom and insight you need to make smart decisions? What if these experts could teach you what you don't know, help you choose the right job, find the right employer and set a course for **LIFELONG SUCCESS** at work and home?

Arlington HealthCare Presents:

ADVENTURES IN MEDICINE: THE RESIDENT'S GUIDE TO LIFE AND PRACTICE

With decades of experience helping over 2,000 physicians find employment, relocate and begin their careers, our team at Arlington HealthCare has engaged a cast of thousands of physicians, CEOs, recruiters, experts, researchers, writers and designers to guide you along the critical steps you must take to find the life you imagined — a life of caring, healing, family, fun and lifelong friends. But this guide isn't for everyone.

WE KNOW YOU'RE SMART, you're busy, and you don't have a lot of free time. We also know you're tired of textbooks and memorization, so we created this book for busy, overwhelmed residents just like you. It hits the high points, allowing you to work quickly through the information and arrive at your own informed conclusions.

So, we made it **EASY**. This workbook is your personal guide to finding the path to the life you imagine. For the first time, everything you need to know and every step in searching, choosing and transitioning into your first job is in this one simple book. We have carefully put together an abbreviated, easy-to-read workbook that walks you through each step, stage by stage. Each stage is provided in sequence so you can walk through the guide as you prepare for the various stages of your job search and transition.

1. **Job search timeline**
2. **Market trends and trials**
3. **Compensation packages**
4. **Life, money and career priorities**
5. **Search strategy**
6. **Interviewing**
7. **Job selection**
8. **Contract negotiation**
9. **Finance basics**
10. **Job transition**

We made it **ENGAGING**. You'll find exercises that will challenge your thinking and help you learn more about yourself and the adventure you're entering — an adventure full of excitement, reward, danger and perils.

We made it **ENTERTAINING**. Along the way, you'll read short stories of other physicians — some who have learned and succeeded and others who have struggled and failed. You'll find colorful charts and graphs full of critical information. And along the trail, we'll point out guide points and roadblocks, and you'll be introduced to trailblazers who have left nuggets of wisdom along the path just for you.

MAKING IT REAL AND GETTING SMARTER

From our experience, we know that having this information in this guide is invaluable. It will help you set your direction and thought, but you'll need one more element — advisors. Working through the process with experts and people you trust will give you opportunity to talk, listen, gain other personally relevant information, and help you consider the consequences. You can't do it alone and be successful.

This team of advisors will help you:

- Learn information you don't know from experts in their field
- Free up time to focus on what you do best, practice medicine
- Brainstorm with like-minded people
- Process opportunities, situations and challenges
- Be even headed, not over-react
- Make wise, fact-based decisions
- Receive emotional and spiritual support

So, before we begin, think through the types of people you need as advisors and confidantes. Here are some examples of people you might ask to be on your advisory team:

Personal: Family members, spouse, siblings, friends

Professional: Physician as Mentor, Financial Planner, Attorney, Coach, Accountant

DR. GOODHOOK'S FIELD NOTES

Introducing the Cantankerous

Dr. Gh.

Along the way, you'll run into the ruminations and writings of the legendary Dr. Goodhook – an aging, eccentric physician whose insightful musings are spotted throughout the guide to "forewarn and inform the young resident."

And we can certainly endorse our experts who are contributors to this guide. These people have the expertise, experience, and patience to help you stay on the right track throughout the entire job search process.

Now Is the Time

So for years, even decades, you've worked and dreamed about beginning your first job as a practicing physician. **THE END IS IN SIGHT!** And we couldn't be more excited for you!

So turn the page. Don't let a moment delay.

Let the Adventure Begin!

Your Backcountry Guides

Two physicians who know the terrain

We have been fortunate to have two outstanding physicians play an important role in the development of *Adventures in Medicine, The Resident's Guide*. We think you need to know these two dedicated physician-teachers, who have given time and expertise to help you map your own adventure and career in medicine. To these two generous physicians, we offer our gratitude for their insightful contributions and our heart-felt appreciation for their guidance.

- The editors

"I don't think I realized back then how little I knew. I was so busy just trying to keep up with everything else that was supposedly "more" important that little time was left for preparing for life changing decisions like finding my first job."

— Kenton Lee, M.D.

"I made so many mistakes during my search it was too stressful and overwhelming. I could have used numerous tips from the Guidebook that would have saved a lot of time and even money."

— Adriana Tobar, M.D.

Kenton Lee, M.D.

Clinical Assistant Professor, University of Illinois College of Medicine

Interim Program Director, University of Illinois Rockford Family Medicine Residency

M.D., University of Hawaii, John A. Burns School of Medicine

Kenton Lee has devoted his career to educating physicians, having spent 15 years as full-time faculty at the University of Illinois Chicago. He now directs the Family Medicine Residency in Rockford, the only program of its kind, where M2-M4 students have direct interaction with patients and responsibility for their care through the University's primary care clinics. The University of Illinois College of Medicine currently serves some 2,600 medical students on four campuses. His professional interests include curriculum development, evidence-based medicine and pediatrics. In his spare time, he enjoys swimming and time with family.

Adriana Tobar, M.D.

Family Medicine Physician, Dean Health System

M.D., Pontificia Universidad Catolica del Ecuador, Quito;

Family Medicine Residency, University of Illinois College of Medicine, Rockford

Adriana Tobar practices the full scope of family medicine, with a special focus on adolescents and women's health, with the Dean Health System, one of the nation's largest integrated healthcare delivery systems. Owned and governed by physicians, the Dean Health System encompasses a network of clinics in southern Wisconsin, health insurance, and clinical research and education. She is a community preceptor for fourth-year medical students at the University of Wisconsin. Previously, she was Assistant Professor of the Family Medicine Residency program at the University of Illinois, Rockford. She spends her free time with her husband and two children.

From the Publisher

After working with thousands of physicians over the years, we've found that residents like you possess rare personal qualities of drive, intellect, problem solving and focus that propel them through the unusual rigors of becoming a physician. You have given a decade of your life to this pursuit, steeling yourself physically and emotionally to achieve this goal. **CONGRATULATIONS!** You have made it!

Soon your passion to heal the sick and bring life and hope to many will become reality. But don't be mistaken — completing your residency or fellowship is not the end, but just the **BEGINNING**. While graduating is a major milestone, beginning your career wisely and thoughtfully is the next, and most critical, step.

What do you want from your career as a physician? What type of life do you want to lead?

Recently we've researched thousands of physicians and residents and discovered a shift in priorities. We've found that you, the new resident, want something more than a career — you want a **QUALITY OF LIFE**!

Frankly, a few years ago I was searching for this same quality of life and balance between work and home. And while I had piled up achievements of personal success, I realized I needed perspective, purpose and focus. I didn't want to look back in 10, 20 or 30 years with regret. I wanted to make smart, thoughtful decisions that I knew would lead me and my family to the quality of life I desired. How could I navigate this? I needed someone to guide me through it.

As you begin to step out on this next phase of your career, you need experts to educate you, to help you, guide you and protect you from the **MISSTEPS**, **DANGERS** and **PITFALLS**. This book, *Adventures in Medicine: The Resident's Guide to Life and Practice*, is a gift from our subject matter experts, creative team, values-based sponsors, and me.

This book is an invaluable key to a successful career in medicine. Priceless counsel is found within the pages of this amazing, one-of-a-kind book. In addition, you'll want to talk this through with good advisors who can listen and guide. Now it's up to you to set aside the time, to prepare, consult, decide and take the first step.

So for years, even decades, you've worked and dreamed about beginning your first job as a practicing physician. **THE END IS IN SIGHT!** We hope you'll find this book useful, but even more, a life-guide to the wonderful, rewarding Adventures In Medicine!

Sincerely,

Todd Skertich
Chief Executive Officer, Arlington HealthCare

The Sponsors for Your Adventure

Unusual organizations you'll want to know

As fellow adventurers, we know you want to work for organizations you can trust.

These organizations are different from most. Their vision and commitment to their physicians sets them apart. They are invested in the pyhsicians' lives and families, who share their community and walk their halls.

On the following pages, you'll read their stories and discover information that may pique your interest. As you discover your true values, evaluate the fit and consider making contact with them.

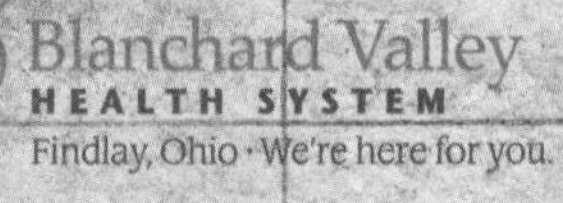

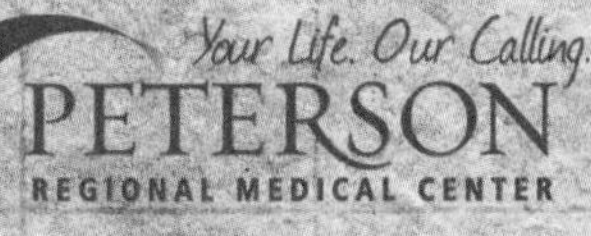

Books can't talk. Experts can.

Bring the guide to life with complimentary Residency Workshops!

We created the *Adventures in Medicine* Guidebook and Online Resource Library to prepare you for life after residency, but we're firm believers that learning is an interactive process. That's why we launched our Residency Workshops — lively presentation and discussion sessions with industry experts. They're ready to answer your most pressing questions about the business and personal sides of medicine at no cost to your program.

Highlights

- ★ We provide Residency Workshops at no cost to your program!
- ★ Each workshop lasts 45-60 minutes
- ★ Perfect for medical students and 1st, 2nd and 3rd year residents
- ★ Over 85% of 2010 attendees said workshops exceeded their expectations

For more information about bringing Residency Workshops to your program, contact Nicole at 847-649-2621 or e-mail nicole@AdventuresInMedicine.net

Workshop Topics

From financial planners to life balance coaches, our speakers specialize in supporting the medical community. Our Residency Workshops delve deeper into specific topics from each chapter of *Adventures in Medicine.*

Job Search Timeline	Interviewing
Market Trends and Trials	Job Selection
Compensation Packages	Contract Negotiation
Life, Money and Career Priorities	Finance Basics
Search Strategy	Job Transition

INTERACT. EXPLORE. ENLIGHTEN.

Dig Deeper.

Take your adventure beyond the page with the Adventures in Medicine Online Resource Library!

Your journey doesn't end here. Our Online Resource Library is packed with interactive tools and information to help you uncover a purpose-driven career and life. In addition to a virtual copy of the guide, members receive exclusive access to financial planning tools, podcasts, webinars and so much more.

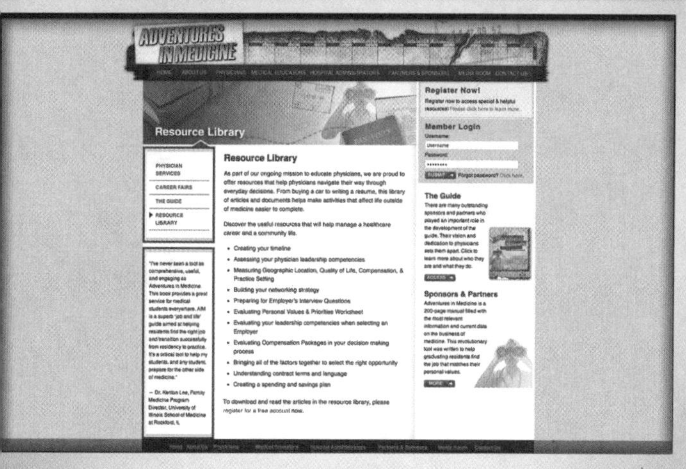

Your one-stop shop for career and life strategy.

Below is a glimpse of what's available in the Resource Library. Register today for membership and full access!

- Position Papers
- Financial Planning Tools
- Industry Links
- Market Commentary
- Suggested Reading
- Personal Career Tracker
- Podcasts
- Calculators
- Whitepapers
- Webinars
- Worksheets
- Newsletters

Ready to start exploring?

Just visit www.AdventuresInMedicine.net to register and receive access to the Resource Library and Members' Area. Don't worry — it only takes a couple of minutes. We'll see you there!

Collaborate. Comment. Connect.

Follow Dr. Goodhook and the Adventures in Medicine team of bloggers!

Stories and thoughts from residents like you. The latest topics and advice from industry experts. And yes — a word or two (or seven) from medicine's most persnickety practitioner, Dr. Hypocrates Goodhook. It all comes together in the new blog from Adventures in Medicine. Each week, we'll introduce diverse perspectives on topics that matter the most. Follow along, comment and even ask Dr. Goodhook a question (if you dare). Together, we can build a community to make practice purposeful.

Your ears have not fooled you, young resident. I'm launching a "blog." I've been convinced, in spite of this silly term, that it is a technological advancement worthy of my attention. Ask not how. Fond of quill and ink, I am not often interested in gadgets and tomfoolery. Alas, I digress. Together with respected colleagues and residents, I'll be offering my opinions without filtered tongue. I invite you to join the conversation and toss your own stones into the digital pond.

— Dr. Gh.

Insight in Every Update.

Each week, we'll create posts on topics that are important to you. Here are just a few things you can look forward to:

- ★ Weekly journals written by residents like you
- ★ Tips, advice and news from industry experts
- ★ Q&A with Dr. Goodhook
- ★ Healthcare trends and issues
- ★ Community discussion and interaction

Visit www.ADVENTURESINMEDICINE.net/blog to jump in on the conversation!

www.adventuresinmedicine.net/blog

STAGE 1:

Job Search Timeline

Create a plan and work it!

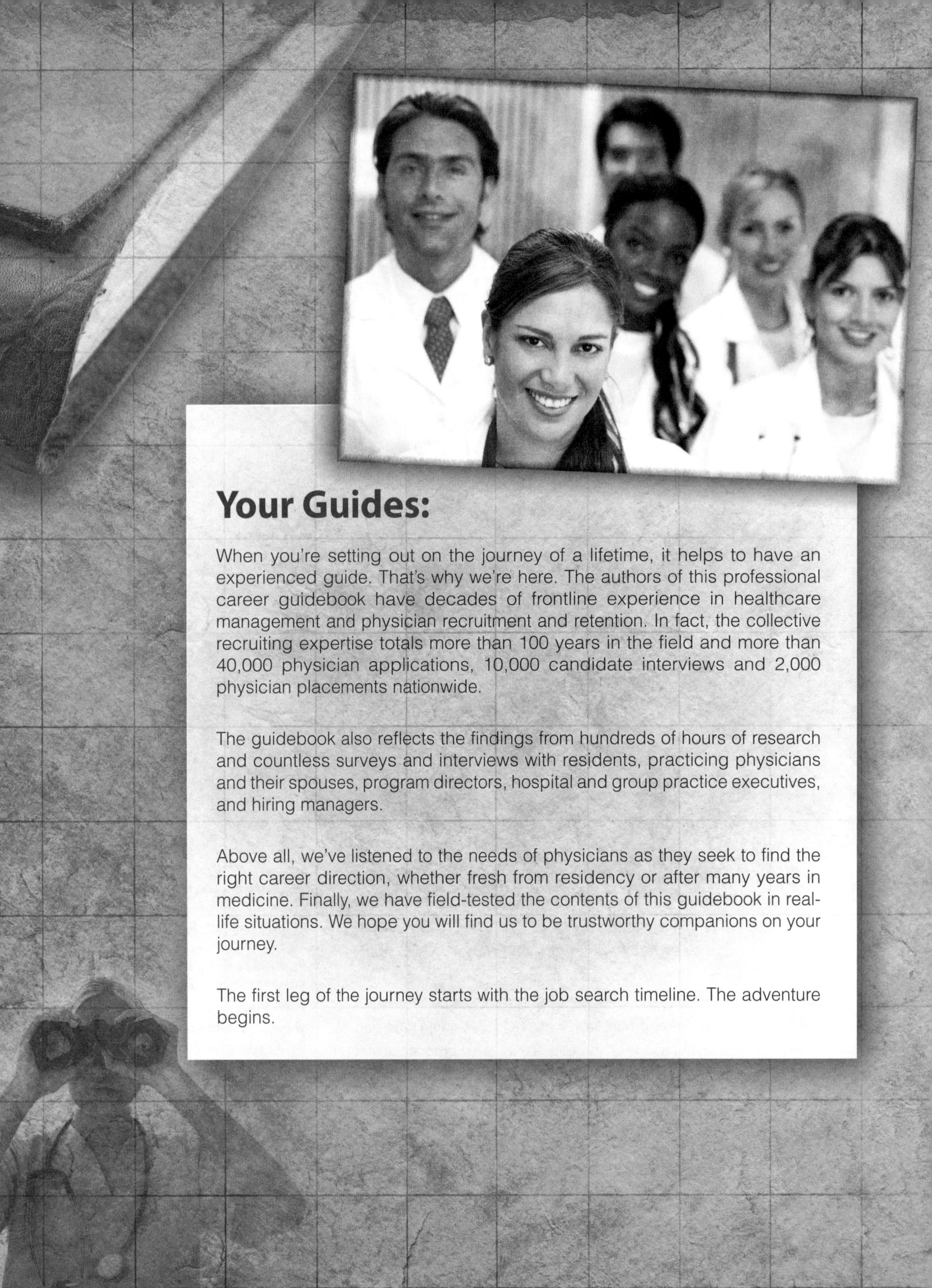

Your Guides:

When you're setting out on the journey of a lifetime, it helps to have an experienced guide. That's why we're here. The authors of this professional career guidebook have decades of frontline experience in healthcare management and physician recruitment and retention. In fact, the collective recruiting expertise totals more than 100 years in the field and more than 40,000 physician applications, 10,000 candidate interviews and 2,000 physician placements nationwide.

The guidebook also reflects the findings from hundreds of hours of research and countless surveys and interviews with residents, practicing physicians and their spouses, program directors, hospital and group practice executives, and hiring managers.

Above all, we've listened to the needs of physicians as they seek to find the right career direction, whether fresh from residency or after many years in medicine. Finally, we have field-tested the contents of this guidebook in real-life situations. We hope you will find us to be trustworthy companions on your journey.

The first leg of the journey starts with the job search timeline. The adventure begins.

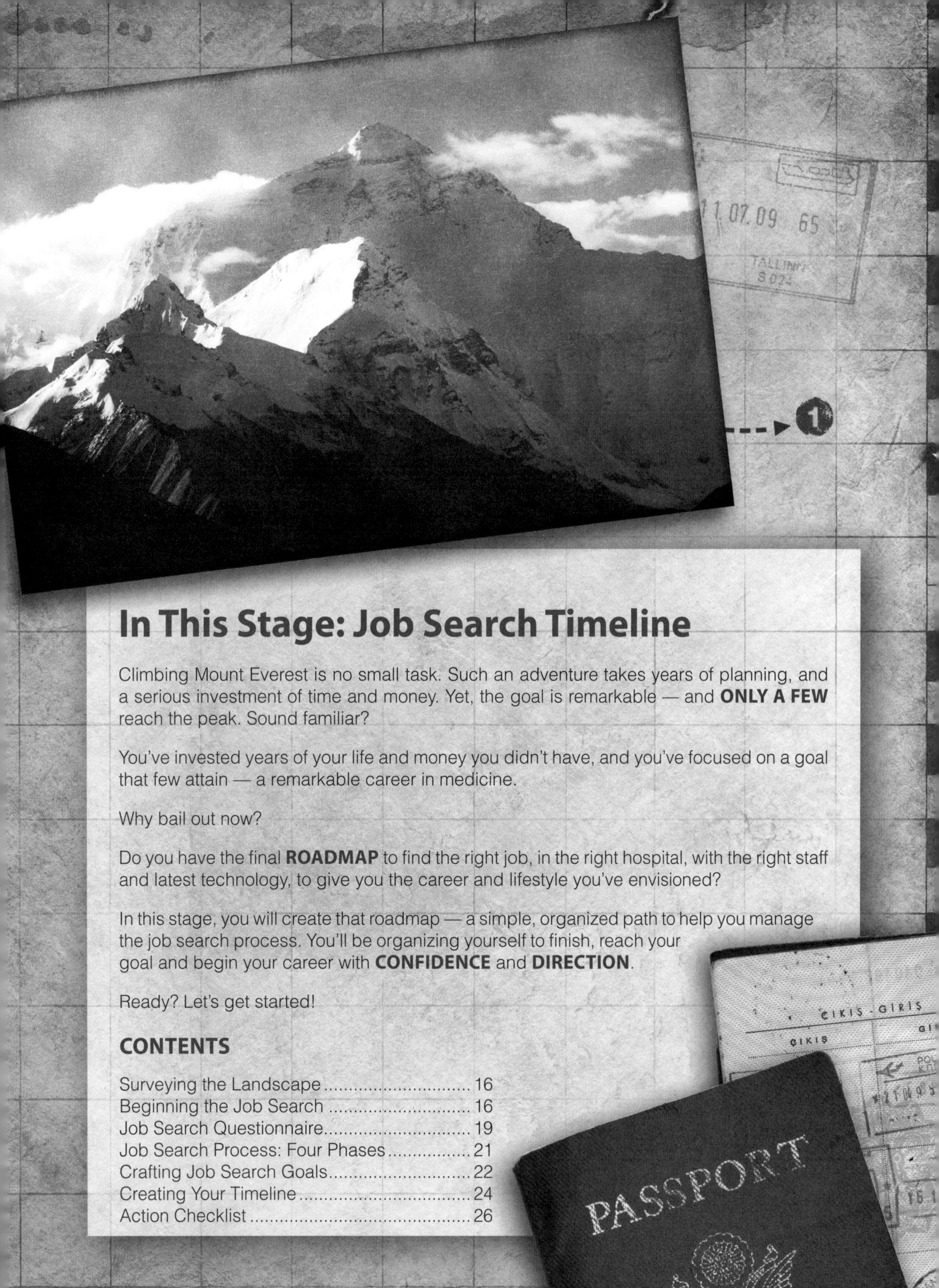

In This Stage: Job Search Timeline

Climbing Mount Everest is no small task. Such an adventure takes years of planning, and a serious investment of time and money. Yet, the goal is remarkable — and **ONLY A FEW** reach the peak. Sound familiar?

You've invested years of your life and money you didn't have, and you've focused on a goal that few attain — a remarkable career in medicine.

Why bail out now?

Do you have the final **ROADMAP** to find the right job, in the right hospital, with the right staff and latest technology, to give you the career and lifestyle you've envisioned?

In this stage, you will create that roadmap — a simple, organized path to help you manage the job search process. You'll be organizing yourself to finish, reach your goal and begin your career with **CONFIDENCE** and **DIRECTION**.

Ready? Let's get started!

CONTENTS

TRAILBLAZERS

"I started the job search in November and I feel that it was **TOO LATE**. I wish I would have started in July. I didn't realize all the steps and things to complete until midway through the process."

"I **LEFT $65,000 ON THE TABLE** because I didn't do my homework. Had I started six months earlier, I wouldn't have felt the pressure to take this job."

"I am separated from my wife because I didn't involve her in the decision-making process and now she feels **LEFT OUT** and **ABANDONED**. She hates the location I picked and hasn't found it easy to fit in to the community."

"I'm from Brazil, so I needed to start 14 months ahead of time because of the work visa situation. The **STRESS** was lifted off my shoulders when I landed a position in September before my final year of residency started."

Surveying the Landscape

The creation of a job search timeline is the foundational — and arguably most important — step in the job search process for a resident. By creating a timeline, you will walk away with a **TACTICAL, STEP-BY-STEP PROCESS** for your job search that will give you a clear roadmap as you move forward. This will eliminate guesswork and redundant effort that wastes your time — time you don't have to spare.

You might be thinking to yourself, "Why do I need to develop a job search timeline? I'm too busy as it is, and I don't have time to do this. There are plenty of jobs for physicians in today's environment, so I can study for my boards instead. What's the rush?"

But think about how many years you've spent studying and preparing to become a physician in the first place. You owe it to yourself, and perhaps your family, to invest time up-front, get organized and take a more clinical, well-thought-out, and planned approach to the job search process, just as you have done during your training.

By creating a job search timeline, you will set your **DIRECTION** and **FOCUS**, gain **CONTROL**, and ultimately spend **LESS TIME** on the search for the right job for you.

Beginning the Job Search

Dr. Kenton Lee, Program Director for Family Practice Medicine in Rockford, Illinois, recommends that residents begin the job search process in their second year by preparing their CV and identifying their options. He assigns third-year residents as mentors for second-year residents to help them learn how to handle non-clinical issues, including the job search.

Dr. Lee shared a story about one resident who started looking three months prior to graduation. The resident didn't think it was a big deal, because he wanted to practice in the Chicago market, which was only 45 minutes away, and he assumed there would be a "plethora" of options to choose from.

Once he started looking in the Chicago suburbs, he realized that most of the opportunities did not match his criteria, such as loan repayment and higher salary. In fact, he found the opposite: the job possibilities paid 20 to 25% less than smaller, rural communities, and he could find no loan-repayment options. To make matters worse, the resident learned that the cost of living — specifically buying a house — was much higher than he had anticipated.

Once the resident realized that he would be working a lot harder for less money, he panicked and took the first offer, settling for the "next best" opportunity because the most desirable positions were no longer available. After two years, he found himself disappointed and frustrated with the job and began the job search process all over again, uprooting his family and damaging the momentum of his career.

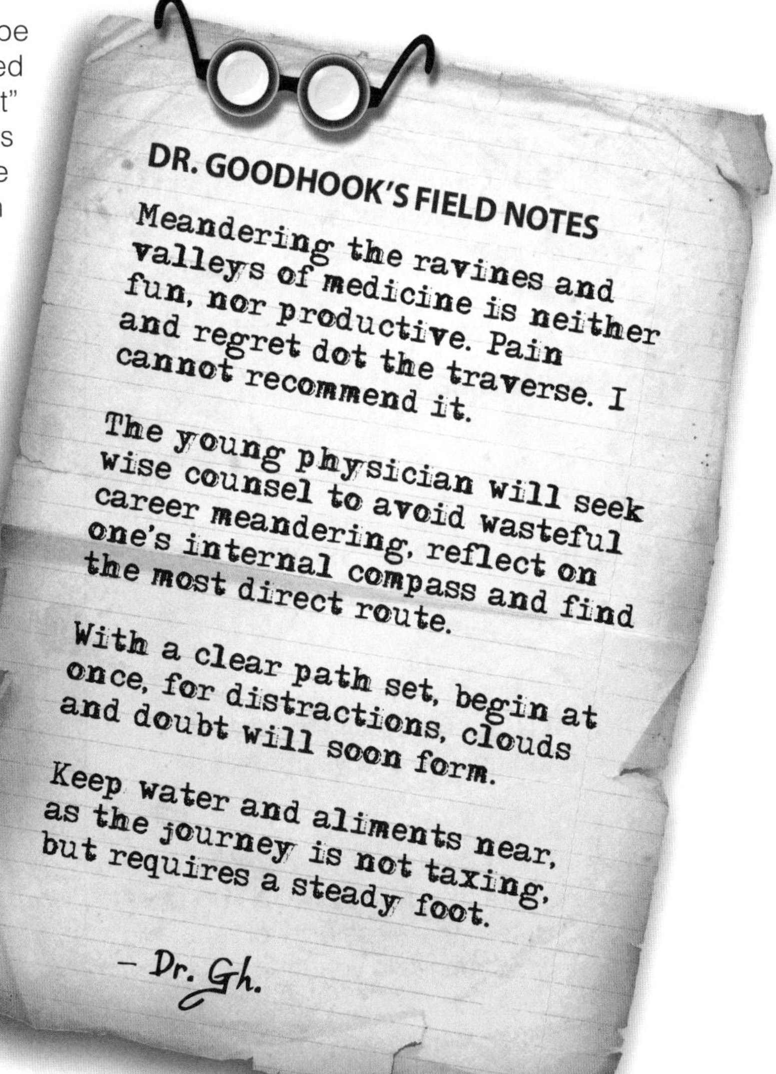

DR. GOODHOOK'S FIELD NOTES
Meandering the ravines and valleys of medicine is neither fun, nor productive. Pain and regret dot the traverse. I cannot recommend it.
The young physician will seek wise counsel to avoid wasteful career meandering, reflect on one's internal compass and find the most direct route.
With a clear path set, begin at once, for distractions, clouds and doubt will soon form.
Keep water and aliments near, as the journey is not taxing, but requires a steady foot.
– Dr. Gh.

Unfortunately, this is not an isolated case. A 2006 Physician Retention Study by Cejka Search and American Medical Group Association reported that **46%** of those physicians who leave a practice are most likely to do so within the **FIRST THREE YEARS** of employment. According to the survey results, a lack of cultural fit with the practice and/or the community was a driving force in turnover. This data is consistent with past reports, stating a "poor cultural fit with the practice" is the single most frequently mentioned reason for voluntary separation (51%). In addition, "Relocated to find a better community fit" was mentioned **20%** of the time.

However, family reasons that required the physician to relocate were also strong contributors to turnover, with "relocating to be closer to own or spouse's family" **42%** and "spouse's job required relocation" **22%** revealing that moving for family reasons is a significant cause for physicians leaving the practice.

Below you'll find a list of implications of starting your job search earlier versus later. Which ones resonate with you? Are you someone who is proactive and takes action, or someone who procrastinates and waits until the last minute?

STARTING EARLIER	STARTING LATE
❑ Planning up front provides you the opportunity to devine your **VALUES** where decision making becomes much more **CLEARER**.	❑ It may take **LONGER** to find the right job with the right fit.
❑ You have **MORE TIME** to evaluate options and negotiate contracts.	❑ You may **LOSE OUT** on the best job opportunities.
❑ You can **FOCUS** on things like preparing for boards, finishing residency, and completing visa requirements.	❑ You may have **LIMITED** options (location, compensation, etc.).
❑ You can complete the licensing application process **ON TIME**.	❑ Your CV and references may be **MISSING** important information that could limit job opportunities.
❑ You're more likely to find a job that meets your **PERSONAL** and **PROFESSIONAL NEEDS**.	❑ You may **NOT BE ABLE TO START WORK** right away because you haven't completed the state licensing process.
❑ Having more time increases your **CONFIDENCE** and ability to make decisions that are right for you and your family.	❑ You risk taking a job that pays the bills but leaves you **UNHAPPY**, **DISSATISFIED** and **QUITTING** after a short time.
❑ You may be able to sign a contract with a hospital or practice **MANY MONTHS** prior to the start date with a possibility of receiving a stipend while you finish your training.	❑ You could become **REACTIVE** and **PANICKY** often leading to poor decision making.

Job Search Questionnaire

Complete this questionnaire that contains thoughts and perspectives related to the job search process.

	Very True	True	Some-what True	False, Not at All
1. I started the job search already.				
2. There's so much to do and not enough time to complete everything.				
3. The job search process is overwhelming. I've never had to find a "real job" before, and I don't know where to begin.				
4. I'm excited about the possibilities that are out there. I can't wait to get started or keep searching.				
5. My spouse or partner is assisting me in this process.				
6. I expect to have 5-10 job offers given the demand for my specialty; therefore, I'm in the driver's seat, and I can call all my own shots.				
7. I have a solid network of people whom I can turn to for help.				
8. Searching for a job is a lower priority for me right now.				

REFLECTION

What do your ratings of these statements indicate about your **ATTITUDE** toward the job search process?

Are you **SATISFIED** with your attitude at this point? If not, what is one action step you can take to begin to address this?

GUIDE POINTS

1. Started job search — If you have, what benefits are you seeing? If you haven't, when do you plan to begin? How will you make this a priority? How do you feel about the process? Confident, scared, anxious?

2. So much to do and not enough time — How much time will you devote to the job search process? Finding the right position takes time. Plan on spending three to four hours a week for a period of three to six months, especially during the initial stages of identifying the type of position you want to pursue.

3. Job search is overwhelming — At the end of this stage, you'll fill out a job search timeline that captures all the activities and critical decisions that you must make. When you look at the big picture, it can be overwhelming, but when you break it down by phases and steps, it's easier to work through the process.

4. I'm excited about the possibilities — How's your attitude? A positive attitude is a must when it comes to a job search. If you view it as a chore or a hassle, this attitude will be translated into how you present yourself on paper and in person.

5. Spouse or partner is involved — If you have a spouse or partner, it's critical that they are part of your team and involved in the decision-making process. Your decisions impact their lives as much as yours.

6. Keep your values close — Verify your assumptions by conducting research online and/or by networking, learning about the salaries as well as the supply and demand for a particular area. Even if you determine that there may be several offers to consider, there may be 1 or 2 that align with your values.

7. Solid network — The job search process is lengthy and filled with unexpected twists and turns. Find a mentor and/or a team of people you trust who can offer advice and tips for success. Check with your program director and/or attendings to get the help that you need. Don't work alone or in a vacuum, because this decision is one of the most important that you will face in the months and years to come.

8. Make your career a Priority — re-entering yourself back into life after dedicating your life to medicine over a decade is no easy feat and it takes time.

Job Search Process: Four Phases

There are four distinct phases to work through that encompass all 10 stages of the job search process. Working through each phase will guarantee the best outcomes.

PLAN — DO YOUR HOMEWORK

Stage 1: Develop your job search timeline.

Stage 2: Know the medical market conditions and practice options.

Stage 3: Understand compensation structures, productivity formulas and geographic implications.

Stage 4: Align job options with your life, money and career priorities.

SEARCH — WORK YOUR PLAN

Stage 5: Build your search strategy.

Stage 6: Prepare for and conduct interviews.

DECIDE — CHOOSE THE JOB WITH CONFIDENCE

Stage 7: Analyze and select the best job offer for you.

Stage 8: Negotiate your employment contract.

IMPLEMENT — START THE JOB

Stage 9: Implement healthy financial disciplines early on.

Stage 10: Transition into your first job.

GUIDE POINTS

Goal Setting

1. **MORE THAN ONE** goal associated with the job search process is acceptable.

2. Make sure you use the **SMART** criteria to create goals that make sense and provide focus and direction.

3. Don't confuse **ACTION ITEMS** with **GOALS**. Action items are related to goals in that they are specific activities that you will complete in order to achieve the goals.

4. **SHARE** your goals with the people in your network (program director, attending physicians, colleagues, friends, family members) and get their opinions: Ask them to evaluate your goal(s) on the SMART criteria. Ask if they are relevant and realistic based on what you've described, and talk about your ultimate job-search objective.

5. Do not short-change this task! When you write down and verbalize goals, you're likely to **ACHIEVE** them — as long as they follow the SMART criteria, especially being **REALISTIC** and **TIMEBOUND**.

Crafting Job Search Goals

Goals in life and work are very important. Obviously, you have worked hard toward the goal of completing medical training. Now you are at the point of creating the goal that addresses: **"NOW WHAT?"** Goal setting involves a simple formula that is widely used in business, professional and personal settings. This model is called **SMART GOALS**. In case you're not familiar with SMART goals, the acronym stands for:

S **SPECIFIC**

M **MEASURABLE**

A **ACHIEVABLE**

R **RELEVANT**

T **TIMEBOUND**

Follow this formula and create a SMART Goal for your job search:

DATE: By this date...

ACTION: my job search goal is to...
(list actions)

RESULTS: resulting in...
(describe the outcome).

EXAMPLES:

By January 1, my job search goal is to complete phase one (plan) and phase two (search) activities that result in a minimum of five on-site interviews and three job offers to consider.

What makes this SMART?

DATE: January 1

ACTION: Complete phase one and phase two

RESULTS: Five on-site job interviews and three job offers

By June 1, my job search goal is to complete phase three (decide), resulting in choosing a job offer and signing a contract for hire with a preferred employer based on my top two choices.

What makes this SMART?

DATE: June 1

ACTION: Complete phase three

RESULTS: Choosing a job offer and signing a contract

My Job Search Goal(s):

By this date...

my job search goal is to... (list actions)

resulting in... (describe the outcome).

Now that your job search goals are established, it's time to evaluate each phase of the job search process and identify specific activities that you plan to complete. Taking a more systematic, planned-out approach to the job search process increases your odds of landing a job that is right for you.

Creating Your Timeline

PLAN *(Stages 1-4)*			
TIMEFRAME *(Month(s)/Year):*			
	START	**FINISH**	✓
Complete/update CV, cover letters and reference letters.			
Identify your core values.			
Create your life-purpose statement.			
Identify your life, money, and career priorities.			
Apply for licenses, visas (international students).			
Identify "must-have" physician leadership competencies.			
Build your advisory team (mentor, professionals, family, etc.).			

SEARCH *(Stages 5-6)*			
TIMEFRAME *(Month(s)/Year):*			
	START	**FINISH**	✓
Identify job opportunities.			
Mine your network.			
Research job postings.			
Select recruiters.			
Research and contact employers.			
Respond to postings.			
Schedule interviews.			
Prepare for interviews.			
Conduct phone interviews.			
Conduct in-person interviews.			
Evaluate outcomes.			
Follow up with employers.			

The purpose of this timeline is to provide a roadmap of your job search journey. For each of the major phases, indicate the timeframe you will spend on that phase by writing the month(s) and year in the space provided. For each activity, identify a desired start and finish date. Finally, when a particular activity is complete, check it off and move on. (Some activities may overlap with other phases.)

DECIDE *(Stages 7-8)*

TIMEFRAME *(Month(s)/Year):*

	START	FINISH	✓
Receive and evaluate offers.			
Assess offers based on priorities, compensation and "must-have" physician leadership competencies.			
Select a job offer.			
Negotiate your contract.			
Provide verification of necessary documents.			
Complete pre-employment requirements (credentialing, background checks).			

IMPLEMENT *(Stages 9-10)*

TIMEFRAME *(Month(s)/Year):*

	START	FINISH	✓
Get your finances in order with a spending, savings and investment plan.			
Protect your life and career with a healthy dose of work-life balance.			
Know the job requirements.			

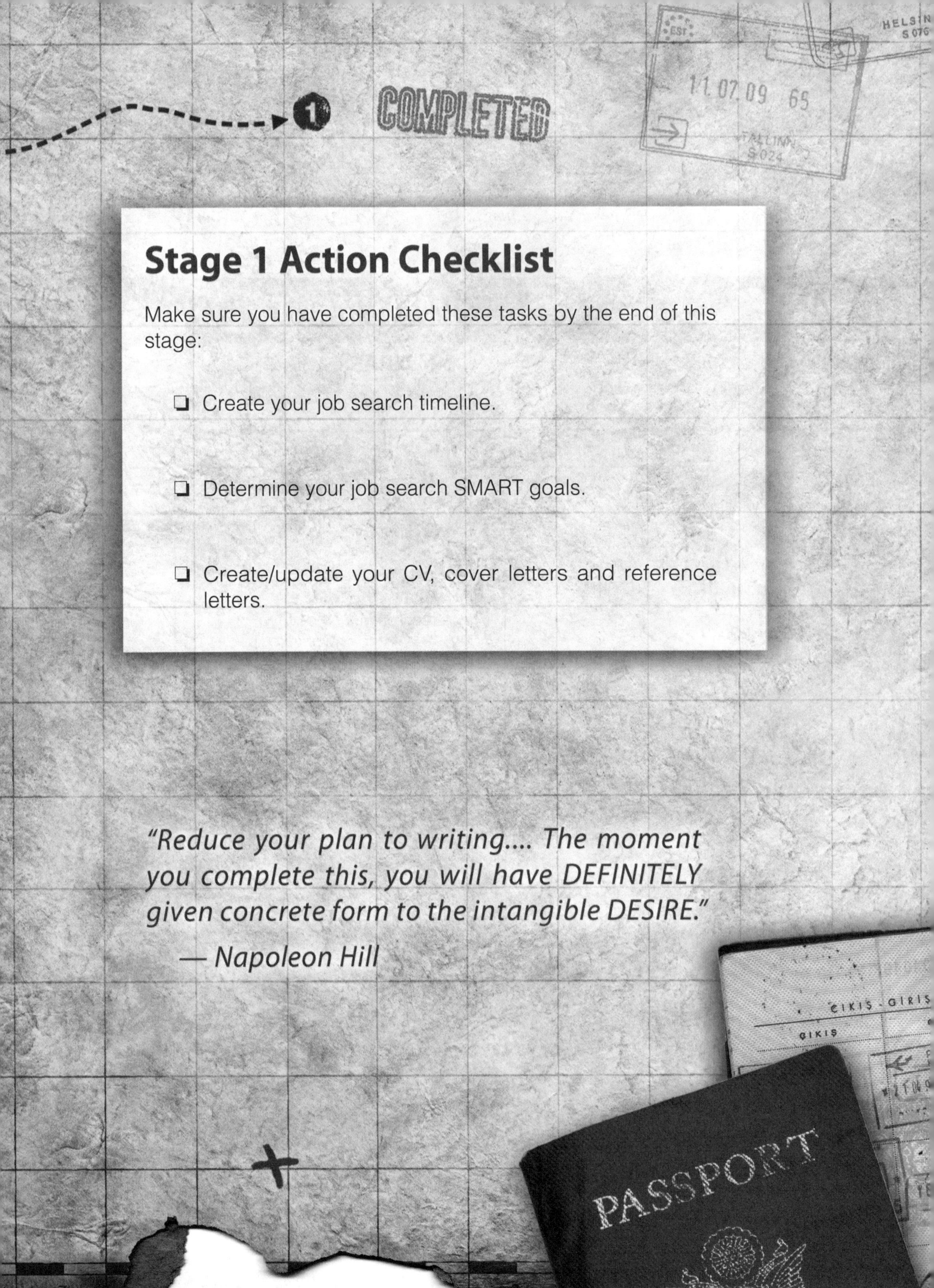

Stage 1 Action Checklist

Make sure you have completed these tasks by the end of this stage:

- ❑ Create your job search timeline.
- ❑ Determine your job search SMART goals.
- ❑ Create/update your CV, cover letters and reference letters.

"Reduce your plan to writing.... The moment you complete this, you will have DEFINITELY given concrete form to the intangible DESIRE."

— Napoleon Hill

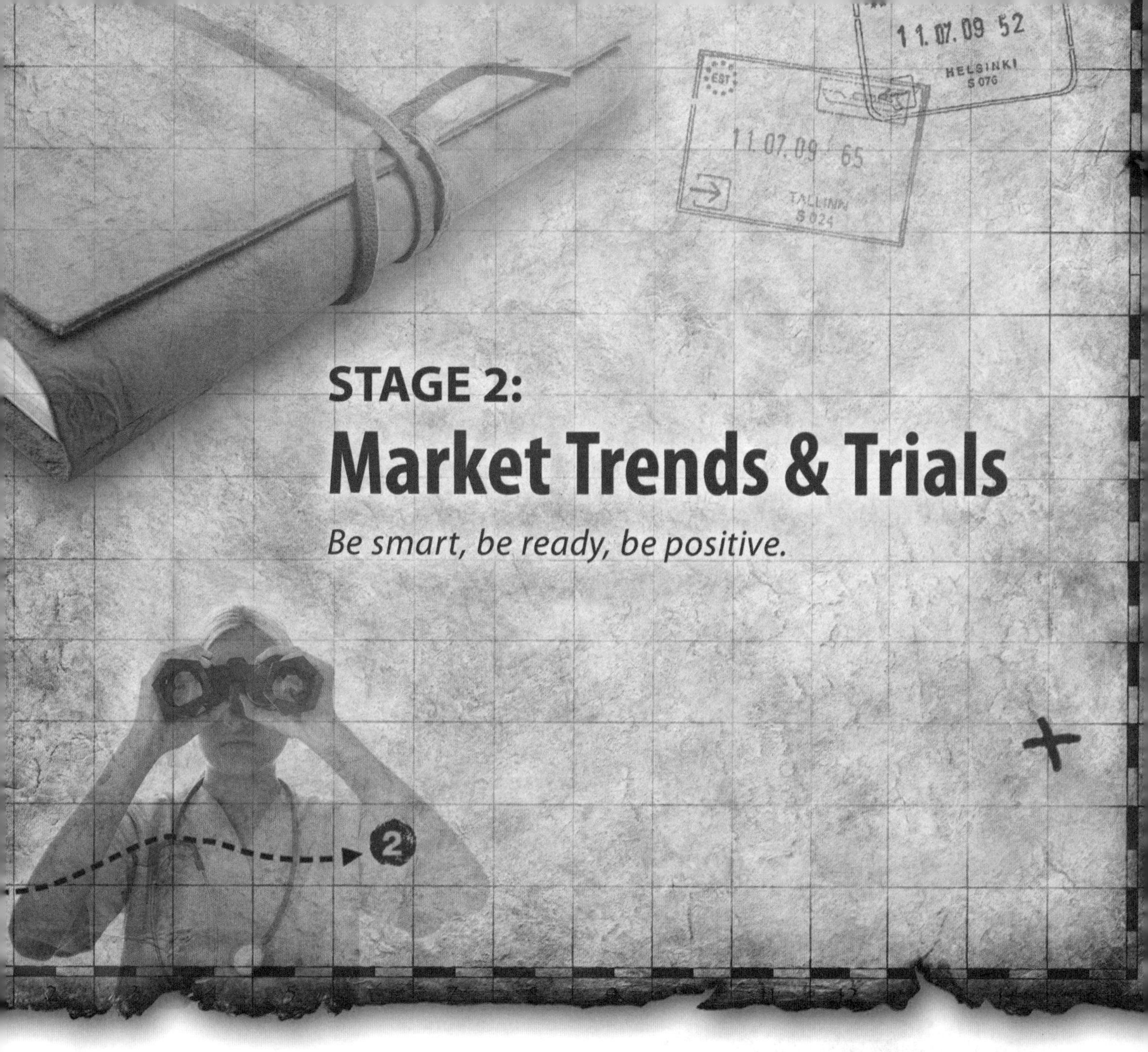

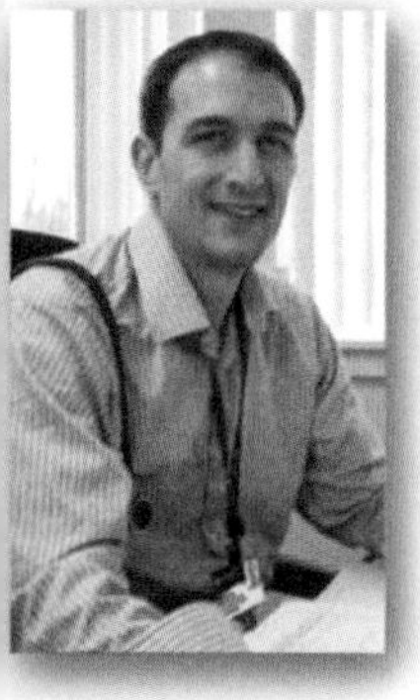

Reilly Coch, MD
Primary Care
Guthrie Clinic

"I interviewed at more than a dozen hospitals. Guthrie stood out as my clear choice because I was impressed by the quality of care. Doctors just seemed to go out of their way for patients.

I wanted the benefits of working in an integrated medical practice. As a primary care physician, I recognized the difficulties of starting a new practice and wanted the backup of an integrated system - both the specialists and the administrative help. In addition, Guthrie has a world-class medical records system that has been really helpful in starting my new practice. I also like the team approach as I can refer to a specialist and have them refer back to me within a short period of time in a way that is easily accessible. It was clear to me that having the support and collaboration of an integrated system was important.

The rapid pace of change in medicine has forced us all to be more nimble and it is difficult to do that as a solo practitioner. Most of us who have come out of residency or medical school have been trained with the team approach, the system approach, and I looked at a lot of different places before I chose Guthrie. I feel confident that the way the system is run here is outstanding; in short, the best thing for a colleague to know is that the system at Guthrie works."

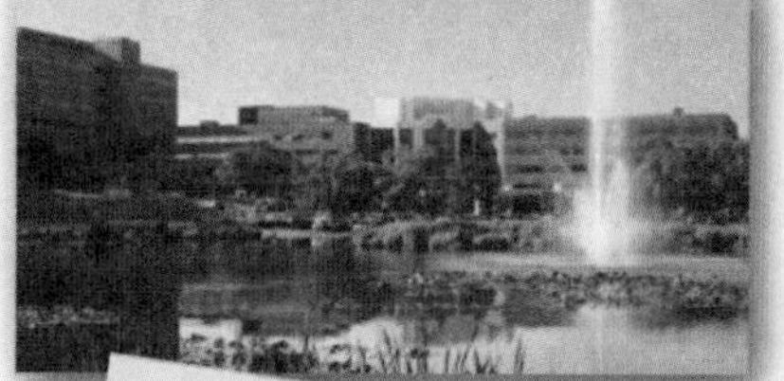

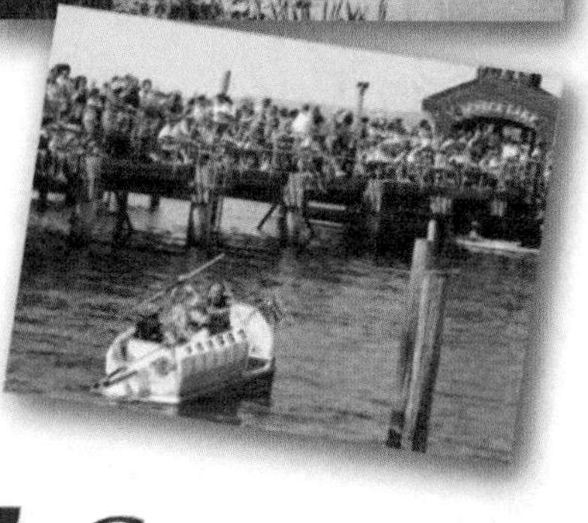

Look for Guthrie Physician Recruitment:

www.ichoseguthrie.org

GUTHRIE

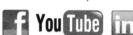

Your Market Guides:

James A. Rice, Ph.D.., FACHE

Vice Chairman, The Governance Institute
Executive Vice President, Integrated Healthcare Strategies
Faculty/Lecturer, Cambridge, Harvard, University of Minnesota, Thunderbird
M.A., Ph.D., Management and Health Policy, University of Minnesota

As a senior leader of The Governance Institute, James Rice plays an influential role with the Institute's members, who represent the leadership of healthcare systems nationwide. He is also a practice leader on compensation for hospital systems and medical groups for Integrated Healthcare Strategies and active in strategic capital planning with U.S. hospital systems through LarsonAllen. He is a former senior officer of Allina, a $2.2 billion integrated health system. James draws upon his extensive experience in integrated system development, managed care, and HMOs.

Kathryn C. Peisert

Managing Editor, The Governance Institute
B.A., University of California, Los Angeles;
M.M., Boston University

Kathryn Peisert is responsible for all Governance Institute publications, both in print and online, which number more than 150 publications, as well as DVD/video programs, webinars, and e-learning courses. She works closely with the Governance Advisors and Governance Institute faculty to ensure that members receive timely and accurate information to help arm them for better decision making in the boardroom. Kathryn is also a classically trained flutist and performs private recitals and concerts around the San Francisco Bay Area.

The Governance Institute

The Governance Institute serves as the leading, independent source of governance information and education for healthcare organizations across the United States. Located in San Diego, The Governance Institute serves over 11,000 trustees and CEOs through its membership services.

In This Stage: Market Trends & Trials

As any good anthropologist will tell you, understanding the people, landscape, language and culture you'll encounter on this adventure is a prerequisite for success.

You'll want to know the location of **DANGERS** and **PITFALLS**. The peaks and valleys. The smooth, safe path and the treacherous, rough rock.

In this stage, you'll learn how hospitals and medical groups are changing, about the roles and responsibilities of those you'll be working with and the pressures and economics that drive hiring decisions. You'll learn how to enter the changing world of healthcare and map your **PATH TO SUCCESS**.

So let's dig in.

P.S. Oh, by the way, they've had some rough luck recently, with a major earthquake impacting the landscape of healthcare.

Be alert. It's a jungle out there.

CONTENTS

TRAILBLAZERS

Actual physician testimonials as reported to Press Ganey:

"In the past few years, hospital administration focus has been on the 'business' aspect of healthcare, with 'token' concern and emphasis on the quality of healthcare delivered at this institution. **QUALITY** is not the priority, but the **COST** is!"

"Doctors are becoming increasingly **ISOLATED** from one another. We're too busy trying to see too many patients. We don't have enough time for interaction and there are few opportunities."

"Leadership is locked in to their own vision/agenda with seemingly very **LITTLE REGARD** for the opinions of those who directly provide patient care. Most members of leadership don't actually practice medicine and thus have a very superficial understanding of the day-to-day problems/issues regarding patient care and physician needs. The role of hospital leadership is supposed to be to support healthcare providers in their delivery of patient care."

Changing Landscape of Healthcare

Throughout medical school and residency, you may have been exposed to or even experienced for yourself the **POLITICAL TURMOIL** and **SILO MENTALITY** that have been beleaguering many physicians in the hospital setting for a long time.

With the onslaught of rapid-fire change occurring within the healthcare industry, let's gain a basic understanding of hospital structures that exist today and briefly discuss the new structures of tomorrow.

TODAY: SILOS

For decades, healthcare organizations have been operating essentially as **INDEPENDENT UNITS WITHIN A LARGER WHOLE**. With a few exceptions, hospitals and physicians function in separate worlds. Hospitals provide practice privileges for physicians seeking access to practice in the hospital setting. Those physicians make up the "independent medical staff," and largely function as a group of individuals. The medical executive committee (MEC) typically is the interface between hospital administration and the medical staff.

This independence has been encouraged over the years since the advent of managed care in the 1970s, with the traditional payment structure in which physicians and hospitals are reimbursed separately for services, based on a fee-for-service payment schedule. This encourages doctors (and hospitals) to provide more services in order to get paid more — volume, not value. It does not provide incentives for hospitals and doctors to coordinate care.

Though physician employment in hospitals has increased over the past five years, the healthcare system overall is still very fragmented today, with thousands of independent providers — many in the same market area — duplicating services.

TOMORROW: SYSTEMS

Going forward, the need to **WORK TOGETHER** will cause the physical makeup of the hospital and medical staff to go through many changes and transitions, some of which have already begun. New physicians will find themselves in organizations in the midst of forming a new direction, with existing physicians seeking to protect their autonomy, and administrations seeking to engage physicians in care coordination.

Recently, The Joint Commission published new leadership standards in its *2009 Comprehensive Accreditation Manual for Hospitals* that refocused the leadership structure of healthcare organizations from silos to a comprehensive system:

> *"For many years prior to 1994, the standards included chapters on 'Management,' 'Governance,' 'Medical Staff,' and 'Nursing Services.' In fact, each department in the organization had its 'own' chapter of standards, as if the good performance of each unit — governance, management, radiology, dietary, surgery, and so forth — would assure the success of the organization. The Joint Commission sought the advice of some of the nation's leading healthcare management experts and clinical leaders from both practice and academia to redesign this unit-by-unit approach. They were unanimous in their advice: stop thinking of the healthcare organization as a conglomerate of units and think of it as a 'system.' A system is a combination of processes, people, and other resources that, working together, achieve an end.*
>
> *"If we want a healthcare organization to succeed, it must be appreciated as a system, the components of which work together to create success. It is not possible to determine what each component should be and do unless it is examined in the light of the goals for the system and the rest of the system's components. For a healthcare organization, the primary goal is to provide high-quality, safe care to those who seek its help, whether they are patients, residents, clients, or recipients of care. While there are other goals for a healthcare organization, including financial sustainability, community service, and ethical business behavior, The Joint Commission's primary focus is on the organization's goals of providing high-quality, safe care to patients."*[6]

As a result of this shift in thinking about the structure of leadership for healthcare organizations, The Joint Commission created a recommended leadership structure that not only included the governing body of the organization (Board of Directors or Board of Trustees) and an administrative staff (C-Suite), but also a team of physician leaders (licensed independent practitioners) who could speak uniquely to the clinical aspects of care that drive quality of patient care and safety. According to the white paper, "In a hospital, this third leadership group comprises the leaders of the organized medical staff. Only if these three leadership groups work together, **COLLABORATIVELY**, to exercise the organization's leadership function, can the organization reliably achieve its goals."

With the need for collaboration among the three leadership groups of a healthcare organization, the function and makeup of the medical staff will be very different. Hospitals will continue to be required to have a medical staff (of some form or another) to meet Joint Commission standards. The question will be how to comply with these regulations while making the transition to clinical integration and accountable care.

Medical Market Trends

There are many emerging trends impacting the business side of medicine. Whether you allow these market conditions to impact your relationships with your employer, patients, and/or your family will be determined how you react. Will you be a victim to the market conditions or be known to rise above by any market condition to fulfill your life and career goals?

TREND	IMPACT ON:		
	Hospital Organization	**Physician**	**Patient**
Shortage of physicians • 39% are Baby Boomers • Not enough physicians to replace demand • 50% are women and work on average of .8 FTE.	• Access to care will be an acute issue as more uninsured and underinsured patients are able to obtain health insurance and begin seeking care. • Recruitment efforts and integration models/incentives for physicians need to be a top priority to attract needed physicians to the community.	• More stress • Burnout • No moment to themselves • Stretched to the limit • Working in a crisis mode • No work/life balance • Carry over to home life	• Patients may experience longer wait times to see the doctor. • Less access to the doctor as more mid-level practitioners step in to fill certain care-delivery roles.
Malpractice insurance • Shortage of physicians increases patient load, which increases mistakes and malpractice. • Too many malpractice cases in a litigious society, which raises premiums, raises costs of business, and lowers profits, which puts strain on everybody.	• Hospitals have been implicated in malpractice suits for allowing the physician in question to have practice privileges. Hospitals are burdened to prove that they went through a rigorous credentialing process and show proof of documentation. • Hospitals and physicians must work together to educate patients about their care options and help them select appropriate care, rather than promoting overutilization of services simply to protect against malpractice.	• Facing rising premiums, decreased income. • Medical malpractice linked to inefficient interpersonal skills. Doctors hold back due to fear of being sued.	• Overall costs of care go up when malpractice premiums are a factor. • Patients are already paying indirectly to alleviate these costs on providers.

TREND	IMPACT ON: Hospital Organization	Physician	Patient
Failed economy • More unemployment which means either no insurance or Medicaid. • For people who do have insurance, companies are increasing deductibles, so patients don't go because they don't want to pay deductibles, and when they do go, hospitals have a harder time collecting the money. • Business closures, bankruptcies and foreclosures are all adding to the mix.	• Possibly tighter pressures on local hospitals to prove their tax-exempt status, especially if affiliated with a system corporation located in another region, as local governments may be seeking more revenues in places where they did not seek it before.	• Working more and making less, increasing pressure on the physicians. • Physicians moving into employee role versus solo practitioner.	• Everyone feels the cost crunch in a down economy. • Patients will avoid seeking care until the last moment to delay any out-of-pocket costs.

REFLECTION:

What impact might these trends have on your decision to practice medicine in your chosen specialty?

What's your understanding of these trends? What have you heard or been exposed to?

The Big One: Healthcare Reform

There are three major **SHIFTS** occurring related to healthcare reform: substantial increase in covered population, shifting Medicare and Medicaid financial risk to providers, and reduction in Medicare payment rates.

SUBSTANTIAL INCREASE IN COVERED POPULATION

About **16 MILLION** Americans will be added to the Medicaid program, and Medicaid reimbursements will be raised to Medicare levels for general internists, family physicians and pediatricians in 2013 and 2014.

Still, many doctors have no interest in this new pool of Medicaid patients. Throughout the country, some doctors are trying to lower their percentage of Medicare patients or even eliminate them entirely. Some doctors will also avoid the new Medicaid patients because they say that dealing with government insurance programs is a snarled tangle of frustrating paperwork.

Most physicians don't have that choice. A lot of physicians operate on very short margins and are unable to cut their overhead. They get paid relatively little per patient visit and need to have volume. Yes, there are premier practices that won't accept insurers offering less than Medicare rates, but they are the exception rather than the rule.

Although many primary care doctors are eager to start seeing these new patients, specialists may get the short end of the stick. The Medicaid reimbursement rate for them will not rise to Medicare levels.

SHIFTING MEDICARE AND MEDICAID FINANCIAL RISK TO PROVIDERS

The exploding interest in **ACCOUNTABLE CARE ORGANIZATIONS** (ACOs) sparked by the health reform legislation represents a sea change in the way hospitals and physicians currently function. An accountable care organization is a clinically integrated healthcare provider (various models, including hospitals with an employed physician group, or a physician group that has contracted in some way with a hospital or health system) that assumes responsibility for the quality of patient care as well as the cost decisions behind that care, for a certain population.

The ACO will receive one "bundled" payment for an entire episode of care (from the initial doctor visits to the procedure in the hospital, to the follow-up visits, etc.). The ACO is then responsible for dividing that single payment across the various providers involved in the episode of care. In the short term, this will be played out as a pilot program for Medicare, and the bundled payments will vary depending on patient outcome (i.e., positive outcomes will receive higher payment; thus the ACO is accepting risk). In the long term, most experts assume that this will be the primary direction most payers will move towards, not just Medicare.

It will open up new **CHALLENGES** and **OPPORTUNITIES** for physicians in practice, and those in new leadership roles. Physician career paths will reflect calls to move into a new mix of clinical practice and leadership roles for such diverse positions as:

- Traditional medical staff leadership
- Health-system clinical care councils
- Care-management committees
- Clinical service-line management in hospital systems
- Health plan care management
- Medical directorships for many functions within integrated healthcare systems

GUIDE POINTS

Understanding Market Conditions & Healthcare Reform

- Rapid change will continue to be constant. Stay as informed as possible.
- Conduct your own research.
- Surround yourself with positive people. Remember to look for the "**SILVER LINING**" in every challenge.
- Don't fall prey to negativity you may hear and experience from other doctors.

REDUCTION IN MEDICARE PAYMENT RATES

Hospitals will receive lower reimbursements across payers. Immediate challenges are **MAXIMIZING EFFICIENCY** and **ELIMINATING WASTE** in care-delivery systems to maintain operating revenue and credit rating. They must position themselves to accept bundled payments and risk-based payments.

With regards to **INSURANCE**, changes in managed care, rising medical costs, and government regulations will no doubt impact insurance costs as well. In the short term, Medicare patients may find fewer doctors willing to accept them. In the longer term, payments will likely level out, and physicians will need as many patients as they can get, so fewer will be turned down based on insurance/payment levels.

Notably absent from healthcare reform was any mention of fixes to the **SUSTAINABLE GROWTH RATE** (SGR), which determines physician reimbursement. Medicare reimbursements cuts — whether or not made at the full 21.2% as proposed — would be disastrous. Markets would lose long-term attraction of physicians into medical school, access to physicians could be constrained, and stand-alone physician practices would fall by the wayside as practices merge and join hospitals to gain economies of scale and to secure working capital for enhanced technologies, process improvements and staffing support.

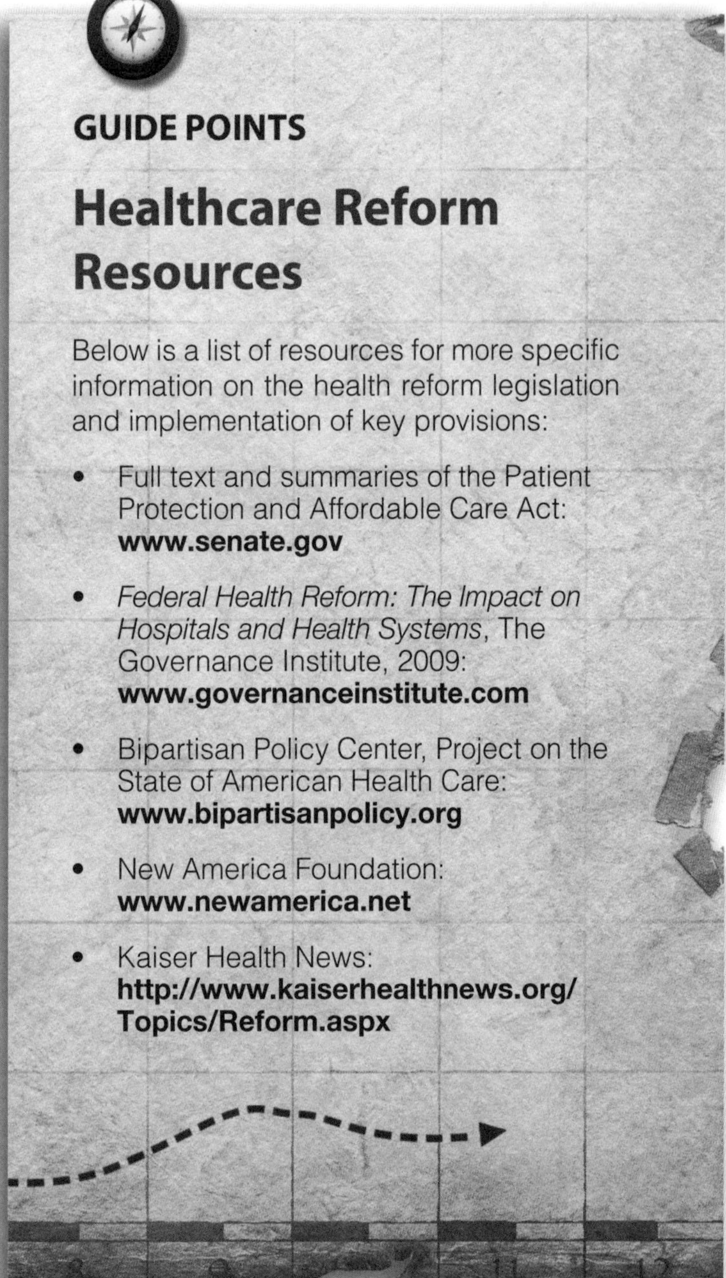

GUIDE POINTS

Healthcare Reform Resources

Below is a list of resources for more specific information on the health reform legislation and implementation of key provisions:

- Full text and summaries of the Patient Protection and Affordable Care Act: **www.senate.gov**
- *Federal Health Reform: The Impact on Hospitals and Health Systems*, The Governance Institute, 2009: **www.governanceinstitute.com**
- Bipartisan Policy Center, Project on the State of American Health Care: **www.bipartisanpolicy.org**
- New America Foundation: **www.newamerica.net**
- Kaiser Health News: **http://www.kaiserhealthnews.org/Topics/Reform.aspx**

OVERALL IMPACT ON PHYSICIANS

What do doctors stand to gain or lose in all of this? As people in a caring profession, many doctors are either truly or theoretically happy that about **32 MILLION** more Americans will soon have health insurance. Yet physicians have every right to be concerned about their own livelihoods and medical practices. For some doctors, the healthcare bill will create benefits and opportunities. Others see no benefits, particularly specialists. And funding the reform — despite what politicians say — could portend an ominous future for physicians.

Although, physicians are likely to face the same pressures from the reform era as their colleagues, this guidebook provides you an opportunity to understand the landscape and take control of your mind and seek the solutions that align with your values.

- More public calls for improvements in **CLINICAL QUALITY** and better **PATIENT SAFETY**.
- More 24/7 **PUBLIC REPORTING** on the Internet of quality and cost-performance metrics.
- More **REGULATORY OVERSIGHT** from state and federal governments that constrains clinical decision making.
- **SQUEEZE IN TAKE-HOME PAY** as practice expenses rise and revenues are constrained.
- More **MULTI-SPECIALTY GROUPS** will be formed by and with hospitals in efforts to prepare for accountable care.
- Exploding demands to rely on **ELECTRONIC MEDICAL RECORDS** (EMRs) across care settings to better manage chronic disease.
- ACOs' demand for clinical integration will move physicians into **LEADERSHIP ROLES**.

- Regulators and governing boards will demand more **FORMAL ACCOUNTABILITY** and development of physician leaders as a means to successful physician alignment.
- Will need more primary care physicians to **COORDINATE** with hospitalists.
- Physicians must be able to **NEGOTIATE** for their fair share around the table of the new ACOs.

The nation may therefore face the challenging irony of offering more coverage for more people, but having fewer physicians ready, willing and able to respond to the new needs and demands for care under the new reforms.

Hospital Organization Structure & Practice Options

- The following provides an overview of the connection points between **PATIENTS**, **HOSPITALS**, and **PHYSICIANS** in regard to hospital organization structure and practice options. By understanding each of the roles of senior leadership teams, Board of Directors, community, and how each practice setting is connected to the hospital will give you an understanding how an organization operates as well as providing you insight on what type of setting is the best fit for you.

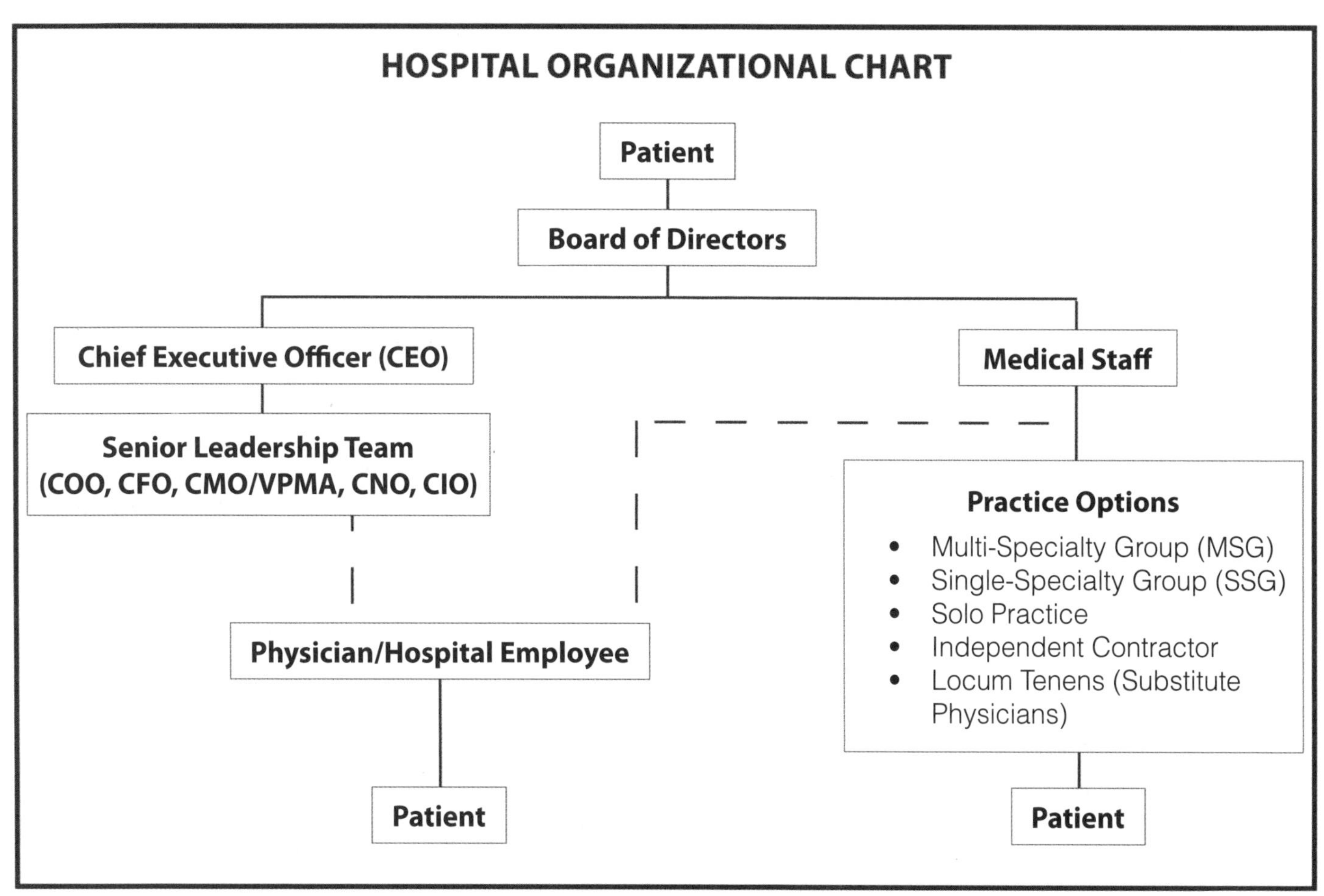

ROLE DEFINITIONS:

- **Board of Directors:** The Board of Directors is responsible for strategic and generative thinking about the organization and its mission, vision and goals, and oversight of the organization's functions, especially its financial sustainability. The governing body has an additional fiduciary obligation to continuously strive to provide safe and high-quality care to the patients who seek health services from the organization. If the Hospital is a 501(c)3 not-for-profit — as most hospitals are — the governing body has a responsibility to benefit the community, often called "community needs."

- **Chief Executive Officer (CEO):** Responsible for quality of care and fiscal responsibility, including:
    - Providing information and support systems
    - Providing recruitment and retention services
    - Providing physical and financial assets
    - Identifying a nurse leader at the executive level who participates in decision making
    - Representing the hospital in the community
    - Speaking for the hospital in matters of regulatory, legislative and accreditation issues

- **Chief Operating Officer (COO):** Responsible for the day-to-day operations (staffing, resourcing, service, plant and clinical equipment) of the hospital.

- **Chief Finance Officer (CFO):** Responsible for the registration and billing of patients, negotiations with third-party payers, and management of all issues related to the balance sheet of the hospital (debt structuring, investment management, accounts payable, etc.).

- **Chief Medical Officer (CMO)/Vice President Medical Affairs (VPMA):** Responsible for the effective organization of the medical staff structure, including the medical executive committee; together with the CNO, assures the quality of care provided and patient safety.

- **Chief Nursing Officer (CNO):** Responsible for the effective organization of the professional nursing structure; together with the CMO/VPMA, assures the quality of care provided and patient safety.

- **Chief Information Officer (CIO):** Responsible for building and maintaining efficient and cost-effective clinical and business information technology networks to support the day-to-day and strategic needs of the hospital.

- **Medical Staff:** Oversees the quality of care, treatment and services provided by those individuals with clinical privileges; self-governing but accountable to the governing body, who approves the medical staff structure, which conforms to medical staff guiding principles. There is a single organized medical staff unless criteria are met for an exception to the single medical staff requirement.

PRACTICE OPTIONS:

- **Multi-Specialty Group (MSG):** A physician-owned group with more than three physicians with a minimum of two different specialties.
  - Pros: Trial period before commitment; less risk up front; minimal administrative and management duties; focus on clinical vs. business
  - Cons: Less autonomy; multiple partners may have different philosophies and priorities; higher stress to drive revenue and perform; chance of not being voted in as a partner; dealing with staffing, administrative and business issues; less stable, more volatility with income

- **Single-Specialty Group (SSG):** Two or more physicians within the same discipline. Generally, physicians are employed for one to three years, with a track to partnership.
  - Pros: Trial period before commitment; less risk up front; minimal administrative and management duties; focus on clinical vs. business
  - Cons: Chance of not being voted in as a partner; dealing with staffing, administrative and business issues; less stable, more volatility with income

- **Solo Practice:** Private practitioner who is solely responsible for decisions. Physicians can be supported by the hospital through an income-guarantee arrangement, or they can set up their own practice if they are self-funded or if they choose to leverage through a bank.
  - Pros: Complete autonomy, high reward
  - Cons: High risk; little back-up; high overhead; less stable, more volatility with income

- **Independent Contractor:** Similar to solo practitioners except that the physician contracts with a hospital or group to provide a service for a specific amount of money per year.
  - Pros: Flexible hours; work when needed or desired; opportunity to write off business expenses
  - Cons: Inconsistent hours and schedule; less security

- **Locum Tenens (Substitute Physicians):** This arrangement allows physicians to choose their own hours and the number of days they would like to work. The locum tenens organization plans out their work schedule and sends them on assignments.
  - Pros: Opportunity to travel; great schedule time; able to experience many different types of practices
  - Cons: Long-term travel can be wearing; many have to travel to undesirable communities; uncertain schedule; unstable income

REFLECTION:

Given current market trends and pros and cons of each practice setting, which one(s) appeal to you right now? Why?

Must-Have Physician Leadership Competencies

The swirling array of pressures for change and calls for medical care that is more accountable, more transparent, of higher value and better quality cannot happen without physicians. But perhaps the physicians of tomorrow will be different than the ones of the past. Physicians entering practice are likely to experience these factors in their practice reality:

- More likely employed in multi-specialty groups within **INTEGRATED HEALTHCARE DELIVERY SYSTEMS**
- Have a new **BALANCE** between the calling of a medical career and the calling of family and eclectic lifestyle pursuits
- Influence the health and healthcare of thousands of people a year through practice, but also through **LEADERSHIP ROLES** in many physician leadership positions
- Rely more on **MULTI-DISCIPLINARY TEAMS** of physician extenders for people with chronic disease
- Need to master **SOCIAL NETWORKING TOOLS** and **EMRs** to manage more engaged and assertive patient populations

Most new graduates will have received little preparation in medical school or residency for these new challenges and opportunities. Life long learning will not only apply to keeping pace with an explosion of **CLINICAL KNOWLEDGE** for the practice of medicine, but also a dizzying selection of **NEW TECHNOLOGIES** and **CONSUMER EXPECTATIONS** to deliver health gain as well as healthcare, as well as provide better value for the money and a superior patient care experience.

There has never been a more important time for physicians to step forward into leadership roles. The healthcare system is transforming and it is critical that physicians shape its future.

When choosing the type of practice and/ or position that comprises the right fit, it's imperative that you evaluate where you are at with each of these **COMPETENCIES** and strategically interview at Employers who can provide you the structure to help you grow into these roles professionally. To self assess these competencies, set some time aside to walk through the exercises on page 48 and 49.

DR. GOODHOOK'S FIELD NOTES

Many an aspiring physician runs into our beloved practice with little common sense.

The bright adventurer, accompanied by ignorance, enthusiasm and self-confidence, runs headlong into pit and peak.

Stunned and lost, the disoriented young resident will oft curse course, blame another and wonder.

A minute of preparation prevents an hour of confusion. Take heed, young doctor, seek to know the land before you tie your shoe.

– Dr. Gh.

- **Patient Centric.** Leaders in healthcare will need to focus more on the patient than ever before, even with the "system perspective." A good physician leader will **UNDERSTAND** and effectively **COMMUNICATE** the impact on the patient for every decision being made.

- **Business Acumen.** Physicians will need a working knowledge of the world of medicine from a business perspective. Cost drivers, financial implications and ability to make decisions that have a **POSITIVE IMPACT** on the organization and patient satisfaction represent key outcomes.

- **Team Focus.** Physicians are part of a team, and a good physician leader is a true **COLLABORATOR** and builds **COHESION** with aligned goals across physicians, administrators, patients, payers and other stakeholders. An important part of this competency is being able to communicate effectively to non-physician leaders the importance of physician input in a large organization such as a hospital or health system.

- **Facilitator of Change.** Like any leader in any type of organization, a physician leader must be able to facilitate change, seek out differing points of view, encourage active discourse, and **BRING OUT THE BEST** in his or her team.

- **Systems / Strategic Thinking.** A physician leaders needs a "system" perspective — understanding the roles of the physicians and other care providers inside a complex system of processes, people,and care delivery. The physician should be able to develop a **STRATEGIC MINDSET** and **METHODOLOGY FOR LEADING COMPLEX ORGANIZATIONAL SYSTEMS**.

SELF-ASSESSMENT: PHYSICIAN LEADERSHIP COMPETENCIES

Complete the following assessment to determine areas of strength and areas of development. This does **NOT** mean that you need to or will be competent in all areas. The goal is to identify areas for **PROFESSIONAL DEVELOPMENT** and determine what type of Employer is most likely going to provide the support for you to grow as a physician. Add the individual items to get a total score for each competency.

PATIENT CENTRIC

I show empathy and match my feelings with those of another person in an interaction.	Weakness 1	 2	 3	 4	Strength 5
I am able to develop a high level of trust with my patients.	Weakness 1	 2	 3	 4	Strength 5
Patients feel comfortable sharing their health concerns with me.	Weakness 1	 2	 3	 4	Strength 5
I can easily meet and initiate conversations with new people when necessary.	Weakness 1	 2	 3	 4	Strength 5
I am a strong communicator (listening, responding, explaining, etc.).	Weakness 1	 2	 3	 4	Strength 5
Total score					
Level of importance to master in the next one to three years	High		Medium		Low

TEAM FOCUS

I am able to effectively work in a team environment.	Weakness 1	 2	 3	 4	Strength 5
I don't allow my ego to get in the way of making team decisions.	Weakness 1	 2	 3	 4	Strength 5
I am a strong collaborator with colleagues, staff, and hospital administration.	Weakness 1	 2	 3	 4	Strength 5
I speak up about the things that I would like others to be open about with me.	Weakness 1	 2	 3	 4	Strength 5
I feel comfortable addressing conflicts as soon as they arise.	Weakness 1	 2	 3	 4	Strength 5
Total score					
Level of importance to master in the next one to three years	High		Medium		Low

BUSINESS ACUMEN

I am able to develop and implement strategies and goals.	Weakness 1	 2	 3	 4	Strength 5
I understand the healthcare industry and the basic structures/ processes of a hospital or health system.	Weakness 1	 2	 3	 4	Strength 5
I understand how a physician private practice connects/aligns with the healthcare system as a whole.	Weakness 1	 2	 3	 4	Strength 5
Total score					
Level of importance to master in the next one to three years	High		Medium		Low

SYSTEMS/STRATEGIC THINKING

I am able to think and make strategic and tactical decisions.	Weakness 1	2	3	4	Strength 5
I think of new ways to approach a problem from a process perspective.	Weakness 1	2	3	4	Strength 5
I am able to work in a complex hospital/practice setting.	Weakness 1	2	3	4	Strength 5
Total score					
Level of importance to master in the next one to three years	High		Medium		Low

FACILITATOR OF CHANGE

I show patience with my staff when implementing a change, knowing that there is an adjustment period.	Weakness 1	2	3	4	Strength 5
I am able to adapt to change in procedures, medical advances, healthcare requirements, etc.	Weakness 1	2	3	4	Strength 5
I am open to the ideas and perspectives of others.	Weakness 1	2	3	4	Strength 5
Total score					
Level of importance to master in the next one to three years	High		Medium		Low

Gaining knowledge and skill in these competencies will enhance your clinical/technical abilities over time. Choose one of the competencies you ranked high in importance to master, and respond to these prompts:

COMPETENCY:		
List concerns you might have with this competency overall:	*What's at stake if you ignore items that reflect areas of weakness?*	*List growth opportunities:*
Identify one to two action items to work on over the next one to three years.		

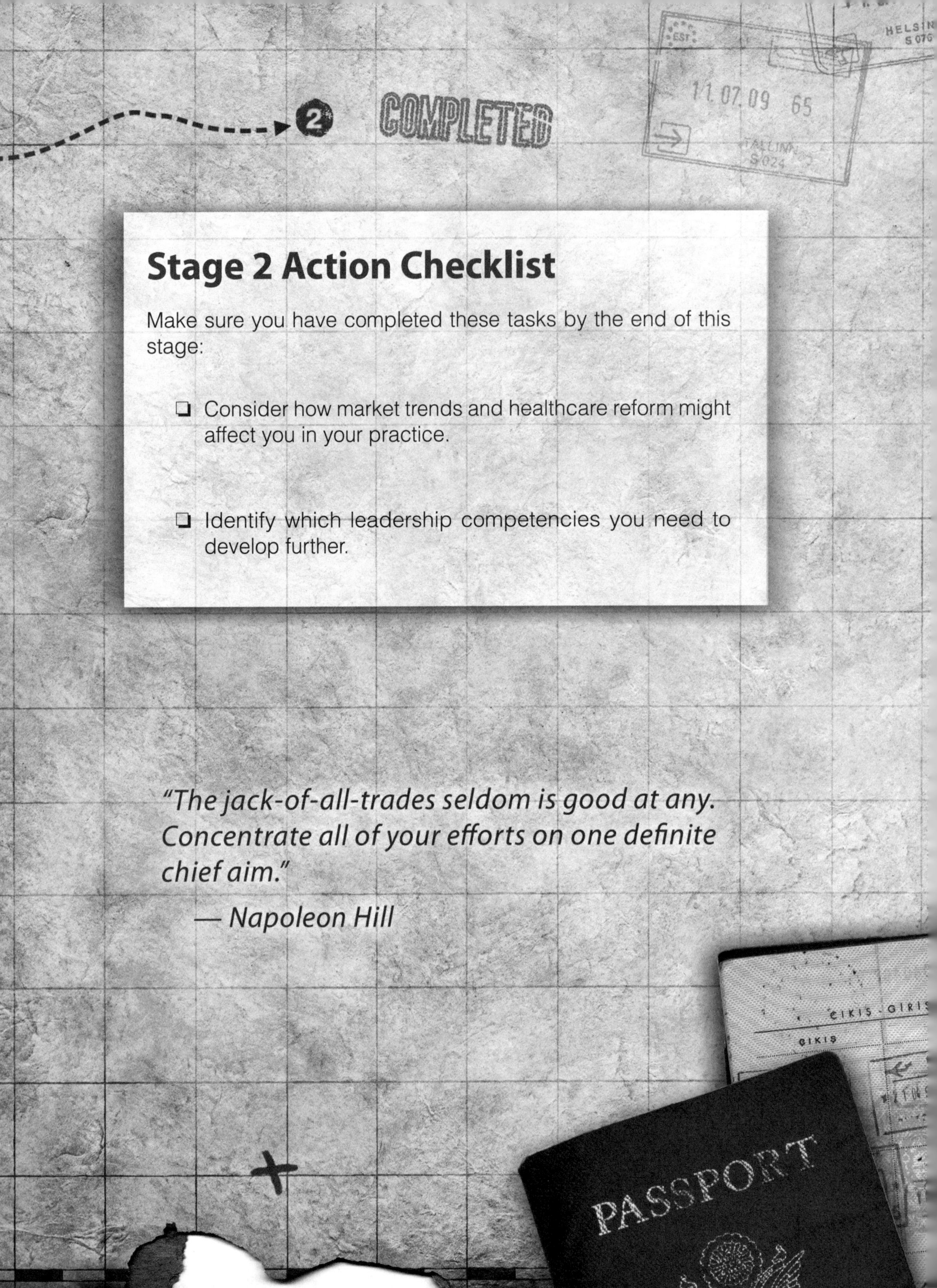

Stage 2 Action Checklist

Make sure you have completed these tasks by the end of this stage:

- ❑ Consider how market trends and healthcare reform might affect you in your practice.

- ❑ Identify which leadership competencies you need to develop further.

"The jack-of-all-trades seldom is good at any. Concentrate all of your efforts on one definite chief aim."

— Napoleon Hill

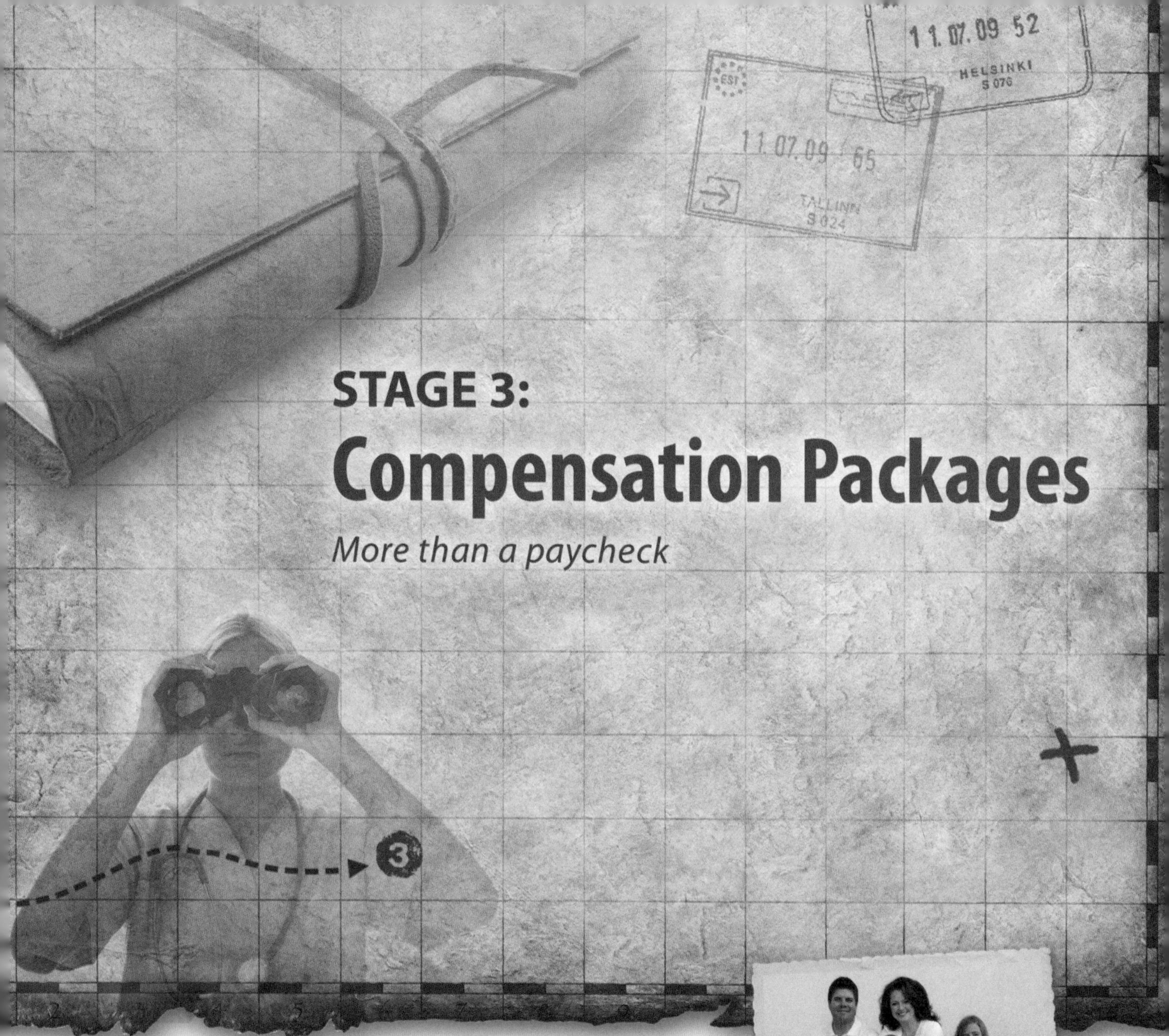

STAGE 3:
Compensation Packages

More than a paycheck

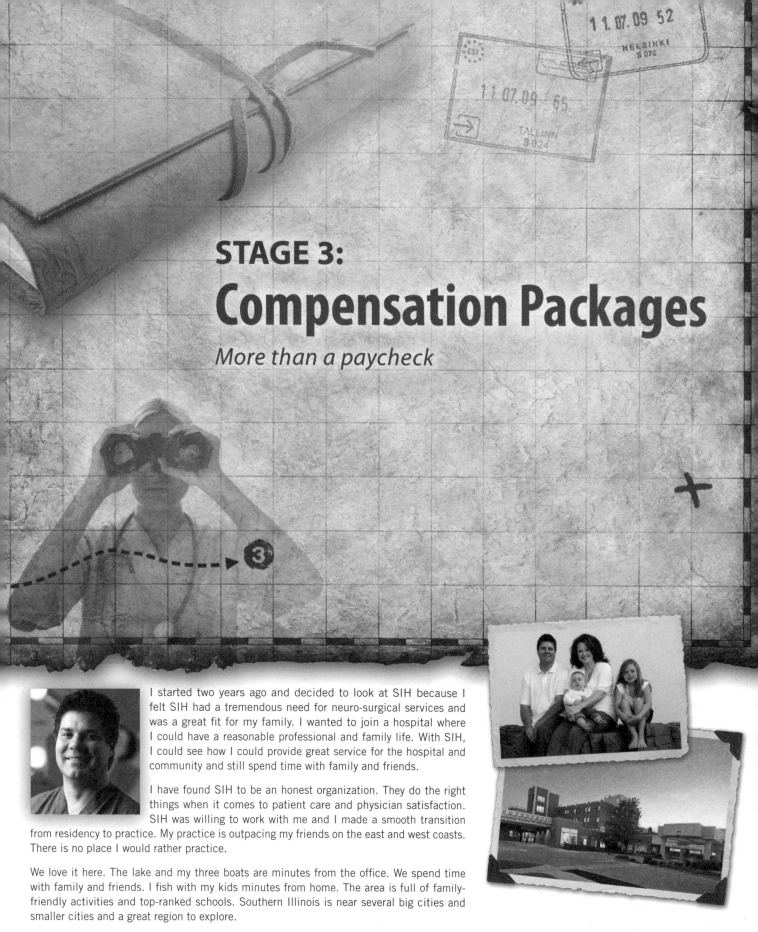

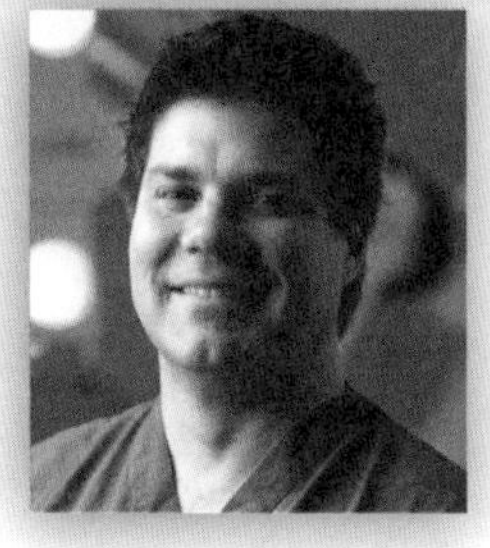

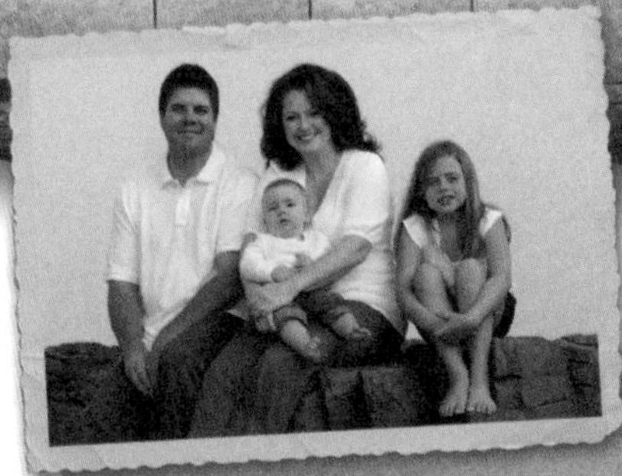

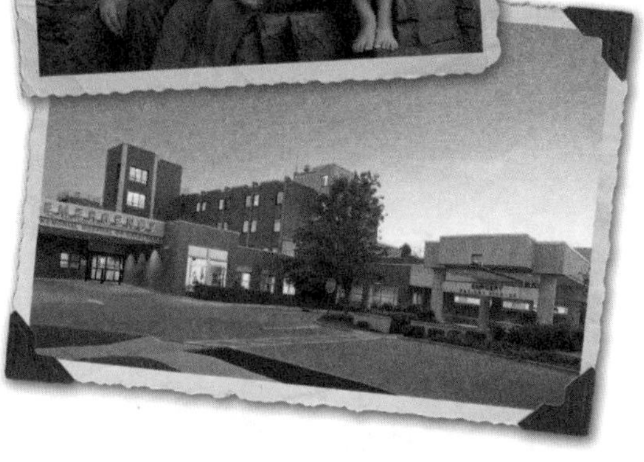

I started two years ago and decided to look at SIH because I felt SIH had a tremendous need for neuro-surgical services and was a great fit for my family. I wanted to join a hospital where I could have a reasonable professional and family life. With SIH, I could see how I could provide great service for the hospital and community and still spend time with family and friends.

I have found SIH to be an honest organization. They do the right things when it comes to patient care and physician satisfaction. SIH was willing to work with me and I made a smooth transition from residency to practice. My practice is outpacing my friends on the east and west coasts. There is no place I would rather practice.

We love it here. The lake and my three boats are minutes from the office. We spend time with family and friends. I fish with my kids minutes from home. The area is full of family-friendly activities and top-ranked schools. Southern Illinois is near several big cities and smaller cities and a great region to explore.

What has my adventure been like at SIH? Good pace of life, supportive environment, honest and friendly.

- Jeff Jones DO, Neurosurgeon

SOUTHERN ILLINOIS HEALTHCARE

To speak to Jeff first hand or to get more information on SIH, call Alexis Depree, SIH Recruitment, at 618.457.5200 ext 67015. Check out the "Introducing SIH" ad on Page 186 and read the SIH CEO Corner.

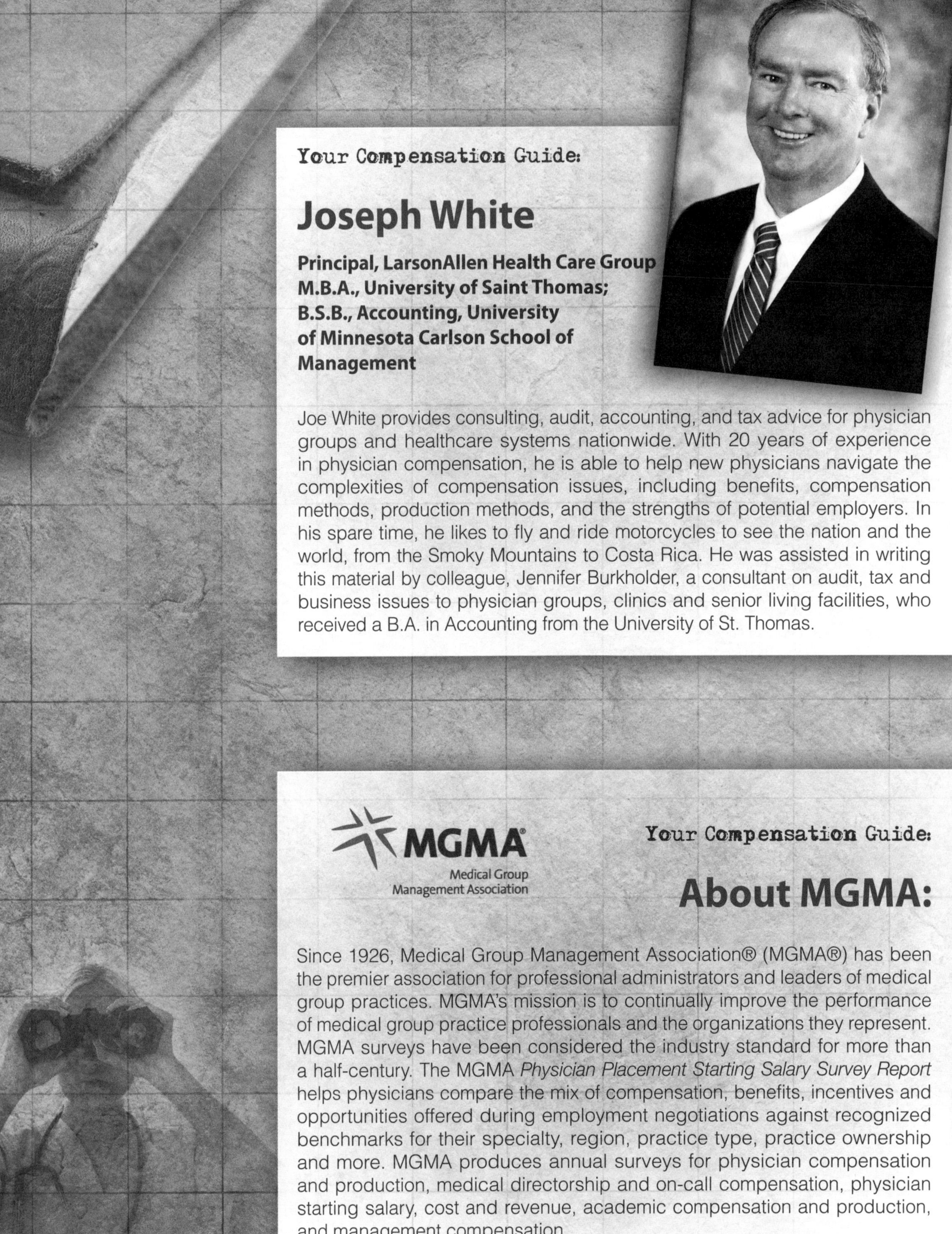

Your Compensation Guide:

Joseph White

Principal, LarsonAllen Health Care Group
M.B.A., University of Saint Thomas;
B.S.B., Accounting, University of Minnesota Carlson School of Management

Joe White provides consulting, audit, accounting, and tax advice for physician groups and healthcare systems nationwide. With 20 years of experience in physician compensation, he is able to help new physicians navigate the complexities of compensation issues, including benefits, compensation methods, production methods, and the strengths of potential employers. In his spare time, he likes to fly and ride motorcycles to see the nation and the world, from the Smoky Mountains to Costa Rica. He was assisted in writing this material by colleague, Jennifer Burkholder, a consultant on audit, tax and business issues to physician groups, clinics and senior living facilities, who received a B.A. in Accounting from the University of St. Thomas.

Your Compensation Guide:

About MGMA:

Since 1926, Medical Group Management Association® (MGMA®) has been the premier association for professional administrators and leaders of medical group practices. MGMA's mission is to continually improve the performance of medical group practice professionals and the organizations they represent. MGMA surveys have been considered the industry standard for more than a half-century. The MGMA *Physician Placement Starting Salary Survey Report* helps physicians compare the mix of compensation, benefits, incentives and opportunities offered during employment negotiations against recognized benchmarks for their specialty, region, practice type, practice ownership and more. MGMA produces annual surveys for physician compensation and production, medical directorship and on-call compensation, physician starting salary, cost and revenue, academic compensation and production, and management compensation.

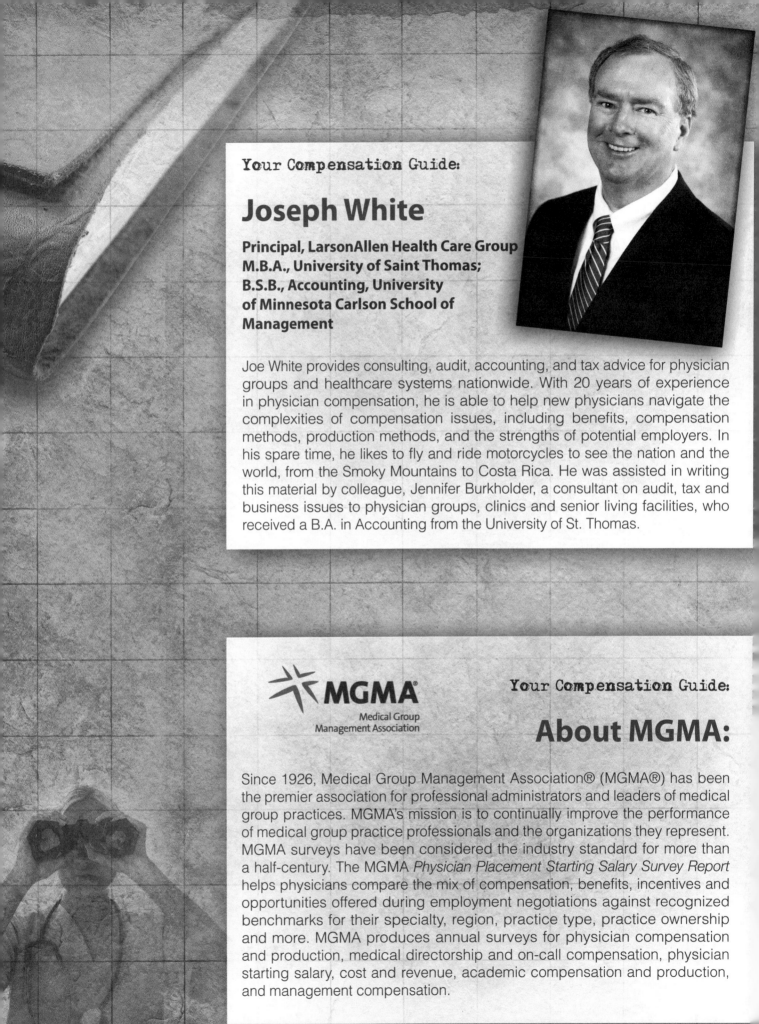

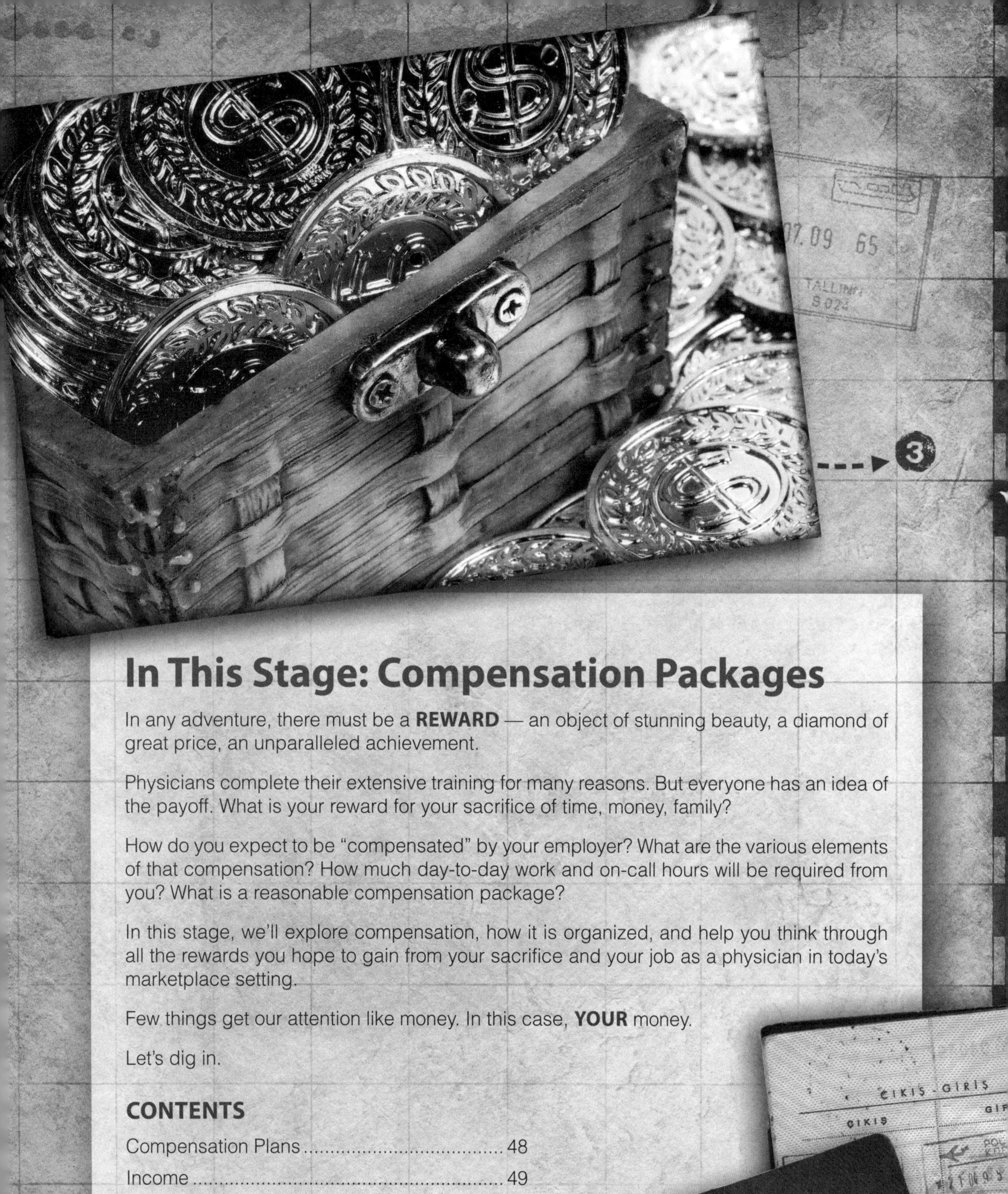

In This Stage: Compensation Packages

In any adventure, there must be a **REWARD** — an object of stunning beauty, a diamond of great price, an unparalleled achievement.

Physicians complete their extensive training for many reasons. But everyone has an idea of the payoff. What is your reward for your sacrifice of time, money, family?

How do you expect to be "compensated" by your employer? What are the various elements of that compensation? How much day-to-day work and on-call hours will be required from you? What is a reasonable compensation package?

In this stage, we'll explore compensation, how it is organized, and help you think through all the rewards you hope to gain from your sacrifice and your job as a physician in today's marketplace setting.

Few things get our attention like money. In this case, **YOUR** money.

Let's dig in.

CONTENTS

Compensation Plans

Based on current medical market conditions, such as physician shortages and changing demographics, you may find yourself inundated with practice opportunities. Sorting through the various offers, with the looming pressure of **REPAYING A MOUNTAIN OF DEBT** ($158,000 for the average resident), can be overwhelming. In this scenario, compensation becomes an important element to consider and assess. Even so, use caution in placing too much emphasis on the "almighty dollar," which can lead to uninformed decisions, impacting other life priorities and leaving lasting consequences.

MORE THAN A PAYCHECK

Compensation plans represent arrangements for how employees are paid. There are many compensation models within the healthcare industry. For physicians, total compensation typically consists of two major components, income and benefits, and may have a third, a signing bonus.

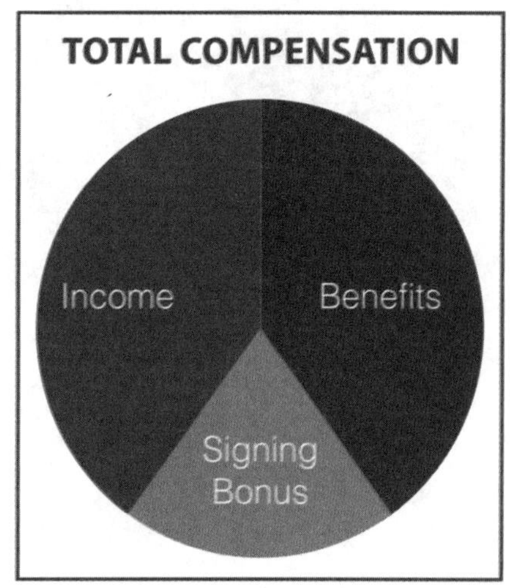

INCOME, or the wages received, can come as a **GUARANTEED SALARY** or **PRODUCTIVITY-BASED COMPENSATION**. Knowing how these are calculated will greatly affect your total pay, so be sure that you understand it.

BENEFITS, which may not have an obvious dollar value attached, are a major part of the overall compensation, and understanding them is vital when assessing opportunities.

Finally, depending on the practice and/or geographic area, you may receive a **SIGNING BONUS**, which can be considerable. The amount is often commensurate with the length of employment spelled out in the contract, and a portion is earned each month you stay with the practice. If you leave the practice earlier than the original commitment, repayment of the unearned amount is required.

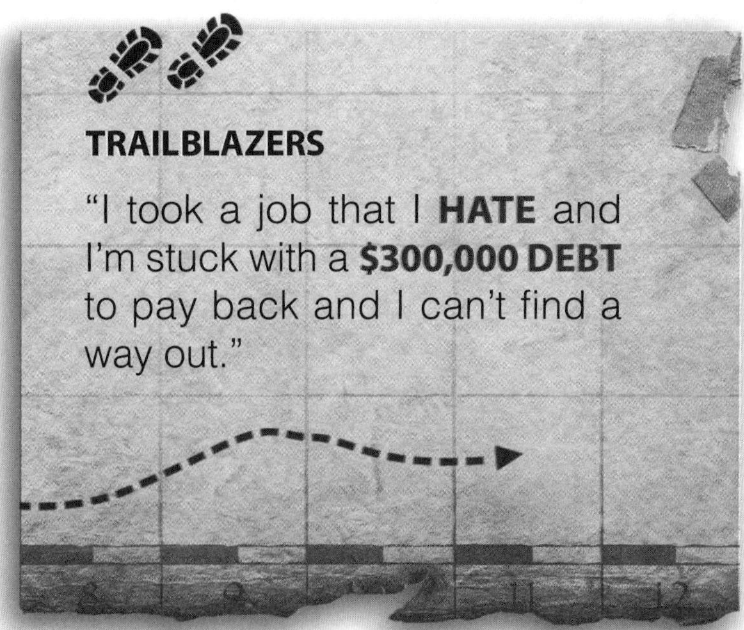

TRAILBLAZERS
"I took a job that I **HATE** and I'm stuck with a **$300,000 DEBT** to pay back and I can't find a way out."

Income

GUARANTEED SALARY

A guaranteed salary is often provided for one to two years before the physician is switched to a productivity-based compensation formula. This guarantee **REMOVES THE RISK** associated with starting a practice as it often takes one to two years for a physician's schedule to become full with new patients. If you do not have a guarantee it means you are paid based upon production: no patients, no production, no money! Typically if you have a guaranteed salary but earn more through production efforts, you would take home the greater amount.

The shortage of physicians has increased the amount that physicians are receiving in salary. For many specialties, employers are sometimes desperate to attract physicians and they rely on higher compensation packages to fill positions that may have been unfilled for months, if not years. In many situations, physicians are being paid **ABOVE-MARKET** salary ranges at the outset.

In the case of a two-year guaranteed salary contract, physicians should take stock of their situation after the first 12 or 18 months. For some physicians, this can be a cold, hard assessment of what their income will be when their compensation becomes production-based. If your production is high, all is well. In some cases, however, physicians realize that their income is going to drop dramatically after that two-year point. Some of them panic and go out and find a new practice and contract that will provide a guaranteed salary once again for another two years. While this may seem like a clever way to keep a steady paycheck, physicians who jump ship every two years **NEVER GAIN THE MOMENTUM** of a long-term practice and their careers ultimately suffer.

PRODUCTION-BASED COMPENSATION

In recent decades, production-based compensation has become by far the most popular way to compensate physicians. While some smaller portion of compensation may stem from patient satisfaction or administrative duties, it is no exaggeration to say that **ALL** new physicians need to know how productivity-based compensation is calculated. While there are various production bases used, in general the physician is paid based on the work he or she performs or the revenue brought in by that work.

Production-based compensation can allow physicians to work the amount that they choose and be compensated accordingly. How it is calculated can change your total pay **DRAMATICALLY**, so know the production base the group uses, and be realistic about how much you will produce in your early years.

The most common methods of calculation are: **GROSS CHARGES**, **NET COLLECTIONS**, and **RELATIVE VALUE UNITS** (RVUs). The specific differences between these methods are described in detail on the next page. You may also encounter a combination method, where there is a combination of a fixed-base amount and a productivity amount. As the method is determined by the organization, specifics can vary from what is discussed here.

Gross Charges

In this method, gross charges (undiscounted rates) for the services provided by the physician are used to determine the physician's percentage of the total gross charges for the group. This percentage is multiplied by the total compensation pool for the group to determine the physician's compensation. The compensation pool is the total amount available to be distributed to all of the physicians. It is what remains of the total receipts after all of the non-physician expenses for the group have been paid. If this method is used to determine productivity, make sure that the fee schedule is reasonable and does not overly reward one procedure over another. If you do not perform a specific procedure, you could be shortchanged.

Net Collections

A second productivity model often used is the net collections method. Net collections represents actual money received for the services provided by the physician and calculates what portion those collections are out of the total collections for the practice. This percentage is multiplied by the total compensation pool for the group to determine the physician's compensation. This method can be a disadvantage for physicians who serve a higher Medicare and/or Medicaid payor mix as these payors tend to reimburse at lower amounts, and patients covered by these payors tend to be the ones who fill up your schedule first as you start a new practice.

Relative Value Units (RVUs)

RVUs represent a third common productivity measure and compensation payout. RVUs are standardized measures of work volume independent of the payment billed or received for the work. Most health systems compensate physicians based the number of work RVUs produced, multiplied by a conversion factor that is predetermined by the practice as a whole and based upon published survey information. The most commonly used survey information is published by **MEDICAL GROUP MANAGEMENT ASSOCIATION** (MGMA) and **AMERICAN MEDICAL GROUP ASSOCIATION** (AMGA). There are entire books written on RVUs, and you will likely want to do additional research on how they may affect your compensation in the future.

Sample Comparison of Production-Based Formulas

	DOCTOR A	DOCTOR B	GROUP TOTAL
Gross Charges	$1,100,000	$900,000	$10,000,000
Net Collections	$600,000	$400,000	$5,000,000
RVUs	5,263	4,486	
Gross Charges Percentage (doctor's percent of total)	11%	9%	
Net Collections Percentage (doctor's percent of total)	12%	8%	
Per RVU Conversion Factor	$45	$45	
Compensation Pool			$2,000,000

For Doctor A, let's look at how the compensation would vary depending on which productivity calculation was used.

DOCTOR A	
11% gross charges percentage x $2,000,000 compensation pool = **$220,000**	Gross Charges
12% net collections percentage x $2,000,000 compensation pool = **$240,000**	Net Collections
5,263 RVUs x $45 per RVU conversation factor = **$236,835**	RVUs

In Doctor A's case, the RVU method and the net collections method would provide about the same income, with the gross charges method falling $20,000 lower.

But for Doctor B, the story is different.

DOCTOR B	
9% gross charges percentage x $2,000,000 compensation pool = **$180,000**	Gross Charges
8% net collections percentage x $2,000,000 compensation pool = **$160,000**	Net Collections
4,486 RVUs x $45 per RVU conversation factor = **$201,870**	RVUs

In Doctor B's case, the RVU-based compensation would be more than $40,000 higher than the net collections method! Possibly this physician has a large number of Medicare clients and the group writes off more of the charges.

Generally an RVU-based formula is seen as **MORE EQUITABLE** than the other measures of productivity. It removes "fee schedule bias" and does not penalize those providers who have more Medicare and Medicaid patients. A practice may choose to reward those who bring in the cash; however, this tends to be less so these days.

Whatever productivity method is used, it is critical that you **UNDERSTAND** how it is calculated. As shown in the example above, it will make a significant difference to your compensation.

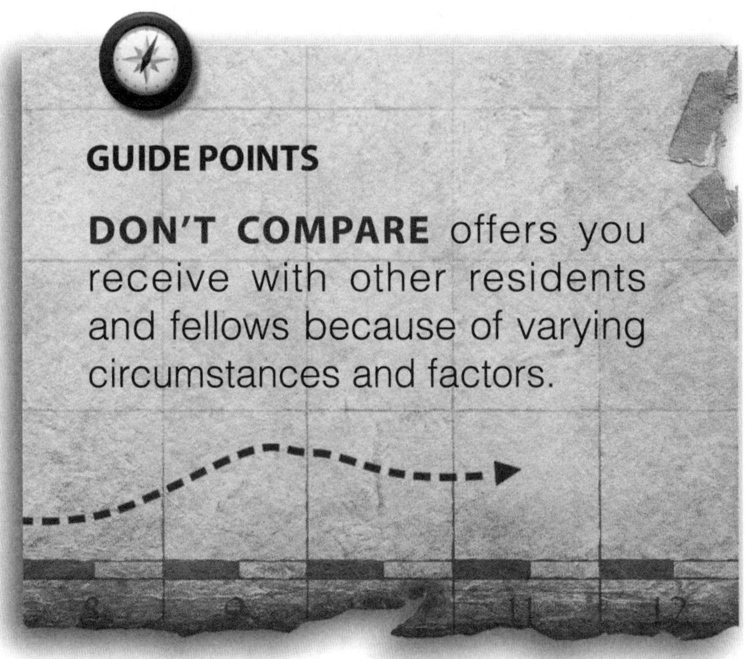

GUIDE POINTS
DON'T COMPARE offers you receive with other residents and fellows because of varying circumstances and factors.

GUIDE POINTS

When looking at compensation during interviews, consider asking these questions:

- Is there a signing bonus? What are its terms? Remember that because of inflation, money today is worth more than money later.
- What is the potential for compensation? Look at both near-term and long-term.
- How long does it take to build a full practice?
- What portion of the compensation is production-based? Does this match your work style?
- What is the compensation per RVU? How does it compare to the market as a whole? How often is this amount revisited?

(For more information about interview questions, see Stage 6.)

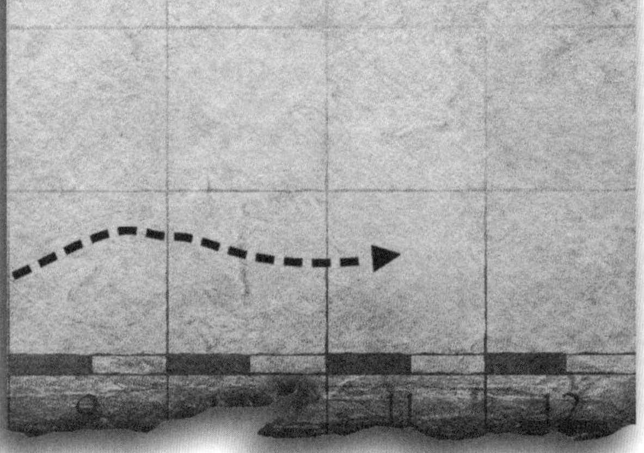

Benefits

While not as obvious as income, benefits can be the difference between a good offer and a great offer. Typical benefits that physicians may receive as part of their compensation package include:

- Pension and/or retirement plan such as 401(k). How much does the practice contribute, e.g., percentage of compensation? Six or nine % annual contributions may result in hundreds of thousands of dollars put aside for retirement if invested properly. Figure out what this amount will be when looking at total compensation. Private practices tend to provide much higher retirement contributions (10% to 15%).
- Relocation
- Paid time off
- Insurance — health, dental, life, disability
- Continuing medical education
- Dues, memberships and licenses
- Malpractice insurance. Depending on the specialty, this can be a large amount.
- Payroll taxes, such as Social Security and Medicare tax
- Automobile — Is a leased car provided by the group? A mileage allowance? Or just straight mileage expenses?
- Cell phone
- Other business expenses
- Temporary housing

In addition to benefits and production-based income, there are other, smaller compensation "pieces" to be aware of. Bonuses are sometimes paid based on **PATIENT SATISFACTION** or various **QUALITY MEASURES**. **IN-SERVICE OR MEETING ATTENDANCE PAY** rewards physicians for attending board meetings and taking on administrative duties within the practice. While common, these forms of pay are typically not a large part of the overall compensation.

Compensation and Geographical Location

Given current medical market conditions, compensation will continue to evolve and change, perhaps substantially more than in previous times. This information reflects current compensation trends based on data extracted from MGMA's *Physician Placement Starting Salary Survey: 2009 Report Based on 2008 Data*. (Visit mgma.com/surveys for more information.)

Depending on the location, population and other factors, there can be **SUBSTANTIAL DIFFERENCES** in physician compensation. Compensation surveys can be a good resource for information, but keep in mind that many of them tally all the participants across the country and provide an average salary.

When researching your specialty's average income, make sure to consider the different markets. In general, salaries are higher in the Midwest and the Southeast than in the Northeast and West Coast states. Income in the Northeast can be 20-30% less than Midwest salaries.

Rural opportunities can be some of the most attractive positions because compensation packages are up to 20-30% higher in rural and medium-sized communities. This is because hospitals and groups often offer signing bonuses, loan repayment and higher salaries.

In addition to looking at compensation data, keep in mind that the cost of living can vary widely across the United States. Major metropolitan areas are more expensive to live in than smaller metros or rural areas. The South and Midwest typically have a lower cost of living than the East or West. To compare specific cities, online calculators like **WWW.BESTPLACES.NET/COL** can show how the cost of living affects your salary.

Five major factors impact a physician's salary and compensation plan:

1. Geographic location
2. Demographic classification
3. Practice type
4. Practice ownership
5. Medical specialty

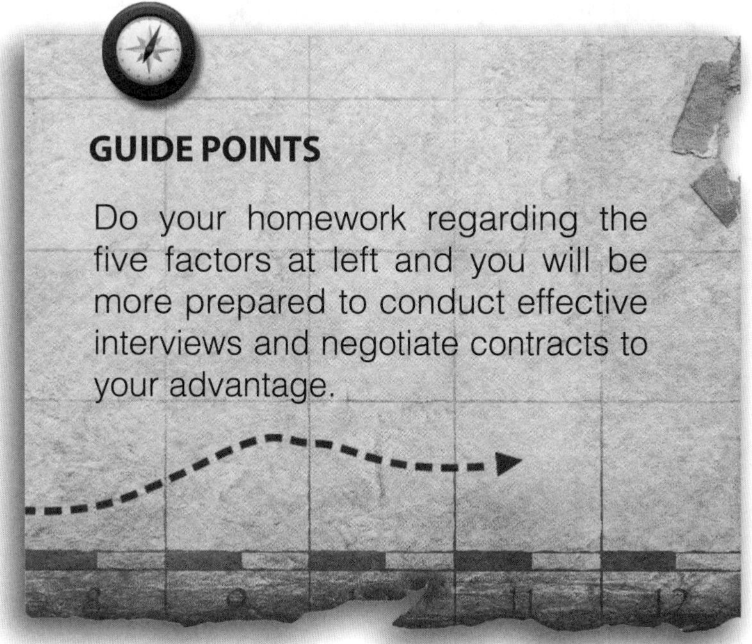

GUIDE POINTS
Do your homework regarding the five factors at left and you will be more prepared to conduct effective interviews and negotiate contracts to your advantage.

The information that follows provides an overview of each factor in terms of trends and resources for which to conduct your own research regarding your specific situation.

1. GEOGRAPHIC LOCATION

Geographic location can make a big difference in compensation levels, as pay can vary dramatically between regions.

Median, First Year Post Residency or Fellowship Compensation by Geographic Location of Placement

(Table 27)[7]	Eastern	Midwest	Southern	Western
Surgery: General	$275,000	$314,000	$300,000	$305,000

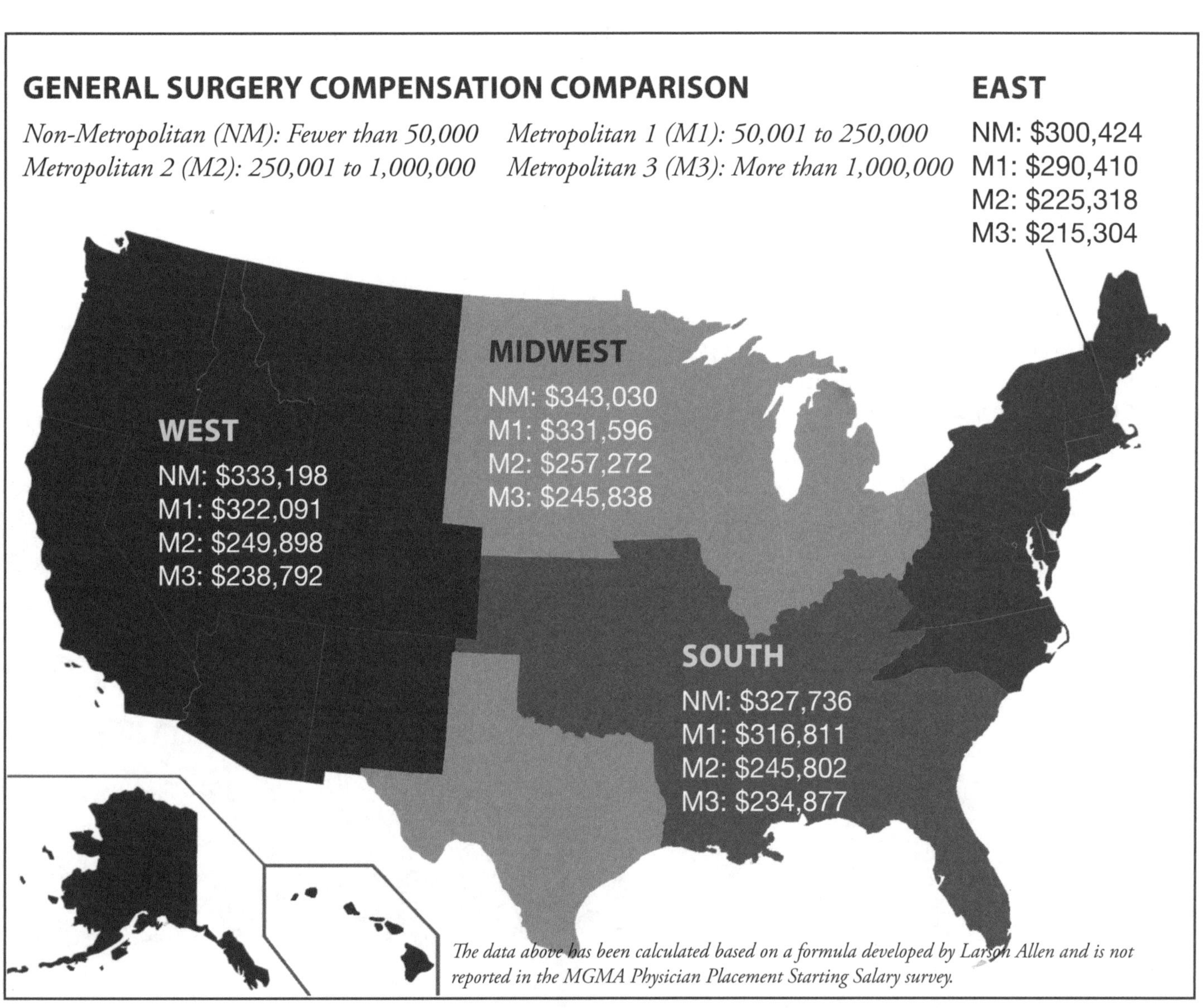

The data above has been calculated based on a formula developed by Larson Allen and is not reported in the MGMA Physician Placement Starting Salary survey.

Eastern

First-year physicians in the eastern United States are, almost with exception, paid the least of any geographic region. The difference is not particularly large in primary care; $10,000 to $15,000 less than the highest paid region, the southern U.S. For some specialties though, the difference can be huge. First-year cardiologists make $150,000 less (33% less) in the East than they make in the South. Other specialties where salaries are significantly lower in the East are dermatology, hematology/oncology, nephrology, ortho and general surgery, physiatry and pulmonary medicine.

Midwestern

The Midwest and South represent the highest paying regions overall for first-year physicians. While primary care doctors fare better in the South overall, many of the specialties do best in the Midwest. Primary care salaries run $5,000 to $20,000 less in the Midwest than the South for family practice, while internal medicine is roughly the same. Specialties that have the highest compensation in the Midwest include surgery (all types), dermatology, gastroenterology, nephrology, ophthalmology and rheumatology.

Southern

The South leads the regions in compensation in a number of areas. Family practice with OB, and OB/GYN doctors are paid $15,000 to $25,000 more than in the other parts of the U.S., while family practice without OB has a much smaller spread. Cardiologists of all types have starting salaries up to $150,000 higher in the South, with the West as the next highest region falling $80,000 behind. Otorhinolaryngology is also much higher in the South, $75,000 more than the East and $130,000 more than the West. Other specialties with higher pay in the South are emergency medicine, endocrinologists, hospitalists, neurology, physiatry, general psychiatry and urology.

Western

The West, along with the East, is notably lower in compensation. There are three specialties that have the highest compensation in the West: anesthesiology, ortho surgery for hands, and neonatal pediatrics. Overall the West runs about 10% higher than the East, but still lags behind the Midwest and the South.

2. DEMOGRAPHIC CLASSIFICATION

In general, as the **POPULATION** increases, the pay **DECREASES**.

Non-Metropolitan (NM): Fewer than 50,000

In virtually all categories, first-year compensation is highest in non-metropolitan areas, roughly 10% above the next highest region. There are a few specialties that are paid significantly more in non-metropolitan areas, namely gastroenterology, cardiology, and otorhinolaryngology. For these, the premium is up to 40% more for the rural areas. The only specialty in which the pay is noticeably less is diagnostic radiology.

Metropolitan 1 (M1): 50,001 to 250,000

The smaller metropolitan areas trail non-metropolitan areas for pay, but are ahead of larger metropolitan areas. The average pay is 8-10% less than the rural areas, and 5-7% higher than the 250,000 to 1,000,000 metropolitan classification.

Metropolitan 2 (M2): 250,001 to 1,000,000

This demographic category is more variable than the smaller populations, with higher pay than the largest metro areas in some specialties, and lower pay in others. On the whole, the compensation is comparable to the largest cities. Specific areas that have higher compensation than the 1+ million category are: cardiology, gastroenterology, specialty OB/GYN, pediatrics of all types, and radiology.

Metropolitan 3 (M3): More than 1,000,000

The largest metropolitan areas tend to have the lowest pay. There are virtually no categories in which these metro areas have the best compensation. There are several that beat out the 250,000 to 1,000,000 population centers, namely hematology/oncology, internal medicine, general OB/GYN, ortho surgery, and physiatry. In all cases, though, the difference is relatively small, roughly 5-10%.

3. PRACTICE TYPE

Physicians in single-specialty practices tend to earn less than those in other practices, while solo practices usually have the highest compensation levels.

Single Specialty

Single specialty has the highest pay in only one area, hematology/oncology. In general, pay in a single specialty practice is 5%-25% less than the market leader.

Multispecialty

Multispecialty practices tend to have the highest compensation in more specialized medicine, such as cardiology, neurology, ortho surgery and radiology. For these, the pay ranges from 5% to 35% higher than in single specialty. Overall, multispecialty compensation is similar to hospital department compensation.

Hospital Department Practice

These practices rarely have the lowest compensation, although it is not necessarily the highest. The areas in which hospital department practices have the highest compensation are anesthesiology, neurology, general pediatrics, psychiatry, pulmonary medicine, specialized surgery, and urology.

Solo Practice

Historically, solo practices have been well compensated. These days, though, they are becoming less common as current trends move toward larger groups. For those areas of medicine that still have sufficient survey respondents, the solo practice has the highest compensation levels, although typically only $5,000-$10,000 higher.

4. PRACTICE OWNERSHIP

Hospital-owned practices tend to have higher compensation than physician-owned practices, from 8% to 50% higher.

Hospital Owned

In general, first-year compensation is higher in hospital-owned practices as hospitals have a higher Medicare reimbursement, and also make money on ancillary services such as x-rays, labs and in-patient. For primary care, compensation varied from 8% to 17% higher at hospital-owned practices. In specialties the range is even greater, stretching from virtually even compensation levels in some specialties to as much as 63% higher in others. The greatest differences were in specialties such as surgery, cardiology and otorhinolaryngology.

Physician Owned

First-year compensation at physician-owned practices tended to be lower across the board, with only a couple of exceptions. Radiology and urgent care were the only categories in which the physician-owned practices paid more than the hospital-owned practices, with differences from 7% to 16%. However, the independent group may have higher earning potential for the physicians in the long run, and

GUIDE POINTS

Evaluating a Practice

Most residents have already selected a specialty and have already graduated as either an American or international graduate, and many have a predetermined area of the country or population size they would prefer. Given that, finding the right job with the right compensation will often require evaluating opportunities within the chosen specialty and area. Finding a well-run practice will help ensure that the compensation will be the best that it can be in the situation. Here are some questions to consider:

- Is the practice or health system stable? Stable is preferable, but if they are growing, some instability is expected.
- What is its business outlook? Do they have a plan to expand? Or are they in a solid niche?
- Is the practice or the system a market leader?
- Are the current physicians busy? If so, that's good, but make sure they're not "too busy," indicating there could be issues.
- How is the leadership structured? Is the practice run by physicians or non-physicians?
- Are there administrative expectations for the doctors?

they may also provide the physician with an opportunity to invest in other areas related to the medical practice including the medical office building, imaging equipment or ambulatory surgery centers.

5. SPECIALTY

In general, specialists have higher compensation than primary care physicians. Primary care physicians, which includes family practice, internal medicine, pediatrics and geriatrics, has a median range of $132,000 to $160,000. Specialists start there and go up to $400,000 depending on the specialty. The highest compensation goes to cardiology, oncology, OB/GYN maternal and fetal medicine, ortho surgery, pulmonary medicine, radiology, surgery of all types, and urology.

MEDICAL GROUP MANAGEMENT ASSOCIATION SURVEY REPORT DATA[7]

MGMA Specialty Names	Total Physicians Count*	Median, First Year Post Residency or Fellowship Compensation (table 13)
Cardiology: Electrophysiology	5	$290,000
Cardiology: Invasive	13	$300,000
Cardiology: Inv-Intvl	17	$350,000
Cardiology: Noninvasive	11	$280,000
Dermatology	15	$230,000
Emergency Medicine	39	$216,000
Endocrinology/Metabolism	10	$180,000
Family Practice (w/o OB)	169	$149,000
Gastroenterology	26	$245,000
Hematology/Oncology	17	$325,000
Infectious Disease	13	$180,000
Internal Medicine: General	71	$150,000
Internal Medicine : Pediatrics	9	$150,000
OBGYN: Maternal Fetal Medicine	5	$300,000
Obstetrics Gynecology: General	59	$210,000
Orthopedic Surgery: General	28	$375,000
Otolaryngology (Otorhinolaryngology)	18	$180,000
Pediatrics: General	66	$125,000
Rheumatology	8	$172,500
Surgery: General	34	$250,000
Urology	22	$250,000

**Total Physician Count=the total number of placements represented in a particular line of a particular table; sample size*

Using the Data

In examining the data presented in the report, practice administrators and other report users should consider the following:

1. What is the difference between your facility's data and the report median (or mean, if appropriate)?

2. By what methods can the compensation indicator be internally and/or externally changed or controlled?

3. How should your medical group measure performance for this indicator? Do your systems and processes allow for the appropriate assessment of the compensation indicator?

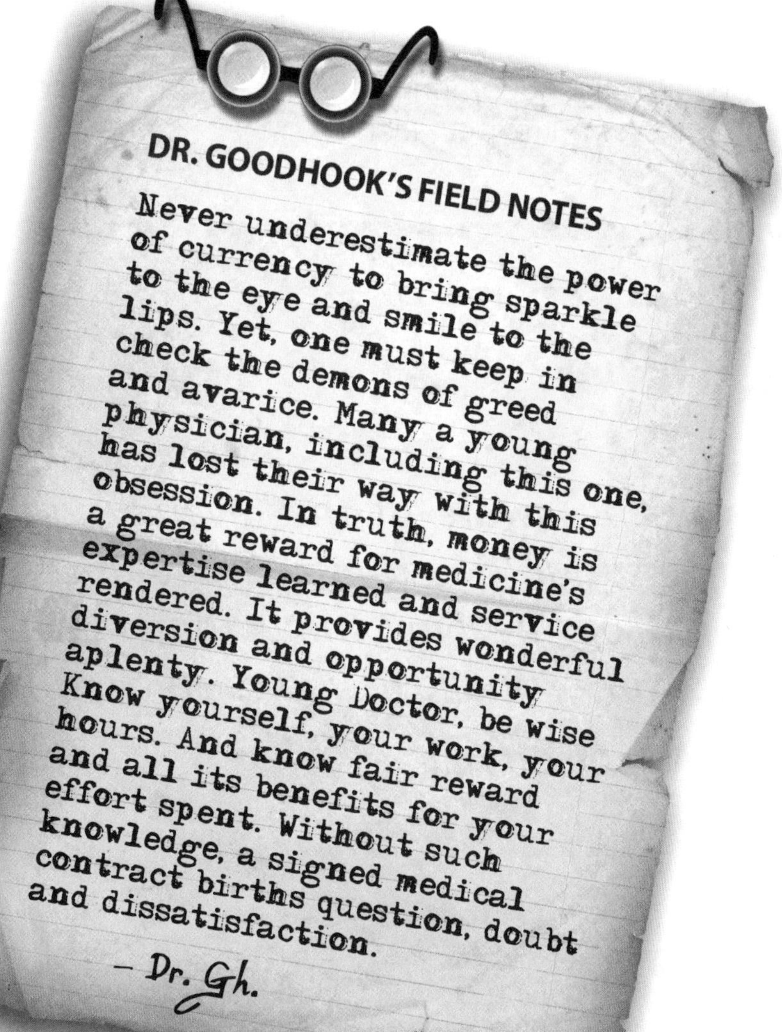

DR. GOODHOOK'S FIELD NOTES
Never underestimate the power of currency to bring sparkle to the eye and smile to the lips. Yet, one must keep in check the demons of greed and avarice. Many a young physician, including this one, has lost their way with this obsession. In truth, money is a great reward for medicine's expertise learned and service rendered. It provides wonderful diversion and opportunity aplenty. Young Doctor, be wise Know yourself, your work, your hours. And know fair reward and all its benefits for your effort spent. Without such knowledge, a signed medical contract births question, doubt and dissatisfaction.
– Dr. Gh.

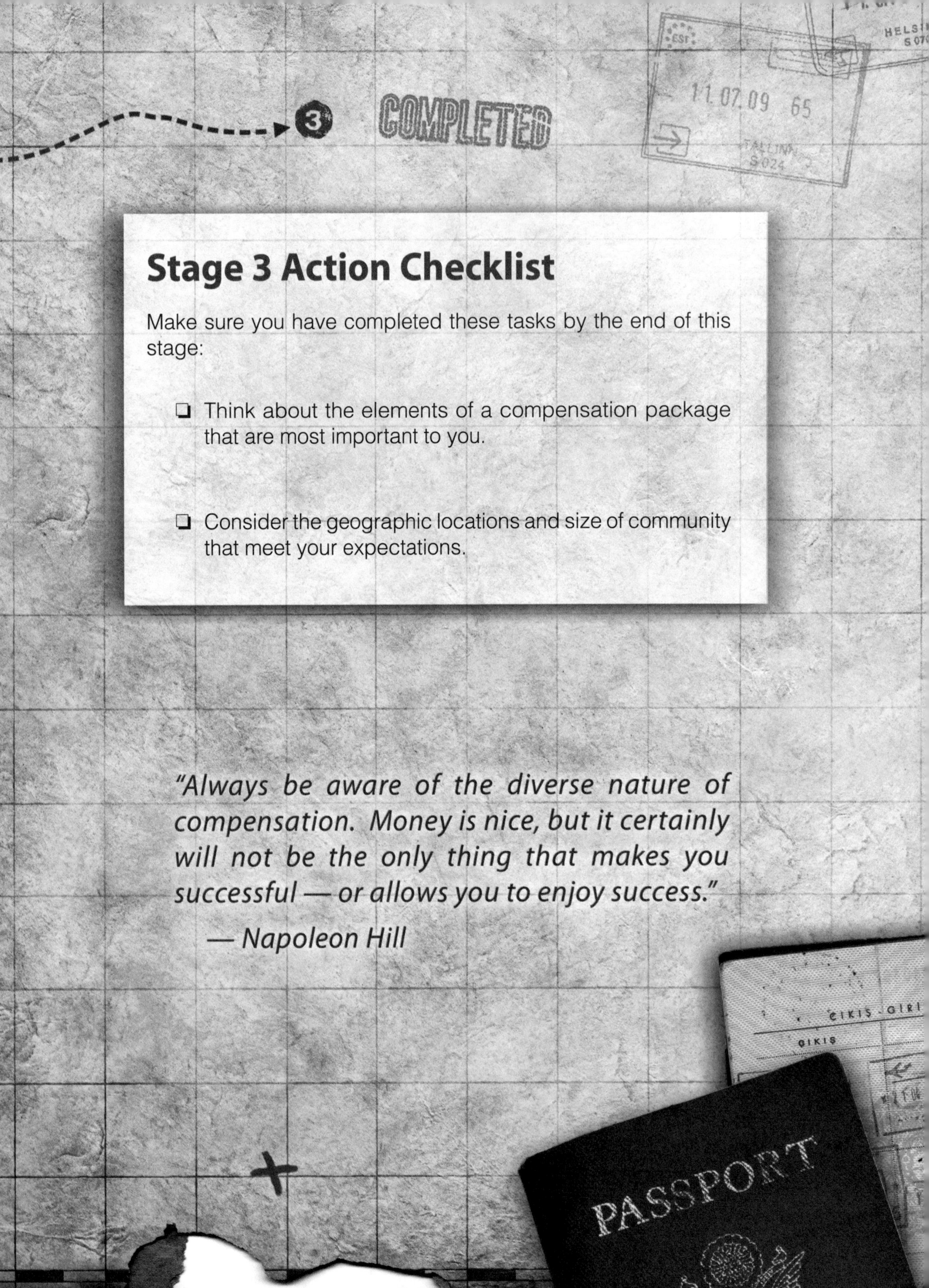

Stage 3 Action Checklist

Make sure you have completed these tasks by the end of this stage:

- ❑ Think about the elements of a compensation package that are most important to you.
- ❑ Consider the geographic locations and size of community that meet your expectations.

"Always be aware of the diverse nature of compensation. Money is nice, but it certainly will not be the only thing that makes you successful — or allows you to enjoy success."

— Napoleon Hill

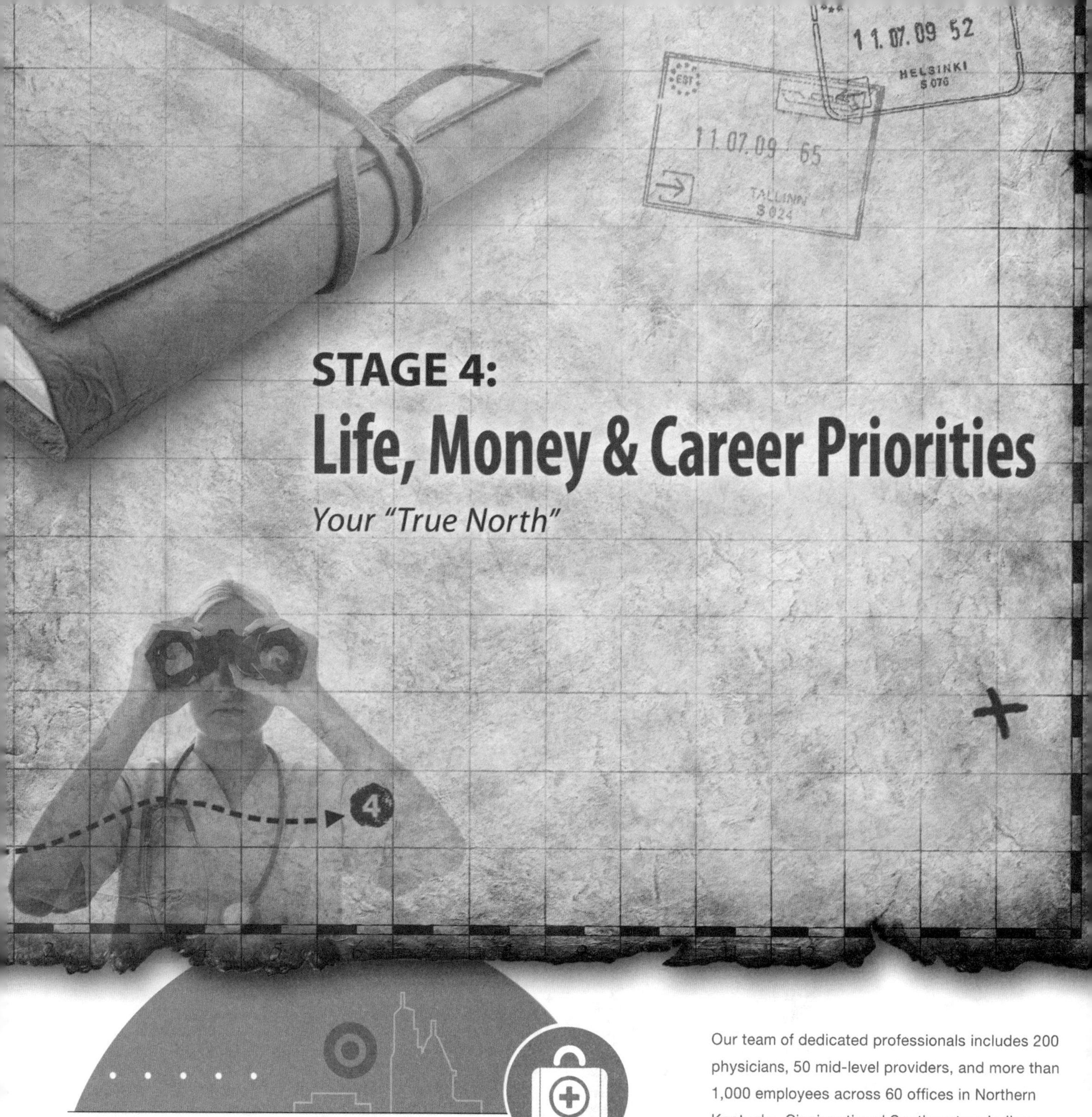

STAGE 4:
Life, Money & Career Priorities

Your "True North"

Your Life Guide:

Brian J. Knabe, M.D., CMP™, FAAFP

Financial Advisor, Savant Capital Management, Inc.
Clinical Assistant Professor, University of Illinois Department of Family Medicine
M.D., University of Illinois College of Medicine, Family Practice Residency; B.S., Marquette University

Brian Knabe, M.D., has a firsthand understanding of the needs of physicians. He practiced family medicine for 14 years, caring for thousands of patients and delivering hundreds of babies. He draws upon his medical and teaching experience while developing comprehensive planning, investment, and tax strategies for professionals - especially doctors. As an Investment Advisor with Savant, he manages client portfolios worth more than $120 million - helping clients work toward the financial stability and security they seek. He enjoys his own family of ten children and outdoor activities.

Your Life Guide:

Michelle Filicicchia, CPLP, RCC

President, Raising The Bar Services
Adjunct Faculty, Roosevelt University, Human Performance Technology
M.Ed., University of Minnesota

Michelle Filicicchia's expertise in learning and performance spans 20 years, focusing on customer satisfaction, communication, leadership, team dynamics, performance improvement, instructional design, and business coaching. Her work has touched the lives of 150,000 employees worldwide and helped to improve revenues for clients by an estimated $40 million. Her mission is to help companies and individuals achieve success by guiding them through an enriching process of defining their life purpose, vision (life destiny), values, priorities, and goals, which helps them to make decisions that provide direction and achieve results. Michelle likes to travel, sing and take walks with her dachshund.

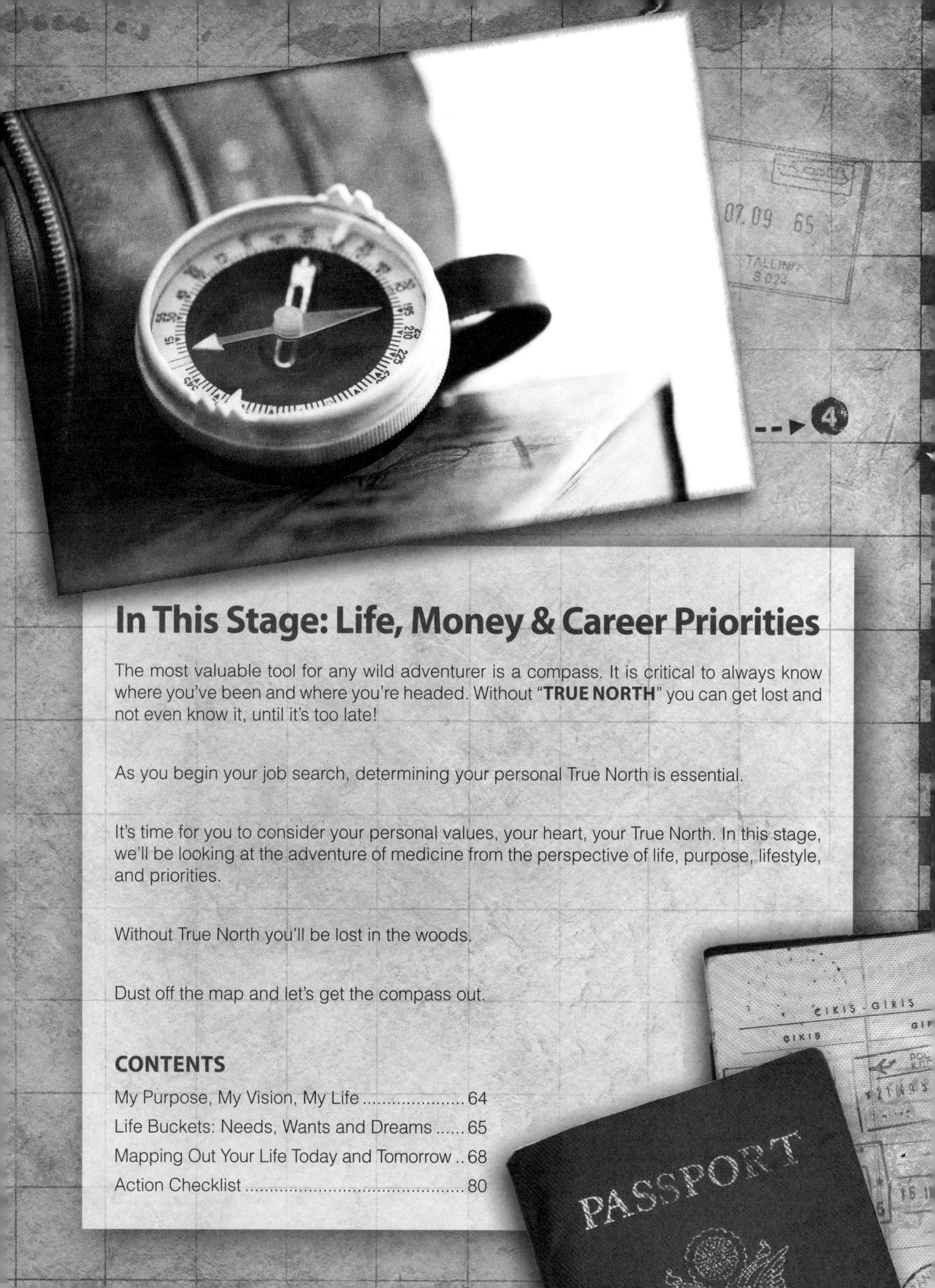

In This Stage: Life, Money & Career Priorities

The most valuable tool for any wild adventurer is a compass. It is critical to always know where you've been and where you're headed. Without "**TRUE NORTH**" you can get lost and not even know it, until it's too late!

As you begin your job search, determining your personal True North is essential.

It's time for you to consider your personal values, your heart, your True North. In this stage, we'll be looking at the adventure of medicine from the perspective of life, purpose, lifestyle, and priorities.

Without True North you'll be lost in the woods.

Dust off the map and let's get the compass out.

CONTENTS

TRAILBLAZERS

"After I graduated from Residency I thought I finally made it — I'm finally a physician. Looking back, ten years later, it took so much out of me becoming a physician that I lost my own identify. I wish I knew now what I didn't know then — although it's an achievement to have earned the white coat, it's meaningless if you lose yourself along the way."

"I wish I had a plan coming out of residency that helped me to make decisions about types of jobs that would best fit **MY LIFE AND CAREER PRIORITIES**."

"I wish I hadn't bought the **BRAND-NEW MERCEDES** and a million-dollar house right out of residency because now I'm **STUCK WITH DEBT** I can't get out of."

"I'm on my **THIRD JOB IN FIVE YEARS**, and if I had done a better job knowing what I wanted in the first place, I wouldn't have gotten myself into this situation."

"I thought I wanted to live in Chicago, a big metropolitan area. Boy, did I make a **MISTAKE** — I didn't realize my commute would be two hours per day."

My Purpose, My Vision, My Life

We've covered a lot of ground thus far. By completing a job search timeline and gaining knowledge about medical market conditions and compensation, your journey takes a detour with a focus on **YOU** — specifically your life's values, purpose and priorities.

Exploring, refining, and articulating what matters most to you will serve you well throughout the search process and beyond. The key is to spend some time alone with an uncluttered mind and **WRITE THESE THINGS DOWN**. The action of writing serves the purpose of taking ideas and turning them into reality. Plus, this information gives you a reference point as you share your dreams and goals with others, interview for jobs and begin working as a practicing physician. Decision making becomes easier when you know what you want, and in the end, you save time and energy and gain focus and clarity.

This **VERY IMPORTANT** stage contains several exercises that help you:

- Define your life buckets in the form of needs, wants and dreams.
- Articulate core values that direct your path.
- Create your life-purpose statement that explains why you practice medicine and what you hope to accomplish.
- Identify your priorities, which pertain to things like: where you want to live, quality of life issues, ideas around compensation, what type of practice setting suits you most, and your preferred work environment.

The ultimate outcome of this stage is to equip you with self-knowledge that will help you make a decision that results in not only a job you love, but a life that has meaning and purpose.

Life Buckets: Needs, Wants and Dreams

A doctor graduating from residency and preparing to start in his or her first position as a practicing physician has important decisions to make regarding financial priorities. The new graduate has usually spent 11 or more years in school and training since high school, and many personal and professional aspects of life have been delayed or put on hold as life has been consumed with studies and work. Gratification has been delayed, and new graduates often go on a **SPENDING SPREE** — buying a big house, a new expensive car, a grand vacation, etc. It is very important at this stage to set priorities for spending, saving and paying down debt. One way to start setting these priorities appropriately is to recognize the difference between needs, wants and dreams. It is helpful to identify expenditures that fit in the following "buckets": basic **NEEDS**, **WANTS** driven by lifestyle preferences, and **DREAMS** related to aspirations, the ideal state or situation.

NEEDS

This bucket includes those items that are absolutely necessary. These expenditures will be made independent of the level of income. Examples include basic housing, clothing, food, transportation and utility bills. Payment on student loans and retirement savings might also be included here. You would continue to spend on these items, even if you were running out of money.

WANTS

Items in this bucket are not absolutely necessary, but life would be quite boring without them. More discretion is involved in determining which items are located here. A modest vacation, eating out on occasion, a new car every few years, and a home in a prestigious neighborhood might be included. You could cut back on items in this bucket, but you would prefer not to do so.

DREAMS

Items in this bucket are certainly not necessary to live a happy and fulfilling life. Dreams, both realistic and over the top, would be included here. Examples include a sports car, a second home or expensive jewelry.

Priorities are unique and different for each individual. For example, where would you put charitable contributions? What about sending your children to a private school? A sailboat might be in the Wants bucket for one person, but in the Dreams bucket for another. These buckets will most likely change over time based on life's experiences, people you meet, etc. At this juncture for you as a resident, it's an appropriate time to be thinking these through **BEFORE TAKING ACTION**, especially the Wants and Dreams bucket.

NEEDS

Item	When

WANTS

Item	When

DREAMS

Item	When

YOUR NEEDS, WANTS AND DREAMS

What are your needs, wants and dreams? Use the list below as inspiration and fill in each bucket. Feel free to add items that aren't on the list. This is your list so make it relevant to your unique situation. Identify a timeframe to experience or acquire each item.

- Accelerated debt repayment
- Annual vacations
- Basic housing (rent or own)
- Basic transportation
- Boat/motorcycle
- Books
- Cash reserves
- Cell phone
- Charitable contributions/tithing
- College funds for children
- Designer clothes/accessories
- Eating out (moderately priced)
- Exclusive club memberships
- Exclusive neighborhood
- Fine dining
- Fine jewelry
- Food and clothing
- Hobbies/interests
- International travel
- Investments
- Live on the water/by mountains
- Luxury car (e.g., Mercedes)
- Luxury house/high-rise condo
- New car (moderately priced)
- New laptop/iPad
- Pets
- Private school for children
- Retirement savings
- Season tickets (e.g., sports)
- Student loan repayment
- Utility bills
- Vacation home
- Work part-time vs. full-time

REFLECTION

What connections do you see between money and the things you think will bring you happiness and contentment?

What can you really afford? Do you know?

Do you know how much the items you listed in the bucket exercise really cost? What sacrifices are you willing to make for each of these items?

GUIDE POINTS

Financial Next Steps

To understand budgets, discretionary income, and how to invest, study Stage 9.

1. Make sure that your chosen position will pay for the items in your Needs bucket. Remember, these are expenses that are required — you must pay for them.
2. You should also ensure you make enough to pay for the Wants bucket. You can live without these items, and you can give these things up temporarily if necessary. But life will be pretty boring if you can't have these items over an extended period of time.
3. Beyond these points, make sure that you manage your debt (paying off and then avoiding "bad debt"), live within your means, and make required payments on your loans.
4. As a simple rule of thumb, save 10% of your income for retirement if you would like to retire at a traditional age. Save 20% of your income if you would like to become financially independent (and have an option to retire) earlier.
5. Following these guidelines, you can be "financially successful" while earning $125,000 per year or $500,000 per year. **YOU WILL BE MOST HAPPY** if you meet these requirements, and also find a position that is in line with your values, interests, and lifestyle expectations.

Mapping Out Your Life Today and Tomorrow

Trying to make a career decision and live life without discovering and prioritizing your **VALUES**, and **PURPOSE** is comparable to you trying to pass your boards without a studying for them — very risky. Most people react to life's circumstances and situations without intentional thought and action related to these items based on their previous habits (pattern of behavior).

As new circumstances arise, your thoughts will impede your actions, and your actions will either have positive or negative consequences. As you move into unchartered waters in your career search and first opportunity you will be making decisions that will impact your life and career. In this chapter, learn how prepare yourself to make good decisions by learning three critical, life-defining, and life-directing elements: **CORE VALUES, LIFE PURPOSE, AND LIFE AND WORK PRIORITIES.**

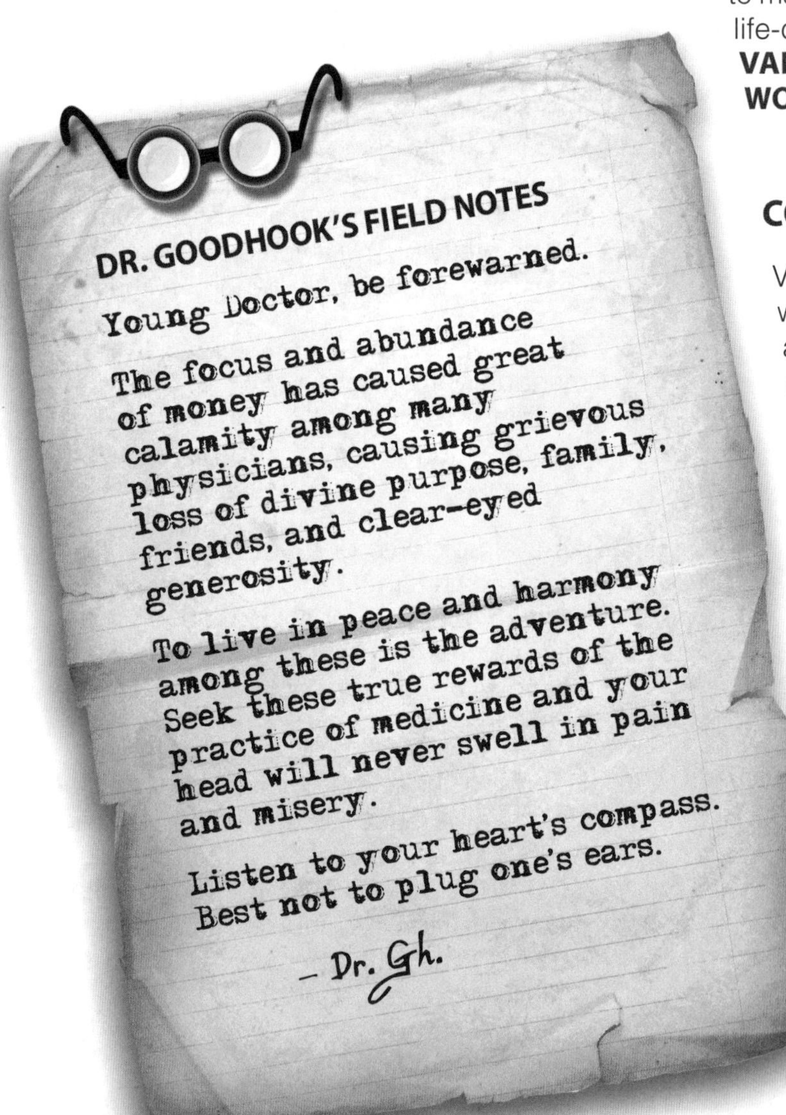
DR. GOODHOOK'S FIELD NOTES

Young Doctor, be forewarned.

The focus and abundance of money has caused great calamity among many physicians, causing grievous loss of divine purpose, family, friends, and clear-eyed generosity.

To live in peace and harmony among these is the adventure. Seek these true rewards of the practice of medicine and your head will never swell in pain and misery.

Listen to your heart's compass. Best not to plug one's ears.

– Dr. Gh.

CORE VALUES

Values represent our internal compass, which guides our actions and behavior. They are that part of us that is "us." People are naturally inclined and eager to take action that aligns with what they value the most. The amount of time and effort you dedicate to a certain activity should be an indication of how much you value that activity or end result. Conflicts in life can be traced back to unshared value systems. Values shape beliefs. We share our value system through our attitude, behavior, work habits and performance.

Articulating your values and integrating them into your career is vital to a fulfilling and successful livelihood. When you make decisions based on your personal values, you feel **STRONGER, HAPPIER AND BALANCED**. After all, your values are those things that, when honored, make you feel good about yourself. In addition, when you are clear about and committed to your values, other people who have the same values are much more attracted and committed to you. Remember: like attracts like.

VALUES EXERCISE

Since values represent core beliefs followed by thoughts and actions, first record your core values in the chart below. Use the list below as a starting point, and feel free to add your own. Be completely honest with yourself and don't worry about what someone else may think. Next, for each value, write down how it plays out in your life and in your career. If you feel comfortable, ask your spouse or significant other (if applicable) to complete this exercise themselves and see where your responses align or differ.

CORE VALUE	HOW IT PLAYS OUT IN LIFE	HOW IT PLAYS OUT IN CAREER
Example: Determination	*Overcame serious sports injury — went through six months of rehab*	*Took MCAT three times — never gave up*

Values

Achievement
Acknowledgement
Advancement
Adventure
Appreciation
Artistic expression
Authenticity
Autonomy
Balance
Beauty
Belonging
Boldness
Caring
Challenging
Collaboration
Commitment
Communication
Community
Compassion
Competition
Contentment
Contribution/giving
Control
Cooperation
Courage
Creativity
Decisiveness
Determination
Devotion
Dignity
Direct
Discipline
Efficiency
Energy
Enjoyment
Enthusiasm
Equality
Excellence
Expertise
Exploration
Faith
Fast-paced
Flexibility
Focus
Freedom
Friendship
Fun
Generosity
Gratitude
Harmony
Healing
Health/well-being
Helping
Honesty
Hope
Humanitarianism
Humility
Humor
Independence
Influence
Integrity
Intellectual status
Justice
Kindness
Knowledge
Leadership
Listening
Love/loving
Loyalty
Mental stimulation
Money/wealth
Openness
Optimistic
Organization
Originality
Participation
Partnership
Passion
Peace
Perseverance
Power/authority
Precision
Productivity
Public service
Recognition
Resiliency
Respect
Risk/risk-taking
Sacrifice
Security
Self-confidence
Sensuality
Serenity
Silence
Spirituality
Spontaneity
Stability
Success
Tolerance
Trustworthy
Truth
Variety
Unity
Wholeness
Winning

Reflection

Why are these values important to you? List three to five reasons.

LIFE-PURPOSE STATEMENT

Some of this material was inspired by The Path: Creating Your Mission Statement for Work and for Life *by Laurie Beth Jones.*

Some individuals wander around for years until they stumble upon a job or life circumstance that brings everything into focus. Many never find their voice or purpose on this earth, and as a result, much time and energy is wasted.

You might be thinking that your life purpose has already been defined. For example: "My life purpose is to practice medicine." This is a simple, well-stated purpose but it doesn't describe the reason and results relative to practicing medicine.

You won't need weeks or months to complete your life-purpose statement. In fact, follow three simple steps and you will be able to develop a strong, relevant statement in less than two hours. You may spend time tweaking your life-purpose statement over time; however, the heavy-thinking, time-consuming part should be behind you.

An effective life-purpose statement is interchangeable for both your personal and professional life. Creating a life-purpose statement is one of the best ways to ensure that life and career decisions align with one another.

What a Life-Purpose Statement Is

A strong life-purpose statement contains a concise and clear explanation for an organization or individual that:

- Explains why you exist (core purpose)
- Provides a sense of direction
- Guides decision making
- Explains the value provided by your actions and/or services
- Identifies stakeholders, key customers
- Guides the actions of a company and/or individual

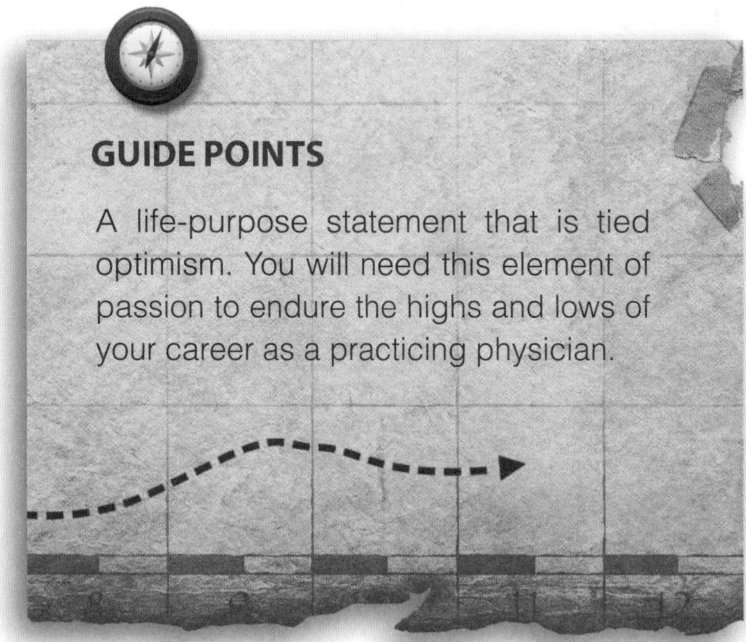

GUIDE POINTS

A life-purpose statement that is tied optimism. You will need this element of passion to endure the highs and lows of your career as a practicing physician.

- Is not about money or something that you can buy

Elements of a Life-Purpose Statement

- Preferably one sentence in length, not more than two
- Simple language and easily understood by those who read it
- Contains words that you buy into
- Applicable for your personal and professional life
- Able to be recited from memory

Examples of a Life-Purpose Statement

As a primary care physician, my purpose is to heal the sick, influence healthy life styles, and serve the low income population in the inner city of Chicago that positively impacts the community where my patients live.

As a cardiologist, my life purpose is to eradicate heart disease through research and utilizing leading edge technologies and treatments which help my patients live long and productive lives.

LIFE-PURPOSE EXERCISE

1. Identify two or three compelling action verbs (see list on opposite page for ideas) that describe the "what" of your mission. It answers the question: What do you do?
2. Describe the audience that you will be serving (e.g., patients, low-income, rural, terminally ill, etc.)
3. Describe the "why" of your actions. Complete the sentence that defines the outcomes of your actions in the context of your life and career.
4. Reread it and recite it out loud three times.
5. Share your life-purpose statement with your spouse, significant other, family members, friends or colleagues. Get their feedback on whether or not this purpose matches their perception and understanding of your interests, gifts and passions.
6. You may want to create your life-purpose statement together with your spouse or significant other.

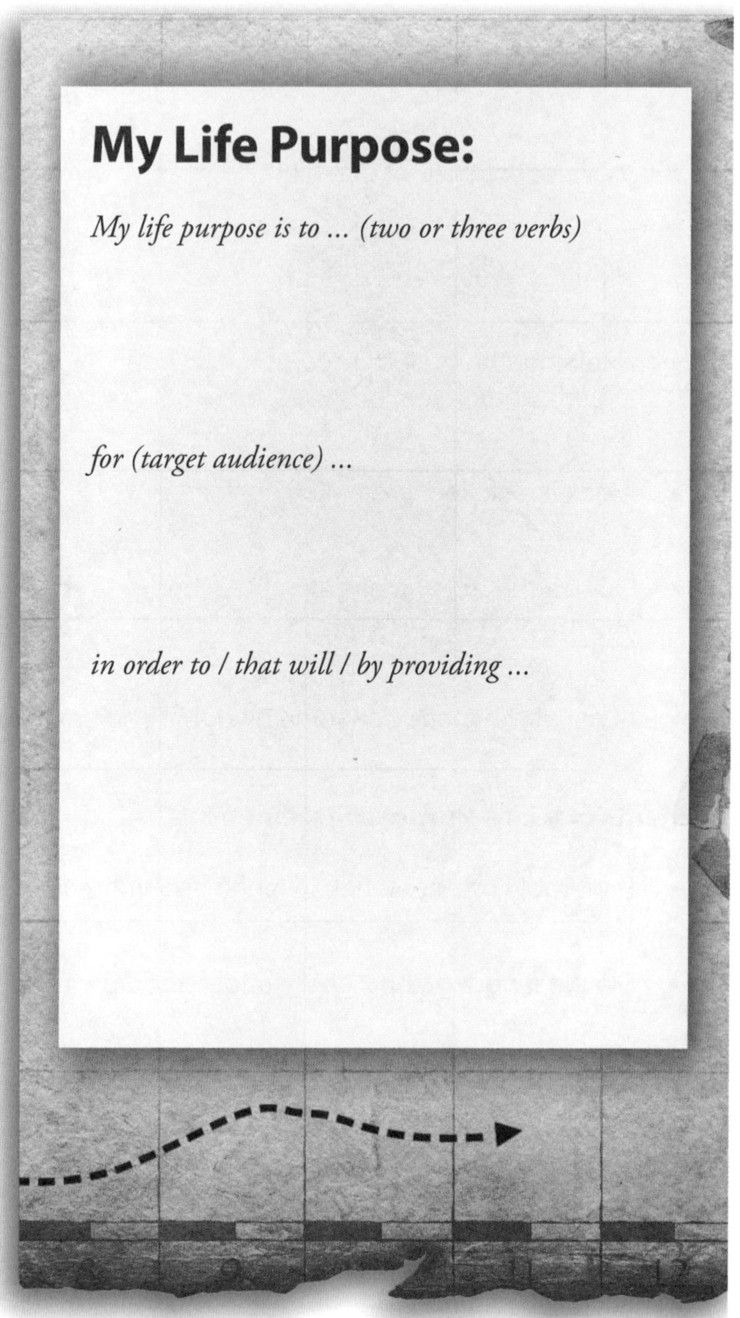

My Life Purpose:
My life purpose is to ... (two or three verbs)
for (target audience) ...
in order to / that will / by providing ...

Action Verbs

Acknowledge	Confer	Divide	Influence	Obtain	Reconstruct
Administer	Consolidate	Eradicate	Inform	Open	Rectify
Advise	Construct	Establish	Initiate	Operate	Register
Affirm	Consult	Evaluate	Inspire	Originate	Reject
Align	Contact	Examine	Instruct	Perform	Remove
Alleviate	Control	Expedite	Integrate	Persuade	Report
Analyze	Convert	Explore	Interpret	Plan	Represent
Assemble	Convince	Extend	Investigate	Practice	Research
Assess	Coordinate	Facilitate	Lead	Present	Review
Classify	Correct	Feed	Measure	Procure	Revise
Coach	Create	Formulate	Mentor	Produce	Save
Collaborate	Design	Gather	Monitor	Project	Scan
Communicate	Determine	Give	Motivate	Prove	Screen
Compile	Develop	Guide	Multiply	Quantify	Serve
Compose	Direct	Heal	Negotiate	Recommend	Supply
Conduct	Discover	Implement	Observe	Reconcile	Support

Reflection

On a scale from 1 to 10 (low to high), how would you rate the effectiveness of your life-purpose statement?

Low									High
1	2	3	4	5	6	7	8	9	10

How does it feel when you say your life-purpose statement?

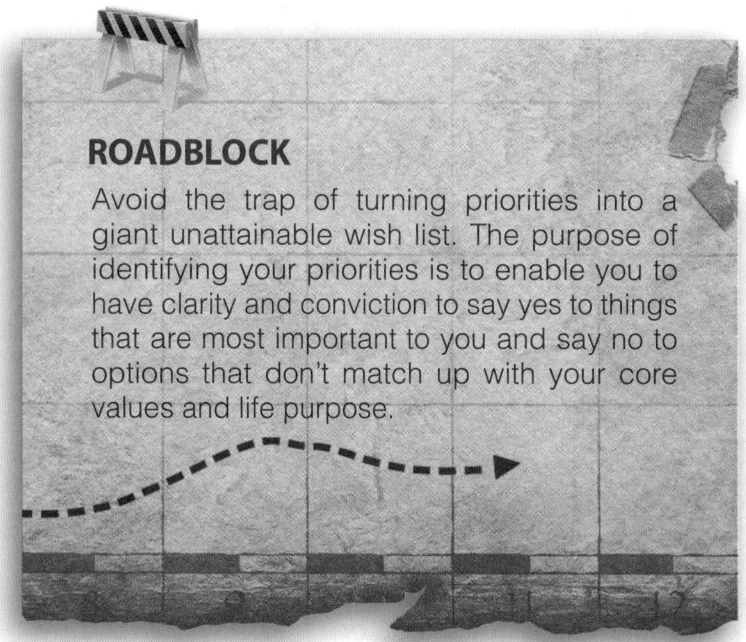

ROADBLOCK

Avoid the trap of turning priorities into a giant unattainable wish list. The purpose of identifying your priorities is to enable you to have clarity and conviction to say yes to things that are most important to you and say no to options that don't match up with your core values and life purpose.

LIFE AND WORK PRIORITIES

Defining priorities prepares you to effectively search for job opportunities and interview for positions with confidence, because you know and can articulate what you want in a **POSITIVE**, **POLISHED** fashion.

PRIORITIES EXERCISE

The following exercises will guide you through the process of establishing and articulating life and work priorities. Work through the following prompts to help you solidify your needs, wants and expectations. With the content provided in Stage 2 (market trends and trials) and Stage 3 (compensation packages), you have access to information that will help you make decisions in these important areas.

GEOGRAPHIC LOCATION

Location represents an important consideration for many physicians. If you are married or in a serious relationship or have children, this category becomes even more critical from a life and lifestyle perspective.

Items to Consider	Your Thoughts	
Current place of residence		
Plans to move to a different location?	❑ Yes ❑ No	
If yes, do you know where?	❑ Yes: ______________________ ❑ Not sure	
If you're not sure, rank the regions you're considering in order of priority. Consider any family ties or spouse requirements.	Eastern ____ Southern ____ Midwestern ____ Western ____	
What size of community would you like to live in? Rank from 1 (most preferred) to 5 (least preferred).	Rural ____ Non-metropolitan (fewer than 50,000) ____ Metropolitan 1 (50,001 to 250,000; e.g., Boise, Kansas City) ____ Metropolitan 2 (250,001 to 1,000,000; e.g., Boston, Nashville) ____ Metropolitan 3 (more than 1,000,000; e.g., Chicago, San Diego) ____	
Place a check by any other geographic features that are important to you.	❑ Warm climate ❑ Cold climate ❑ Seasonal climate ❑ By the water ❑ Near mountains	❑ Wide open spaces ❑ Right in the middle of everything ❑ Other: ❑ Other: ❑ Other:
What challenges or roadblocks might you encounter with the location decision?		

QUALITY OF LIFE

Quality of life represents personal preferences and priorities related to lifestyle (wants and dreams buckets).

Items to Consider	Your Thoughts
What amenities are important to you?	❑ Access to entertainment (e.g., movie theaters) ❑ Access to fine arts (e.g., museums, opera) ❑ Athletic opportunities (e.g., golf courses, gym) ❑ Diverse dining options ❑ Employment options for spouse/significant other ❑ Extracurricular opportunities for children (e.g., sports leagues, music classes) ❑ Good schools for children ❑ Good shopping ❑ Outdoor recreation opportunities (e.g., parks, camping) ❑ Religious opportunities (e.g., church, synagogue, mosque) ❑ Personal services (e.g., spas, salons) ❑ Social/nightlife options (e.g., festivals, clubs) ❑ Other: ❑ Other: ❑ Other:
How would you prefer to commute to work?	❑ Drive ❑ Walk ❑ Public transportation ❑ Other:
What is your maximum acceptable commute time?	❑ Less than 15 minutes ❑ 15-30 minutes ❑ 31-60 minutes ❑ More than 60 minutes

COMPENSATION PLAN

As discussed in Stage 3, compensation is comprised of base salary, productivity-based output, benefits and bonuses. In Stage 7, you will have an opportunity to compare the compensation plans of the offers you receive. In this space, you can jot down your hopes and expectations for these areas, realizing that you may have to compromise in some areas.

Items to Consider	**Your Thoughts**
Base salary (first year)	
Signing bonus	
Productivity compensation (net collections, gross charges, RVUs)	
Benefits • Paid time off	
• Relocation package	
• Pension and/or retirement plan such as 401(k)	
• Health insurance (single vs. family)	
• Dental insurance	
• Life insurance	
• Disability insurance	
• Continuing medical education (CMEs)	
• Reimbursement of dues, memberships and licenses	
• Malpractice insurance, including tail coverage upon termination of employment	
• Automobile allowance	
• Cell phone allowance	
• Other business expenses	
Non-compete agreement	
Term of employment	

PRACTICE SETTING

Place a check next to the practice settings you are most interested in pursuing, and note the reasons why and the pros and cons.

Practice Type	Why?	Pros	Cons
❑ Partner/shareholder in a single- or multi-specialty group			
❑ Employed position in a single- or multi-specialty group			
❑ Solo Practice			
❑ Academic/teaching hospital			
❑ Independent contractor			
❑ Locum Tenens (substitute physician)			
❑ Hospital employee			
❑ Other			

WORK ENVIRONMENT

The environment in which you spend a majority of your time can impact your attitude, motivation, quality of life, work relationships, and more. Check off the environmental descriptors that are most important to you, and note the reasons why.

Descriptors	Why
❑ Autonomy — working primarily by yourself	
❑ Collaboration — working and making decisions with other people	
❑ Alignment — core values aligned with employer and colleagues	
❑ Quality — excellent patient care and safety	
❑ High-tech — access to advanced technology and equipment	
❑ Fun — enjoyable place to work	
❑ Collegiality — positive relationships among administrators, physicians, and staff	
❑ Advancement — opportunities to climb the ladder	
❑ Other:	
❑ Other:	

DAILY WORK

Now we get into the nitty gritty of day-to-day work. For each item listed below, note your preferences and why.

Items to Consider	Your Preferences
Clinical work	
Patient mix	
Support staff	
Schedule (hours, on-call, part-time or full-time)	
Pace of work (frantic or relaxed, number of patients per day)	
Activities in the average work day	
Hospital rounds	
Jeopardy call schedule	
Role of hospitalist	
Electronic medical records (coding)	

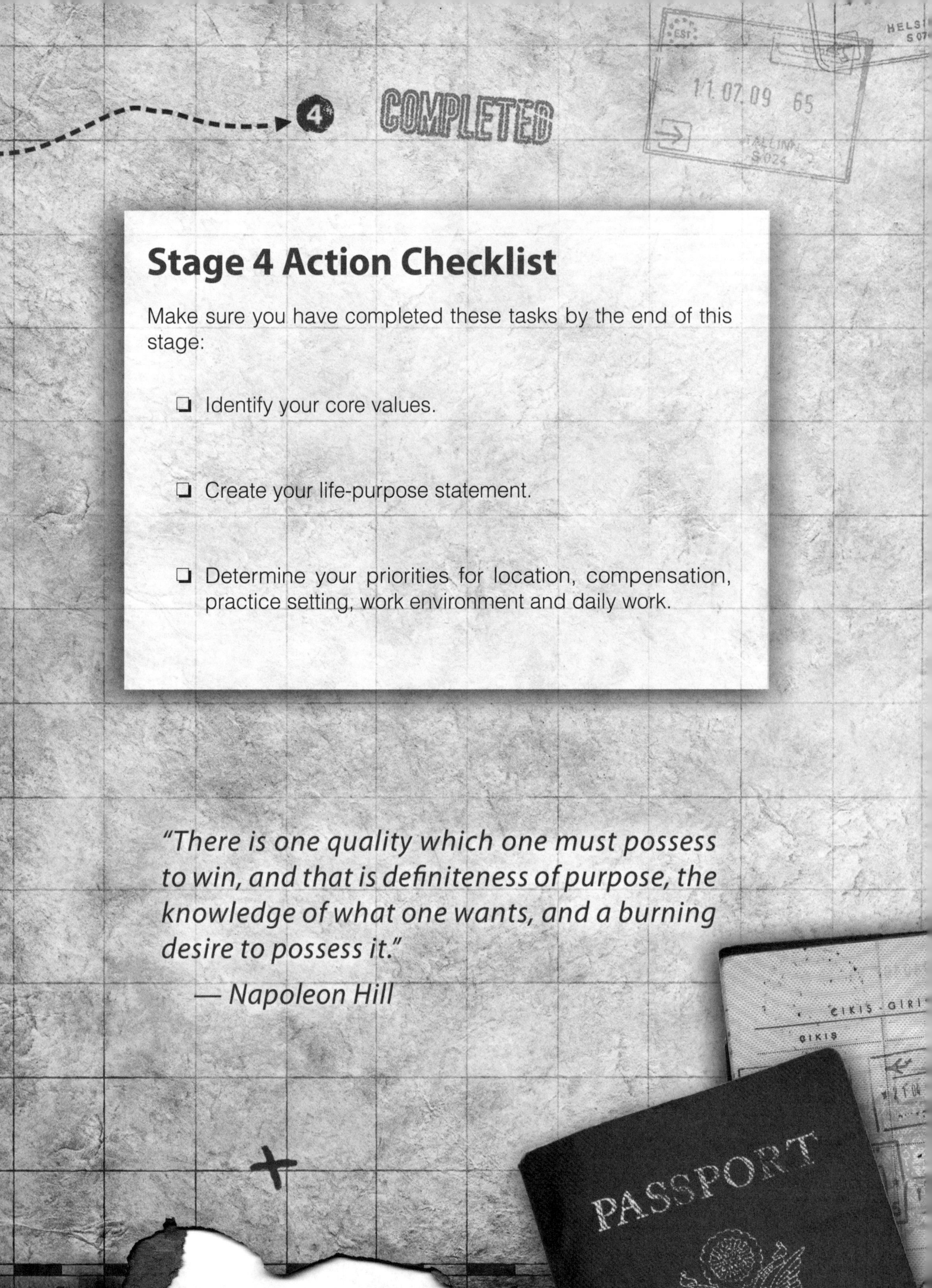

Stage 4 Action Checklist

Make sure you have completed these tasks by the end of this stage:

- ❑ Identify your core values.
- ❑ Create your life-purpose statement.
- ❑ Determine your priorities for location, compensation, practice setting, work environment and daily work.

"There is one quality which one must possess to win, and that is definiteness of purpose, the knowledge of what one wants, and a burning desire to possess it."

— Napoleon Hill

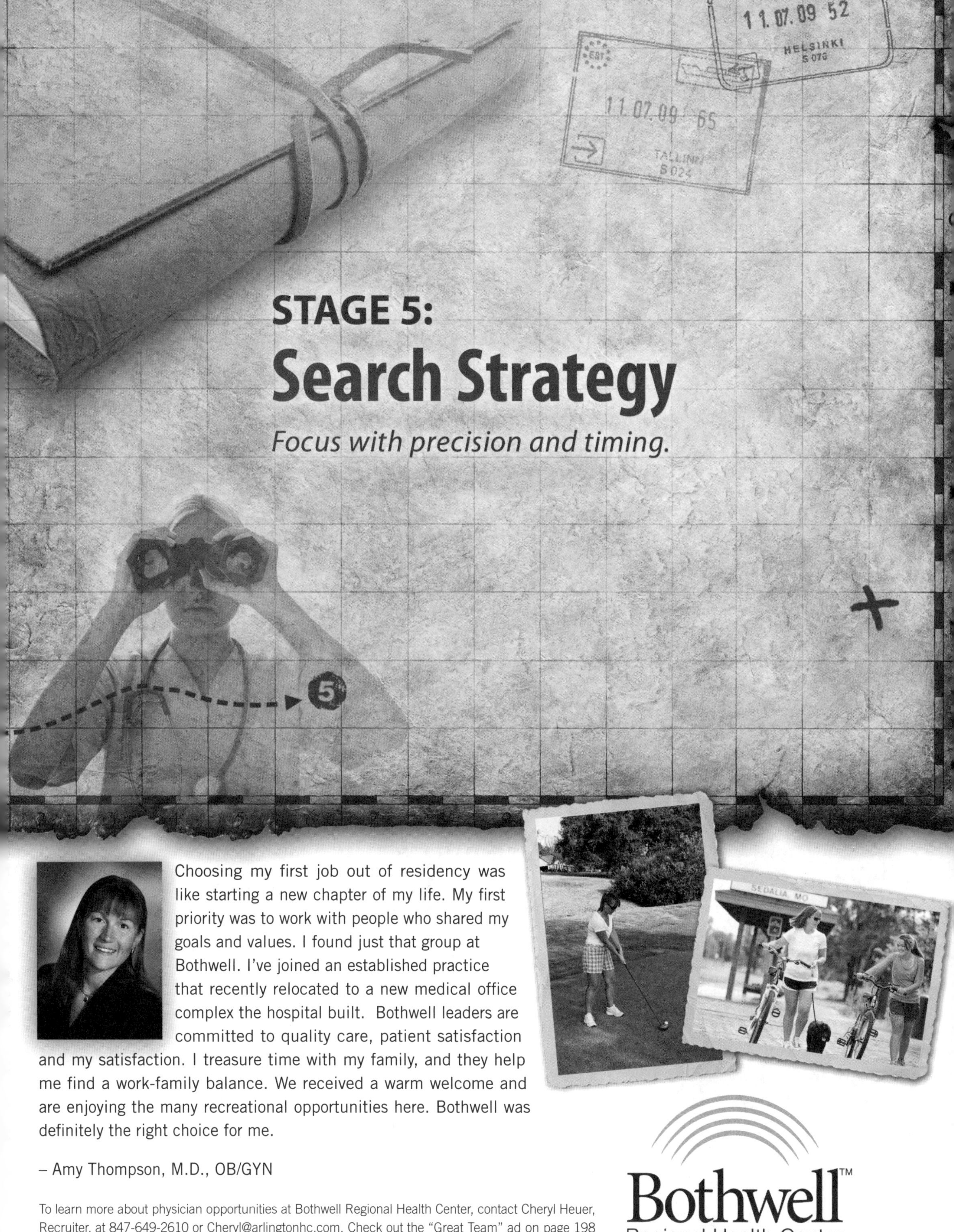
11.07.09 52
HELSINKI
S 076
EST
11.07.09 65
TALLINN
S 024
STAGE 5:
Search Strategy
Focus with precision and timing.
5
SEDALIA MO
Choosing my first job out of residency was like starting a new chapter of my life. My first priority was to work with people who shared my goals and values. I found just that group at Bothwell. I've joined an established practice that recently relocated to a new medical office complex the hospital built. Bothwell leaders are committed to quality care, patient satisfaction and my satisfaction. I treasure time with my family, and they help me find a work-family balance. We received a warm welcome and are enjoying the many recreational opportunities here. Bothwell was definitely the right choice for me.
– Amy Thompson, M.D., OB/GYN
To learn more about physician opportunities at Bothwell Regional Health Center, contact Cheryl Heuer, Recruiter, at 847-649-2610 or Cheryl@arlingtonhc.com. Check out the "Great Team" ad on page 198 and read the Bothwell CEO Corner from John Dawes.
Bothwell™
Regional Health Center

Your Search Strategy Guide:

Julia Zimmerman

Vice President
SwedishAmerican Medical Group – Physician Resources

B.A., University of Wisconsin

As a member of the leadership team of SwedishAmerican Health System, Julia directs physician recruitment and retention and serves as administrator of employed physician services. In 1993, she led the development of SwedishAmerican Medical Group with the acquisition of 23 local physicians. With a focus on physician leadership, the group has grown to over 125 employed providers and is the most-preferred group in northern Illinois. According to Julia, "When new physicians join the group, they become members of the SwedishAmerican family, not just new employees. We foster long-term relationships with comprehensive orientation and mentoring programs, on-site child care and sick-child care, and even a concierge service. These unique benefits attract great candidates and help them balance success at work and at home."

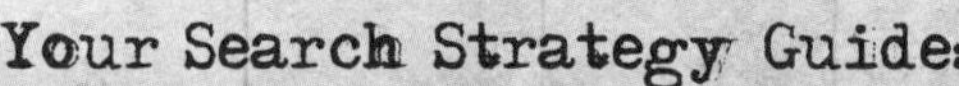

Your Search Strategy Guide:

Vickie Austin

Speaker, Business and Career Coach, and Founder, CHOICES Worldwide

B.A., Arizona State University; Executive Master's in International Management, Thunderbird School of Global Management

Vickie Austin founded CHOICES Worldwide in 1997 to offer strategic marketing planning to entrepreneurs, executives and individuals in career transition. She is a frequent speaker and trainer on career success, networking, negotiation and professional services marketing. She began her career as a healthcare journalist. Her articles have appeared in *National Business Employment Weekly*, *New Perspectives*, and the career sites of the *Wall Street Journal*. She is the author of the e-book *Your Golden Rolodex: How to Network For Results!*© When she isn't in front of an audience speaking, she's singing, songwriting and spending time with family.

5

In This Stage: Search Strategy

When following an adventure trail, a straight line is always the easiest route from Point A to Point B, but when planning your job search, you must blaze a new trail. Without a well-developed plan, you may end up traveling in circles, running into dead ends, or finishing last in line.

Your journey is unique and you must identify your resources, understand your obstacles, and organize the tools at your disposal to reach your final destination quickly and efficiently. In this stage, you will learn who and what can help you on your journey, what may block your path to success, and how to develop your own "golden" opportunity.

Let's get to work.

CONTENTS

Validating Your Values and Purpose

At this point, you have laid out a road map (stage 1) to secure the right opportunity—having a better understanding of all of the elements in a job search. You have studied and learned how today's landscape is changing, how a hospital operates, self assessed your professional competencies (stage 2), gauged how physicians within your specialty get paid by market (stage 3), and dived deep within your soul to discover and prioritize you **CORE VALUES**, **LIFE PURPOSE**, and **LIFE AND WORK PRIORITIES** (stage 4).

Prior to embarking on the "Search" phase, we recommend asking yourself the following questions:

- Can I articulate my core values, life purpose, and my life and work priorities?
- Can I define what type of employer can help me grow professionally based on my professional competencies?
- Can I define the type of community in which I want to live and practice?
- Am I okay with the compensation packages within that territory?
- Do I have a good understanding of how hospitals/groups operate?
- Can I define what type of practice setting in which I would best thrive?
- Do I understand the pros and cons to each type of practice setting?
- Am I prepared to make concessions when choosing a position?

If you cannot answer these questions specifically, you are not alone. After all, you have dedicated a decade of your life to becoming a physician, and re-entering life and choosing a career for the first time is no easy feat. Remember that there is a big difference between acing your exams and applying the information you've learned into diagnosing your first few patients, or performing surgery on your first few cases. The difference is that you've had teachers, professors, and seasoned physicians to help guide you each step of the way.

You can study the job markets, discuss the type of opportunity you're seeking with loved ones, and do the heavy lifting to map out the rest of your life; however, the fact is, you don't know what you don't know—which is another reason to use your resources wisely.

Just like when you were in your internship, you had an opportunity to experience several different specialties to see where your interests lie, searching and interviewing is an opportunity to test pilot the elements you have identified as your search criteria.

GUIDE POINTS
Join your specialty association in order to gain access to current job postings.

Search Methods

There is no one right way to secure an opportunity; instead, it may be a combination of multiple methods. Whether you look online, respond to direct mail or a journal ad, network, or contact a physician recruiting firm directly, the key is to leverage each search method, so you can make the right decision for you and your family.

DR. GOODHOOK'S FIELD NOTES

I'll not soon forget the encounter with old Doc Robert. In truth, he instructed me in the art of fishing for employment. Many young physicians fish wildly, without strategem. The wise student will seek the old scout, with hooked hat and wrinkled eye, to instruct in the ways of fishing for employ. The resident, said he, must know his fish, read rock and stream and, placing bait to hook, work line through calm and eddy.

Prepare, young resident. The job you desire requires more than putrid worm.

– Dr. Gh.

ONLINE RESOURCES

Job Boards and Postings

Everyone is familiar with job-hunting sites like Monster.com and Careerbuilder.com. Similarly there are an overwhelming number of physician job boards to choose from. How do you know which site will actually lead you to the type of position you are looking for?

The best online resource is your specialty-specific organization — for example, the American Academy of Family Physicians or the American College of Physicians. Specialty organizations represent the physicians in your specialty and limit access to job postings to members of the organization. Positions are posted by physicians looking for partners, by hospitals and medical groups offering employed positions, and by universities and residency programs filling academic positions. Several specialty associations also offer online journals that include a classified section where you will find job ads.

Caution: There may be organizations who post their opportunities on job boards and journal ads whose main purpose is to entice you to contact them (e.g., to build their database). These sites may post legitimate positions; however, jobs may be occasionally outdated and/or fictional. As you inquire about these positions, ask specific questions and listen carefully to their responses to avoid an unproductive job search path.

Social Networks

You are the Facebook, MySpace, Twitter generation, so you know well the vast jungle of social networking. What you may not know is that you are being Googled, tracked, and pursued by healthcare organizations and others vying for your personal information. Many in-house recruiters routinely "Google" candidates when they receive a CV, so it is important to keep an eye on what the Internet says about you.

There are over 500 healthcare organizations now with Facebook accounts and most are there to attract physicians and other providers. Nurses, physical therapists, and even physicians are connecting with new employers via social media, so it may be a valuable resource as you look for your ideal position. Most hospitals include links to their official website and may post videos of current physicians and leadership. Use this tool to research the facility, the physicians they employ, and the culture they project and compare these to your ideal practice.

The big question with social networking is how to stay connected with your friends while also projecting a professional image. The answer is perhaps obvious – keep your personal page private and create a second, professional page that will allow potential employers and networkers to see the physician to whom they would entrust their grandmother's care. Use caution with social networking and always keep in mind that your potential employer may be reading your latest post.

CAREER FAIRS

Many physicians know career fairs as a great place to pick up freebies – the gadgets, treats, and gift cards given away by recruiters to entice physicians to their booths. Career fairs can be a great resource, however, because they provide job seekers an opportunity to network with multiple employers within a short period of time and in a single location. They are a place to gather information and to meet people who may help you in your search, even if you don't find your ideal position.

There are downsides with career fairs, but if you understand the terrain, your visit can be productive. Recruiters are looking for candidates and you are looking for a position. They will have their selling points ready and you should too. Be prepared with copies of your CV and your list of priorities. Prepare questions in advance. Dress to impress because you may end up interviewing with a key player. And most importantly, be respectful. If you visit a booth, take a minute to talk with the recruiters – don't just grab the freebie and run. You may not be interested in their position, but recruiters network too, and if their opportunity isn't right for you, many are happy to share your CV with colleagues.

ALUMNI AND MEDICAL ASSOCIATIONS

It's important to network with faculty advisors and residents from previous years. If possible, you should speak with physicians you trust and who know you because they will lead you down the right path. Medical associations represent another opportunity to network with physicians with the same career and clinical focus. These contacts often have knowledge about openings that aren't advertised or posted anywhere. Also, most employers post positions on the job boards of specialty associations. The primary challenge with this resource is carving out time to meet with these people or attending association meetings.

PROFESSIONAL RECRUITERS

There are two types of professional recruiters: Those that work for a health system, hospital, or medical group, known as in-house recruiters, and agency recruiters, or those that work for a placement firm. In some ways they are competitors in search of candidates. In spite of the competition, many in-house recruiters and agency recruiters work together to source quality physician candidates.

In-house Recruiters

In-house recruiters represent solely the physician needs of their organization. In-house recruiters work directly with their physicians and senior leadership and manage the entire recruitment process from candidate selection to contract signing. They are very knowledgeable about their physician practices, organization, and community and will provide you with the detailed information you need to evaluate an opportunity. Most in-house recruiters are also responsible for retention, so they work very hard to find the physician with the right fit for a position. On the flip side, contract negotiation can be more difficult because there is no mediator to lead both parties to middle ground.

Agency Recruiters

Agency recruiters sometimes represent many different organizations at the same time. There are large, national organizations with hundreds of recruiters and clients all across the country, and there are small, one-person offices. Both will connect you with multiple opportunities and may offer valuable advice for gathering references, formatting CVs, coaching for interviews, and contract negotiation. It is important to note that agencies may have limited knowledge of the hospitals and communities they present. Agency recruiters are liaisons between you and the hiring organization, who will pay a placement fee if you are hired. Remember that some may be motivated more by money than by your ultimate job satisfaction, so choose carefully.

GUIDE POINTS

How to Work With a Recruitment Firm

A recruitment firm can be a valuable tool if utilized properly:

- Before you entrust your CV and your reputation to a recruiter, determine how they will identify positions that meet your criteria and how they will help you during your search.
- Work with only one or two firms/recruiters. Working with multiple firms will not increase your chances of finding your ideal position; on the contrary, it may work against you. An employer who receives your CV from multiple recruiters may see you as a desperate candidate no one else wants.
- Give your recruiter a concise, up-to-date CV, three recent letters of reference, your list of priorities, and your "elevator speech." This will allow the recruiter to represent you with detail and accuracy.
- Establish phone call guidelines with the recruiter including the best time to reach you, and a designated number. Return calls promptly and at least once per day.
- Make it clear to your recruiter that they must discuss a position with you before submitting your CV. Your CV should not be presented for a job in which you have no interest. If the employer is interested in you, the recruiter should tell you who will call and when, so you can be prepared to ask and answer questions.
- Consider your recruiter a coach who can provide valuable advice on interviewing, asking and responding to questions, identifying red-flag situations, and negotiating contracts.

PERSONAL AND PROFESSIONAL NETWORK

Most professionals in any industry understand the concept of "networking." Successful professionals network on a continual basis, expanding their networks with each new person they meet. People network on the golf course, at Chamber of Commerce meetings, their children's soccer games, church, and even at the grocery store. They understand that each new contact may provide links to more new contacts, thereby expanding their contact base exponentially.

Few physicians, on the other hand, understand networking. They tend to think only in terms of building a practice, but in reality, building a practice is networking. You see one patient, who then tells a friend, who tells a family member, and pretty soon you have a full schedule. That is the power of word-of-mouth advertising, and it can help you find your ideal practice in addition to filling your waiting room. In spite of the multitude of resources available, the actual mechanics of networking elude those in career transition, including most residents entering the real job market for the first time. Unfortunately, networking carries a stigma and a host of misconceptions.

COMMON MISCONCEPTIONS OF NETWORKING

NETWORKING IS ONLY ABOUT...	FALSE
• Using people	✓
• Attending a group event	✓
• Meeting only new people	✓
• Lots of hard work and time	✓
• Being an extrovert	✓
• Knowing a lot of people	✓

The Real Truth of Networking

If you're like most people, you may fall prey to these misconceptions and potentially miss out on the power and magic of networking. Let's look at the other side of these misconceptions.

First of all, many people think that in order to network, they have to use people, and they are, understandably, uncomfortable doing so. Or, while they've heard the saying that "it isn't what you know; it's who you know," they focus on the "who" instead of the "you." They assume that they don't know anyone — at least, not anyone important. Some are too proud to ask others for help.

Additionally, many people think that networking is a group dynamic, best done at trade shows, business-after-hours events and conventions — in essence, what may be called a "group grope." Nothing could be further from the truth. Networking is a one-on-one phenomenon, built one relationship at a time; and when the art of networking is positioned this way, folks heave a tremendous sigh of relief. Relationships you've made with attending physicians, professors and peers can be the most valuable resources during your search.

Due to the misconception that networking is hard, onerous work comprised of attending a lot of bad cocktail parties and dreary conventions, many avoid networking and miss the gold that's right under our noses — **THE PEOPLE WE ALREADY KNOW.**

Your Golden Rolodex

Networking on a professional level with people you see every day – program directors, attendings, nurses, hospital administrators, and even those in your own circle of friends – can help you create something business and career coach Vickie Austin calls your "Golden Rolodex." For the graduating resident looking for a first job, this is the first place to begin. Your "Golden Rolodex" is comprised of everyone you know. This collection of contacts is your most important tool, but you may be hesitant to use it. You may worry that people will think you are just using them, or you may believe that networking is a group dynamic to be done only at conferences or trade shows. Networking is more about developing one-on-one relationships with others and honoring the people you already know.

To create and grow your Golden Rolodex, you must first understand **HOW** to network. The following guidelines have been adapted from the e-book, Your Golden Rolodex: How to Network for Results! © by Vickie Austin, founder of CHOICES Worldwide (www.choicesworldwide.com).

1. **Be yourself.** Whether you are an introvert or an extrovert, reflective or outgoing, the most important skill for successful networking (as well as interviewing) is to be yourself. When you try to portray yourself as someone you're not, others will sense it and pull back. You must be authentic and comfortable, no matter what your personality type. When you can be yourself, engage in a conversation with someone and be interested in what they're up to, style ceases to be an issue. Substance is the key.

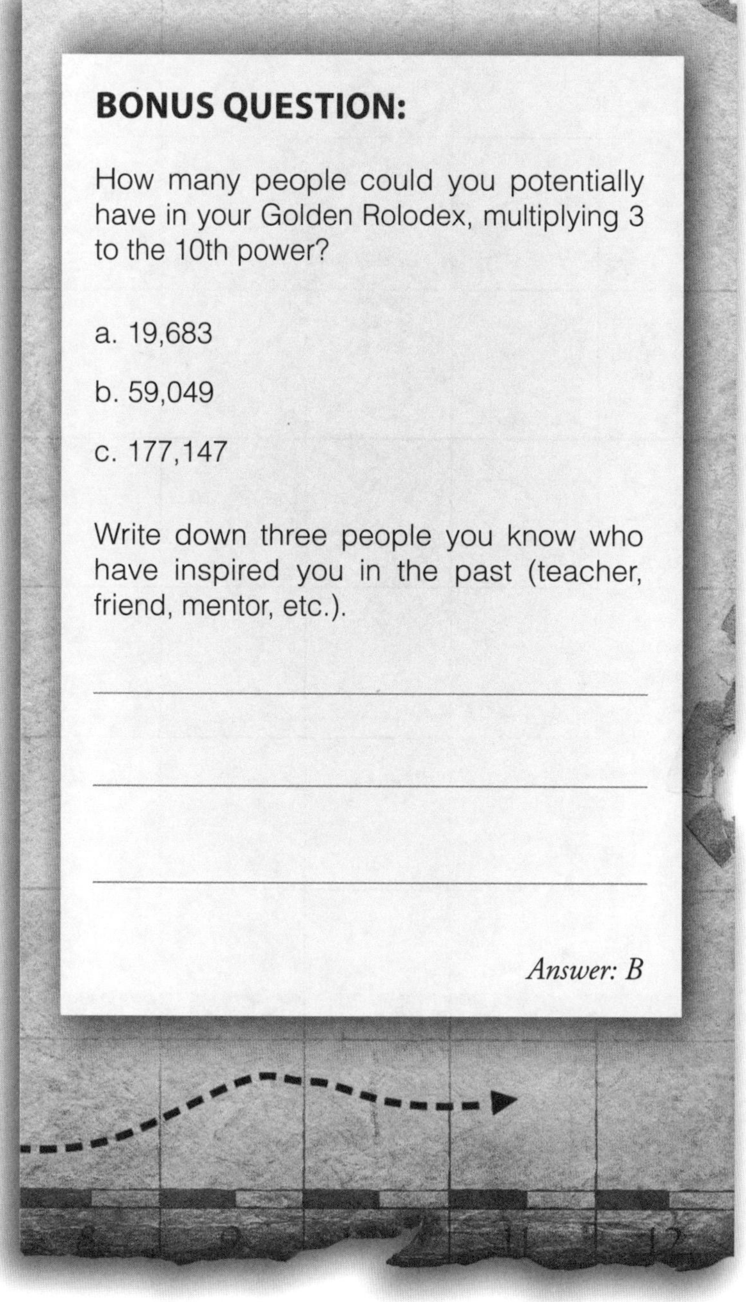

BONUS QUESTION:

How many people could you potentially have in your Golden Rolodex, multiplying 3 to the 10th power?

a. 19,683

b. 59,049

c. 177,147

Write down three people you know who have inspired you in the past (teacher, friend, mentor, etc.).

____

____

____

Answer: B

2. **Start your "Golden Rolodex" with those you already know.** GR = 3^{10}. This equation is the key to building your Golden Rolodex. Think of the three people who wrote your letters of recommendation for residency application. They are already in your list of contacts. With a single conversation, each of those three contacts could connect you with three more contacts, and – well, you get the picture. By the time you add in fellow residents, honor society colleagues, nurses, neighbors, and so on, your Rolodex really does become Golden.

3. **Organize and store your contact information.** As a product of the technology age, you may have never used a Rolodex—a physical collection of business cards or contact information, indexed alphabetically at your fingertips. These days there are all kinds of ways to store that data. Whatever you decide to use, it's important to have a reliable means of organizing your growing list of contacts. This can be your cell phone or an Outlook folder on your laptop. Your contact list needs to be updated continually and easily accessible. And always remember **TO BACK UP YOUR DATA**!

Remember to always ask your new contacts for their business cards or phone numbers, addresses, and email addresses if they don't have cards. With their permission, you can store their contact information, and it's always a good idea to keep some private notes to include something you remember about each person. Perhaps a contact talked about new project, or a new baby in the family. Maybe he or she shared a story with you about a first job or gave you an excellent recommendation for a restaurant. This tidbit will help you remember each contact and often will give you something to mention the next time you talk with him or her.

4. **Create a 30-second "Elevator Speech."** There may be times during networking when you have only a small window of time to introduce yourself and make a good impression. This is why it is important to have a prepared and rehearsed "elevator speech". The best 30-second speech presents the who, what, when, where, and why of your job search.

   To write your speech, begin with the **PAST** (e.g., why you chose medicine), briefly note the **PRESENT** (where you are in training), describe your **DESIRED FUTURE** (you're hoping to establish a traditional practice in the Midwest), and finish with a request of your new contact, such as their ideas for a successful interview or a recommendation of places to apply.

   PAST + PRESENT + DESIRED FUTURE + REQUEST = SUCCESS

   Examples:

   "I received my medical degree from the University of Illinois and just finished my family practice residency at the University of Iowa. I'm now in the process of looking for a position with a family practice group or a clinic based here in the Midwest so I can continue to make a difference with families and their healthcare. I'd be interested in your opinion on how I can position myself for this transition…"

   "My interest has always been in cardiology and I just completed a fellowship in cardiology at Northwestern Memorial Hospital in Chicago. I'm currently exploring opportunities to join a large group practice on the East Coast and looking for ideas on how to do that…"

5. **Take a research approach to networking.** The most successful networkers are naturally interested in other people and they also know that people love to talk about themselves. The desired outcome of networking is to build relationships. The task is much more effective if you give your contact your attention and a real interest in what he or she has to say. Think of yourself as a researcher instead of a nuisance and put both you and your contact at ease.

6. **Develop your "Power Questions."** Your primary goal of networking at this stage of your career may be to gather data that can lead you to your ideal practice. After you and your contact are comfortable and past the "research" stage, you will need to ask questions that can open the door to other contacts or opportunities. The following "power questions" are effective because they flatter and show respect to your contact and the answers may lead you to an opportunity you wouldn't otherwise have.

7. **Request the privilege of someone's time and expertise.** When you have your "Golden Rolodex" ready, your elevator speech rehearsed, and your power questions prepared, you are ready to go after the big prize – a networking appointment. Make a call, send an email, or knock on a door, but remember to ask for the privilege of their time to discuss their ideas, opinions, and recommendations for your job search. Be sure to share your life-purpose statement (Stage 4) that communicates your passion and vision which is much bigger than what you can accomplish alone.

8. **Conduct a "Golden Conversation."** Once you have an appointment scheduled, keep it and arrive on time. If meeting in person, dress professionally, as you would for an interview. When you connect, thank the person for his or her time and reference the source of your connection, be it a friend, relative, or mutual acquaintance.

   Conduct your "research" by asking get-to-know-you questions. Then give your elevator speech and ask a few more questions. Finally, share your life-purpose statement and ask your power questions.

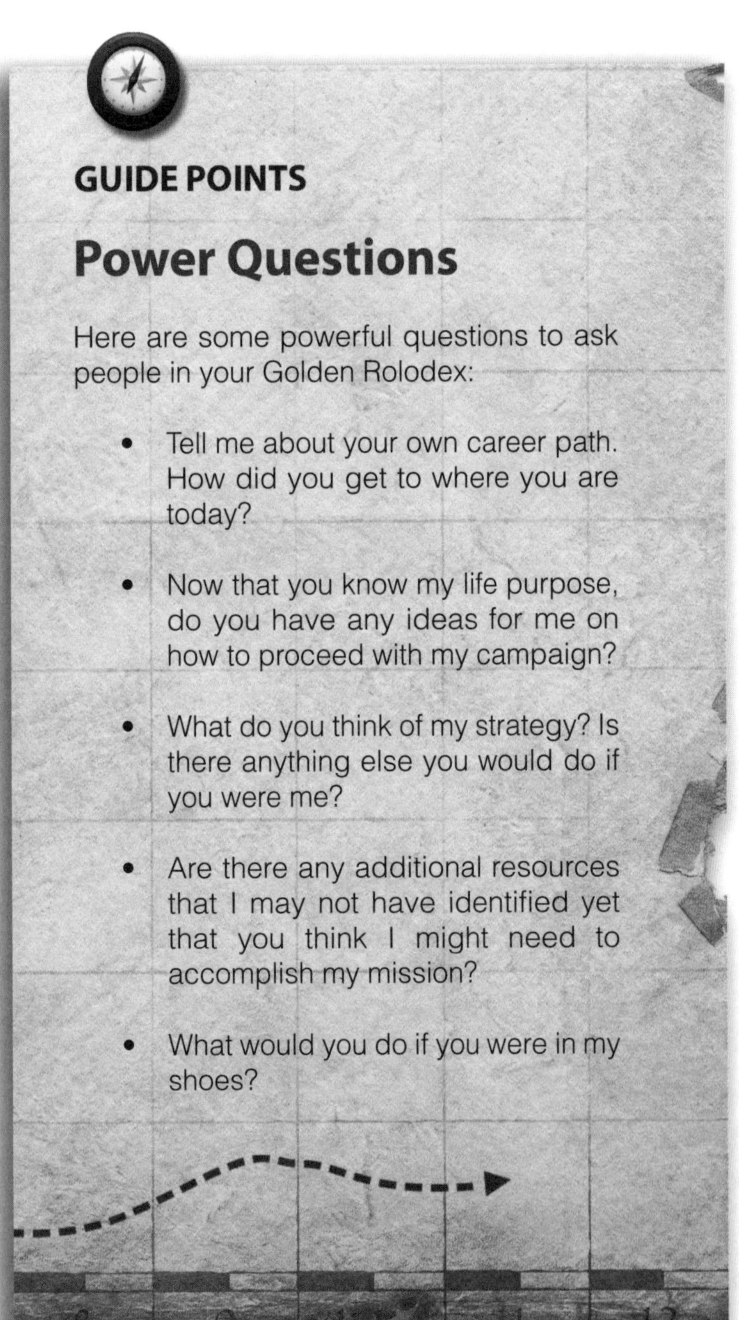

GUIDE POINTS

Power Questions

Here are some powerful questions to ask people in your Golden Rolodex:

- Tell me about your own career path. How did you get to where you are today?
- Now that you know my life purpose, do you have any ideas for me on how to proceed with my campaign?
- What do you think of my strategy? Is there anything else you would do if you were me?
- Are there any additional resources that I may not have identified yet that you think I might need to accomplish my mission?
- What would you do if you were in my shoes?

9. **Mind your networking manners.** Throughout the networking process and the interview process it is important to always exercise good manners and proper etiquette. This is simple common sense, but you would be amazed at how often this is forgotten. Return all phone calls and email promptly. Make formal introductions when meeting people.Don't fidget or talk with your mouth full. Ask for permission to use someone's name or reference. Always send a thank-you note after getting a referral or following a meeting.

GUIDE POINTS

Conduct a Golden Conversation

- Begin with some type of acknowledgement. Thank them for their time, insight and/or expertise.
- Reference the context of your relationship. If you were introduced by a mutual acquaintance, reference that name and your appreciation for the introduction.
- Provide the contact with the reason you're calling or writing — your 30-second commercial.
- Make a request:
  - You would like some time with them (face-to-face or on the phone).
  - You would like their ideas, opinions and recommendations about your life purpose and how you are conducting your search.
  - Ultimately, you would like referrals for people they know who could help you on your continued mission.
  - Ask for permission to use their name, if you are following up with the people they recommended. This may seem too formal but it's an important request to make because people's names are like currency and you're asking to use their name to open doors.
- Follow up.
  - Keep track of the referrals and recommendations.
  - Make those contacts.
  - Let the person who made those introductions know that you made the connections.
  - Acknowledge him or her for the time spent and the contribution to your search.
  - Stay in touch.

EXERCISE: GOLDEN OPPORTUNITY TARGETS

Identify five people in your Golden Rolodex list to talk with before you begin the first round of phone and on-site interviews.

TARGET

Name:

Their position:

When:

Name:

Their position:

When:

Name:

Their position:

When:

Name:

Their position:

When:

Name:

Their position:

When:

EXERCISE: BUILD YOUR NETWORKING STRATEGY

Check off the resources you plan to use. Then identify your planned level of usage (from low to high). Finally, write out your action items for each resource you plan to use.

RESOURCE	USE?	LEVEL OF USAGE	ACTION ITEMS
Online resources (job boards and postings, social networks)	❏ Yes ❏ No	❏ Low ❏ Medium ❏ High	
Career fairs	❏ Yes ❏ No	❏ Low ❏ Medium ❏ High	
Alumni and medical associations	❏ Yes ❏ No	❏ Low ❏ Medium ❏ High	
Professional recruiters	❏ Yes ❏ No	❏ Low ❏ Medium ❏ High	
Personal and professional network	❏ Yes ❏ No	❏ Low ❏ Medium ❏ High	

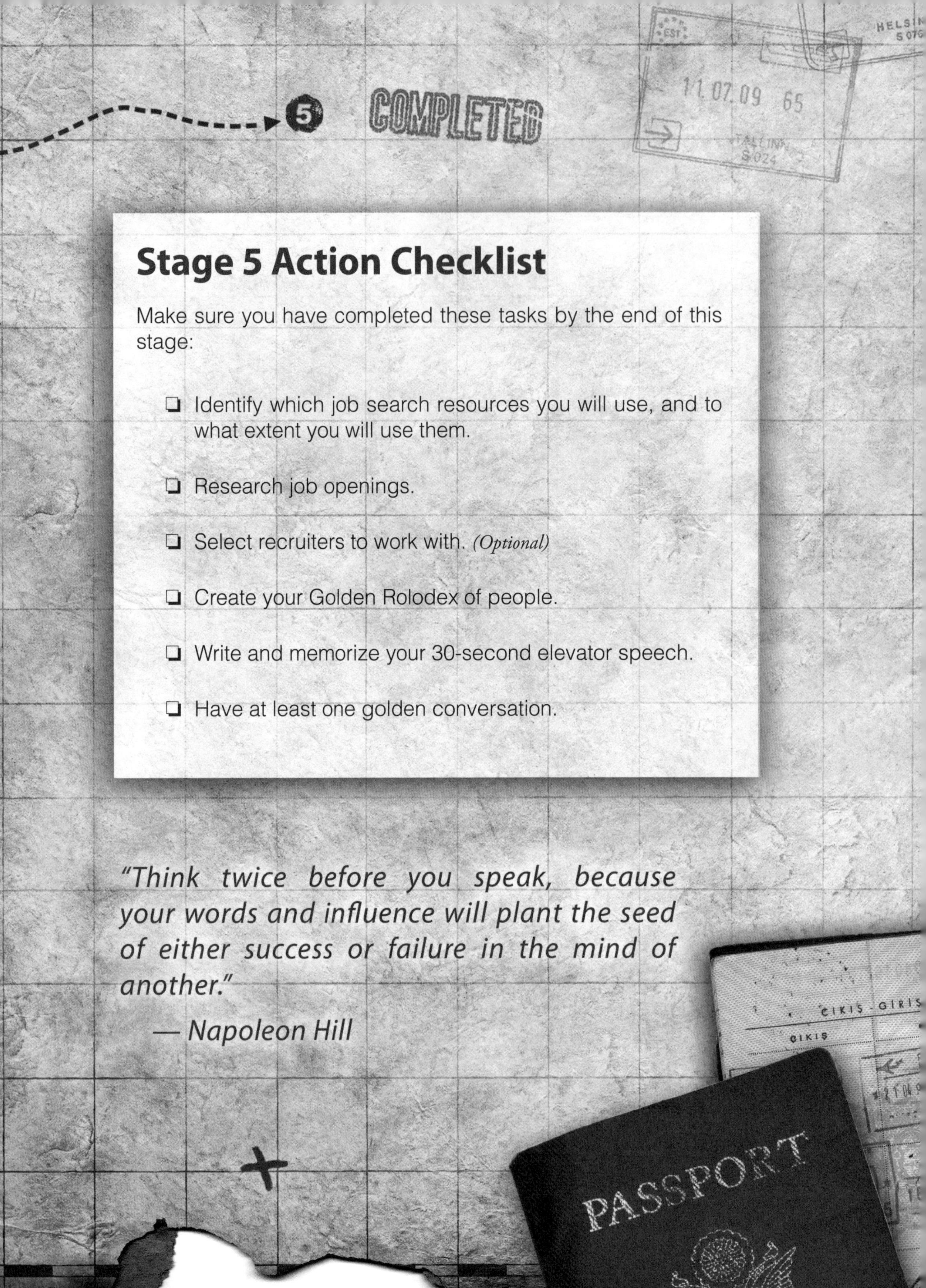

Stage 5 Action Checklist

Make sure you have completed these tasks by the end of this stage:

- ❏ Identify which job search resources you will use, and to what extent you will use them.
- ❏ Research job openings.
- ❏ Select recruiters to work with. *(Optional)*
- ❏ Create your Golden Rolodex of people.
- ❏ Write and memorize your 30-second elevator speech.
- ❏ Have at least one golden conversation.

"Think twice before you speak, because your words and influence will plant the seed of either success or failure in the mind of another."

— Napoleon Hill

STAGE 6: Interviewing

It's a two-way street.

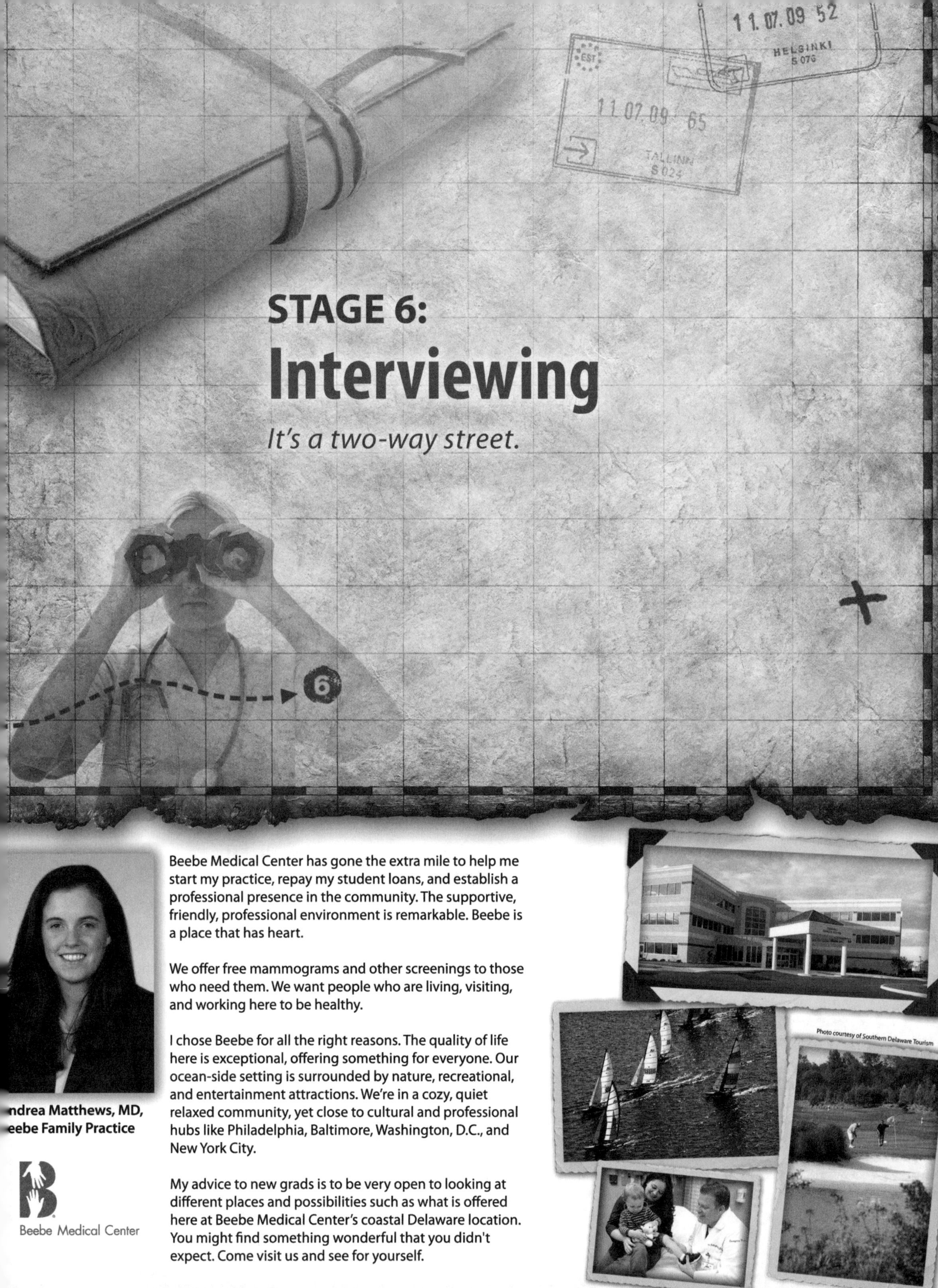

Your Interview Guide:

Alexis Depre, CMSR

Physician Relations Manager, Southern Illinois Healthcare

American Association Physician Recruiter, Diplomat, DASPR

B.S.N., Loyola University Chicago; M.B.A., St. Xavier University

In her efforts to recruit and retain physicians and other medical talent, Alexis Depre has helped Southern Illinois Healthcare significantly grow its services and market share as the regional healthcare system leader. She brings a wealth of experience, including 15 years in direct patient care. She has recruited virtually every medical specialty and assisted physicians in the transition from private practice to hospital employment. She continues to develop breakthrough programs to promote physician satisfaction and retention.

A Board member of the Shawnee Hills Wine Grape Growers Association, Alexis appreciates tending her family's vineyard, winemaking, reading, photography and travel.

Your Interview Guide:

Lorren Pettit

Managing Consultant, Press Ganey
Associate Professor of Sociology, Indiana University South Bend
B.A., University of Winnipeg; M.S. (Gerontology), Baylor University; M.B.A., University of Dallas

Lorren Pettit is a proven strategist at Press Ganey. In his 20-plus years in healthcare operations and corporate planning, he has launched some 70 new products and services for providers, as well as two multi-million-dollar skilled nursing facilities. He has worked to improve relationships between hospital leaders, physicians and employees in over 350 hospitals in North America. In his spare time, Lorren enjoys his family and playing ice hockey.

PRESS GANEY®

With more than 11 million surveys processed annually, Press Ganey provides services to drive healthcare improvement initiatives, based on extensive patient, employee and physician feedback.

In This Stage: Interviewing

There are few moments more awkward or frightening than staring at a grizzly, eye to eye.

While a prospective employer is not a life-threatening adversary like a grizzly, for some unprepared residents, the first interview can be strange and awkward.

How will you prepare for interviews? What questions will **YOU** ask? What questions will **THEY** ask? What do you wear? How will you follow up?

In this stage you will research openings and organizations that may be a potential match with your priorities. Then you'll prepare for interviews by identifying questions and preparing responses to commonly asked questions. By the end, you'll be ready to conduct interviews with excitement and confidence.

While there are always new challenges in any adventure, with good preparation you'll put your best foot forward and identify a good opportunity quickly!

Get your shoes shined. We're going out.

CONTENTS

Interviewing: Two Sides to the "Job Coin"

The interview process represents an interesting dynamic: a two-way street that combines the desires of two parties (physician and employer) to ultimately achieve a win-win outcome (the best fit). Your desire is to find a job and organization that meets your needs and expectations; whereas, the employer is looking for a physician who fits their job requirements and the culture of the organization and contributes to the bottom line. Both parties find themselves on a **FACT-FINDING MISSION** during the interview process. By the end, both parties should feel confident to make a final decision (to hire and to accept). On the flip side, one or both parties may determine that this job might not be the best fit after all. It's OK to come to this conclusion, address the situation and move on.

Hiring Process

The graphic below provides an illustration of common activities associated with the hiring process.

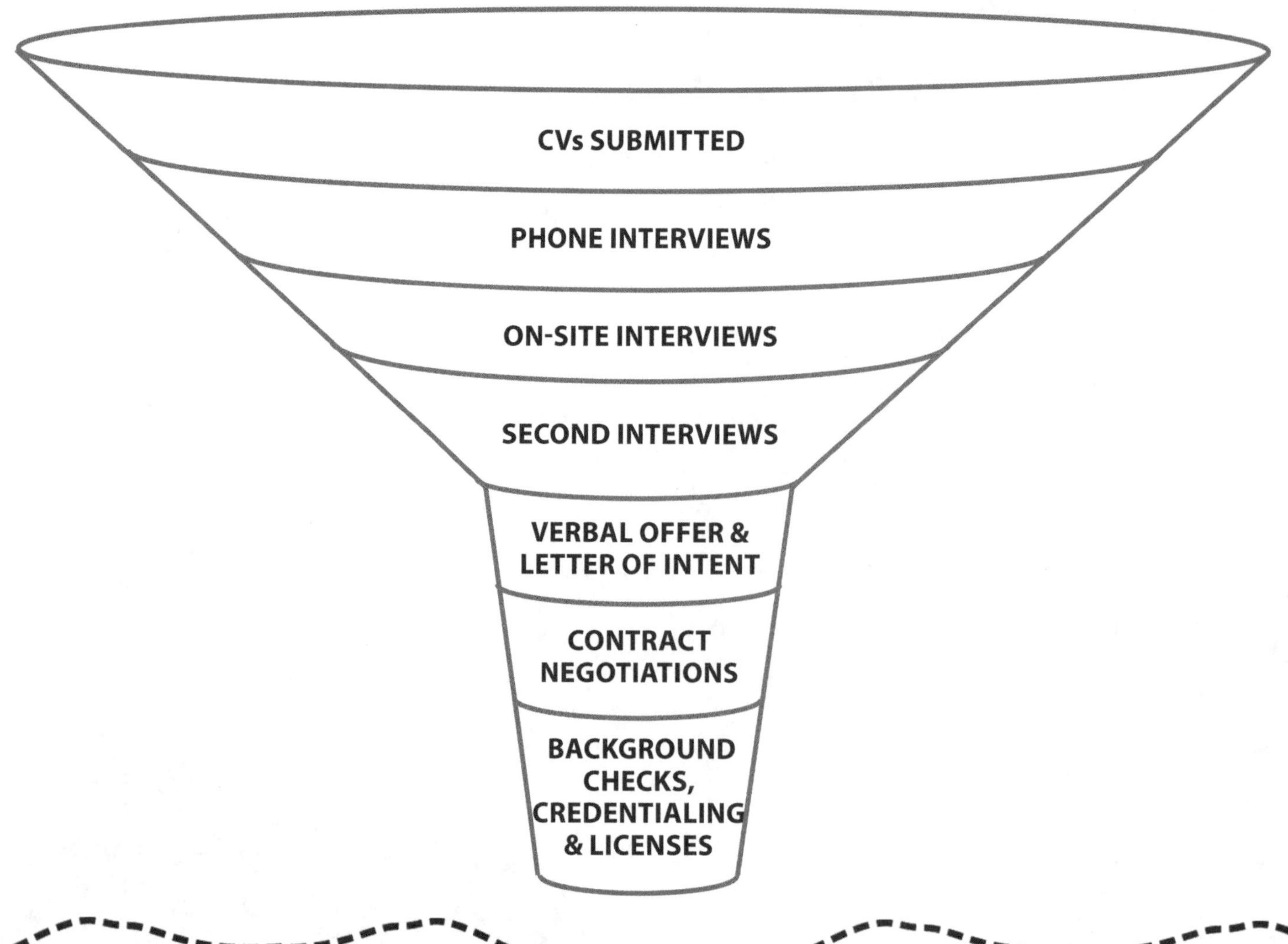

There are two factors impacting the importance of the hiring process and timeline:

- **The significance of the investment.** Hospitals and groups spend a significant amount of money in securing a physician; therefore, they want to minimize their risks before making an investment.

- **The strategic significance of the physician.** Physicians play a significant role to a hospital's or group's strategic success; therefore, the fit must be right. A wrong placement can have many residual implications — financial, physician collegiality, employee perceptions of the healthcare organization, employee perceptions of the medical staff, patient satisfaction, and more.

THE HIRING PROCESS — STEP-BY-STEP GUIDELINES

STEP	WHAT HAPPENS?
1. Candidate targets job opportunities and submits CV.	Using your personal and career priorities list, identify names of potential hospitals, practices, etc. Conduct online search, work with a recruiter, and/or cold call potential employers. For each opportunity that you would like to learn more about, send your CV to either the physician recruiting firm who is representing opportunity or to the in-house recruiter.
2. In-house recruiter receives CV.	In-house recruiter reviews all incoming CVs and identifies the most interesting candidates for review.
3. Selected CVs are forwarded to medical director or hiring physician for further review.	Having received a CV, the medical director or hiring physician will review and assess. The recruiter has a responsibility to the organization and the candidate to make sure the timelines are reasonable to keep the candidate submission top of mind. The goal is placement with qualified, reasonable physicians who are good fits for the organization and community.
4. If CV is approved, the medical director or hiring physician conducts a phone interview with the candidate.	Once a CV has been reviewed and approved, the director or physician contacts the candidate to conduct a phone interview. Although the phone does not replace an on-site interview, basic information can be gained such as clinical expectations, qualifications, organizational culture, and candidate's ideal match for the organization. Phone conduct and etiquette are also evaluated.
5. The medical director or hiring physician determines if the candidate should be brought in for an interview.	After completing the phone interview, the director or physician must determine if they would like to bring the candidate in for an on-site interview. In an effort to consider the best use of everyone's time and resources, it is important to schedule the on-site interview with as many decision-makers as possible.
6. On-site interviews are conducted with the candidate.	Most often, site visits are set at the availability of the candidate. The hiring organizations will continue to interview until it is determined a desired candidate has agreed to sign. Site interviews can take seven days to arrange and last one or two business days. Weekends are a great time to look around the community.

STEP	WHAT HAPPENS?
7. The medical director or hiring physician determines if the candidate should be brought back for a second interview.	The director or physician must decide whether or not to bring the candidate back for a second on-site interview. If both parties are pleased with the initial interview and express an interest in further exploring a potential relationship, then the process continues. Second interviews may be more challenging for the candidate, as they have to take time to travel to the area a second time. Second interviews are necessary if key decision makers were not available on the first visit.
8. An offer is extended verbally or via a letter of intent.	Offers may come in the form of a letter of intent. This is a tool used to negotiate specific terms outlined in the executable contract. After a site visit, it is typical to continue the offer and contract process remotely by phone, e-mail or fax, which means it may take a few weeks to finalize the agreement. Recruiters can help with an understanding of the timeline and keep candidates informed of where they are in the process.
9. Executable contracts are drawn up by the hiring organization and reviewed by the candidate and possibly their attorney.	At this point, the ball is in the candidate's court and the timeframe can vary widely. An attorney's review of the contract can take a few days. After that, there may be requests for changes or revisions that must go back and forth between your attorney and the hiring organization. This process requires more time, perhaps up to 30 days.
10. Organization conducts extensive background checks, credentialing, certifications, etc.	This pre-employment procedure is completed to ensure there are no licensure restrictions or sanctions to practice by the candidate — most notably, sanctions for professional service payment from federal programs. For example, default on federal student loans can exclude a physician from participation in federal insurance programs, primarily Medicare, which is a larger component of most practice revenues and the threshold for all other commercial payors. DUI's or bankruptcy may speak to character. Bad credit may be an indicator of high risk for practice loans, like income guarantee or student loan repayment. Employers must also vet candidates and ensure they have the ability to obtain state licensure and hospital privileges without restriction prior to executing a contract.

You can expect the overall timeframe for the hiring process to vary anywhere from a few weeks to three to six months, depending on the organization, candidate or position.

Do Your Homework

We highly recommend that you **RESEARCH** a hiring organization before you have any phone or on-site interviews with them. Becoming educated about the organization and key people (e.g., medical director, CEO, hiring physician) will help you formulate questions to ask during the interview and communicates to the organization that you are organized, prepared, and above all, interested in the opportunity.

GUIDE POINTS

Tips for Research your Potential Employer

- Visit the organization's website to learn about:
  - Size of facility, number of beds
  - Number of employees
  - Number of years in business
  - Rankings against similar facilities/organizations
  - Organization's mission, vision, and values
  - Who they serve: type of population, patient mix, demographics
- Do an Internet search for the organization's name to check if they have been in the news lately.
- Investigate their reputation using research sites like:
  - **HCAHPS**: www.hcahpsonline.org
    (Organizational, departmental or service line awards or distinction.)
  - **American Hospital Directory**: www.ahd.com
    (Free profiles of hospitals)
  - **Hospital Value Index**: www.hospitalvalueindex.com
    (Free online tool that evaluates and compares hospital performance on multiple factors that go in to providing value)
  - **Top 100 Hospitals**: www.top100hospitals.com
    (Listing of the best clinically and fiscally operating hospitals in the U.S.)
- Check for mentions in scholarly journals and medical association publications.
- Use networking: who do you know who works there or has worked there? Ask them about what it's like to work there and the politics of the organization.

Conducting Interviews

Interviews provide an opportunity to market and promote yourself as the best candidate for the position. Employers interview you to assess how you look, how you interact with people and how you might fit within the organization. Remember, your **PERSONAL SKILLS** — including desire, ambition, attitude, enthusiasm, self-discipline, communication and bedside manner — can be as important in the hiring decision as your **CLINICAL SKILLS**.

Throughout the interview process, the hiring organization is looking for and verifying the following:

- Communication skills
- Emotional intelligence (bedside manner, professional collegiality)
- Attitude as a team player
- Clinical competency
- Productivity
- Operational efficiency

Phone Interviews

The overall purpose of phone interviews is to verify qualifications and determine if this position fits primary requirements on both sides.

HIRING ORGANIZATION QUESTIONS

- Motivation: What are you looking for? Why did you pursue medicine?
- Practice setting: What's your ideal practice setting?
- Experiences: Highlight medical school, internship and residency experiences. What do you like most and least? How did you deal with challenging professional and personal experiences?
- Expectations: What are your expectations relating to your priorities (geographic location, quality of life, work and work environment)?

YOUR QUESTIONS

- How would you characterize the relationship between administration and the medical staff? The relationship amongst the medical staff?
- How do you gather and monitor the concerns of your medical staff?
- Have you conducted a satisfaction survey of your medical staff? What were the main findings? Do you have a plan in place to address these concerns?

Upon completion of the phone interviews and assuming that both parties choose to proceed with the interview process, the next step involves scheduling and conducting on-site interviews.

On-Site Interviews

In preparation for on-site interviews, be aware that there are many details that must be taken care of ahead of time (e.g., travel, schedule, agenda). If you work with a recruiter, their job is to serve as liaison between you and the hiring organization and to coordinate logistics. This saves you a lot of **TIME** and potential **HEADACHES** due to unforeseen changes and situations that may come up (e.g., cancellations, date changes).

Because the selection process usually involves more than one decision-maker, it is customary to meet with several staff members. This should be viewed as a benefit. It gives you the opportunity to meet with people at various levels within the organization, as well as different personality types — allowing you to evaluate your fit in the environment.

The interviewer will ask a lot of questions, so being prepared is essential. Well-thought-out responses should be immediate, but not rote. The more questions you can anticipate and answer, the better the interview will flow. Preparing for potential questions also enables you to identify the type of position and organization you desire. Try **NOT** to answer the questions the way you believe the organization would like them to be answered. This will allow both parties to truthfully determine whether or not there is a good match.

The interview will likely flow along the following outline, although your individual experience could vary.

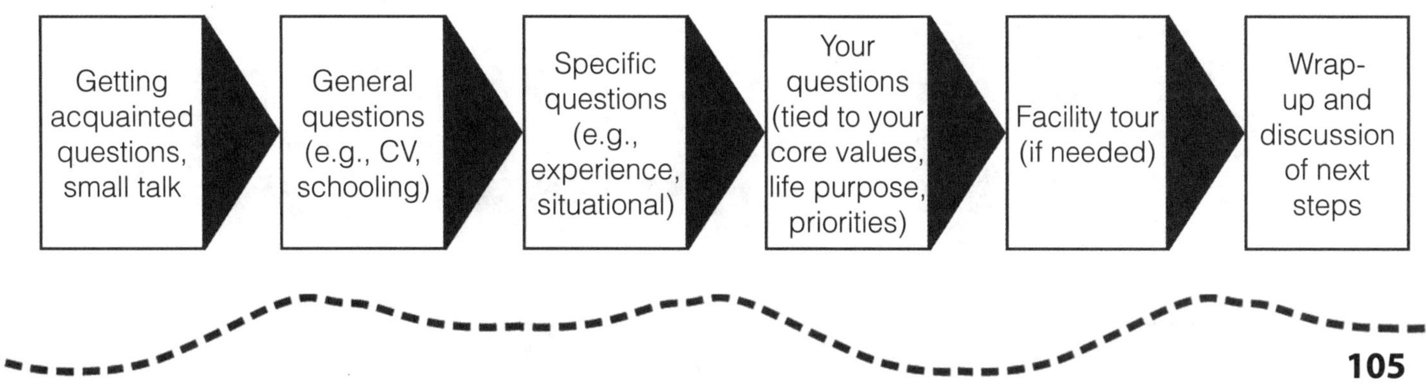

GUIDE POINTS

Interview Etiquette

- Arrive at least 10 minutes early, but not more than 30 minutes.
- Announce your presence to the receptionist, but don't engage in additional conversation unless initiated by them. Jokes and wisecracks may offend them.
- Bring something to read in case there is no reading material while you wait. If there is a delay, be patient and don't show any outward signs of annoyance.
- Listen carefully and be concise with your answers. Ask for clarification but don't ramble on. Be considerate of their time.
- Allow the interviewer to select topics and take the lead in asking you questions. This will help you understand what problems or issues they may be facing, so use this to your advantage. Be polite to everyone you meet and don't take control.
- Be relaxed and appear confident. Comfort portrays that you are smart and puts the interviewer at ease.
- Avoid things that distract from the interview. Fidgeting, playing with your pen, doodling, tapping your feet, leaning on the desk, touching your face or hair, or rearranging things on the desk may indicate your nervousness or lack of confidence.
- Turn your cell phone off or on vibrate if required to leave it on.
- Look like you want the job by having a professional appearance. Have neat, clean, well-trimmed hair. Be discreet with jewelry and wear conservative attire.

HIRING ORGANIZATION QUESTIONS

There are many questions that could be asked by the interviewers and far too many to list them here. Depending on the person conducting the interview, the following factors play into the types of questions they may ask, such as:

- Role in the organization (e.g., CEO, medical staff director, practicing physician, nurse, administrator)
- Personality (e.g., analytical, extrovert, introvert, personable, stand-offish)
- Role in the interview process (e.g., specific qualities, background, qualifications, emotional intelligence)

Many organizations provide their interviewers with a list of questions, asking them to rate the candidate along specific criteria. Typically the last question is, "Do you recommend we hire this physician?" This is the ultimate question you want answered affirmatively.

Each interviewer evaluates and assesses the candidate in his or her own unique way. Bringing these perspectives into discussion is designed to make a good hiring decision for the organization.

EXERCISE: GETTING ACQUAINTED AND GENERAL QUESTIONS

We recommend that you be prepared to answer some of the most commonly asked questions, listed below and on the following page. Record your responses in the spaces provided on the following pages. Be real, be honest, and be sincere. You may want to revisit Stage 4 and review your **CORE VALUES**, **LIFE-PURPOSE STATEMENT**, and **PRIORITIES** to help you answer these questions. Also, you might consider the **30-SECOND ELEVATOR SPEECH** you wrote in Stage 5 to describe who you are and what you're looking for in a job.

QUESTION	YOUR RESPONSE
Tell me about yourself.	

QUESTION	YOUR RESPONSE
Why did you become a doctor?	
Why did you choose this specialty?	
What can you offer this organization / hospital / group?	
What are your strengths and weaknesses?	
What interests you about this job?	

QUESTION	YOUR RESPONSE
What does your ideal opportunity look like?	
What's your ideal work setting?	

Specific Questions

Specific questions often fall into the following categories:

- Experience (past jobs, work experience)
  - I see that you did ________. Could you tell me more about this?
  - What was this experience like for you?
  - What did you like or not like about it?
  - What challenges did you run into with … ?
  - How fluent are you in other languages?
- Situational (Past experiences predict future behaviors.)
  - Tell me about a time when ________. How did you handle it?
  - Describe a situation when you had to work with difficult person. How did you handle the conflict?
  - What three words would your co-workers, program director, or attendings use to describe you?
  - Describe how you handle a difference of opinion with a colleague or superior.
  - How do you handle stressful situations?

GUIDE POINTS

Press Ganey Associates, Inc., a leading healthcare research and consulting firm, considers the following in evaluating physician perceptions of a hospital:

- Quality of patient care that includes:
  - Staff's reliability in recognizing and reporting changes in patients' conditions
  - Teamwork between doctors and nurses at this facility
- Ease of practicing at the hospital, such as:
  - Admitting patients
  - Turnaround time for lab results
- Communication and collaboration with hospital leaders. For example:
  - Degree to which physicians are involved in decision making at the hospital
  - Visibility/accessibility of hospital administration

- Personal (preferences, likes, dislikes, expectations)
  - What's your ideal location? Why?
  - What are your family's and/or spouse's preferences?
  - What are you looking for in a community?
  - Do you plan to take any time off between your residency and your new job?
  - Do you have family ties in this area?
  - What do you like to do in your spare time?
- Growth opportunities (short- and long-term goals)
  - What are your long-term goals?
  - Where do you see yourself in three, five, or 10 years from now?
  - What are your professional goals?
  - What are your research and/or academic goals?
- Concerns (red flags based on your history)
  - Any gaps in your education
  - Anything negative in your records (e.g., DUI, complaints)

YOUR QUESTIONS

Gathering and evaluating as many facts as you can about a potential employer ultimately makes the interview more **WORTHWHILE**. Not only will you gain valuable information to help make your decision, you are also presenting yourself in a more positive light by asking informed questions.

The questions you ask should be linked to the priorities that were identified in Stage 4:

- Core values
- Compensation
- Quality of life (location, community)
- Practice settings
- Work environment
- Daily work (job responsibilities)

In the space provided on the following pages, list questions that you would like to ask during the interviews.

CATEGORY	MY QUESTIONS
Core Values (Alignment) • What's non-negotiable for me when it comes to my values? Sample questions: *I read the mission and vision statement of the hospital. How does that play out in real-life decisions?* *How would you describe the culture of the hospital?*	
Compensation • Salary • Productivity • Benefits • Incentives • Bonuses • Loan repayment Sample Questions: *Please explain the compensation structure.* *Please explain the basic employee benefit package. What about malpractice insurance?* *Does your organization offer a loan-repayment program?* *Describe the process of transitioning from guaranteed salary to productivity compensation. How have other physicians adapted to the change after two years?*	

CATEGORY	MY QUESTIONS
Quality of Life (Location, Community) • Housing • Schools • Health and fitness • Community activities Sample Questions: *What about the schools in this area? I have a son starting first grade next year. Which communities provide quality education programs?* *Exercise is very important to me; does the hospital have a workout facility?*	
Practice Setting • Partner/shareholder in a single- or multi-specialty group • Employed position in a single- or multi-specialty group • Academic/teaching hospital • Independent contractor • Locum Tenens (substitute physician) • Hospital employee Sample Questions: *Describe the personalities of the physicians and some of the staff members. What's it like to work on this team?* *What's the biggest challenge or issue that you're working through right now?* *Describe the partnership arrangements — how does this work?*	

TRAILBLAZERS

The following physician quotes were extracted from Press Ganey surveys. In preparation for your interviews, especially with regards to work environment, take these statements into consideration and assess each opportunity.

"This hospital's greatest strength is the collaborative effort of administration and physicians/nurses particularly regarding patient safety and quality. I believe there has been ample opportunity for physicians to be **ACTIVELY INVOLVED** with administration in all decision-making processes; however, many physicians have not participated."

"Overall, patient care is **SUPERIOR** here compared with other facilities. The system runs smoothly because nearly everyone here, from leadership to ancillary, cares about patients and takes the time to know who works here, which builds a sense of **TEAMWORK**."

"The senior administration is largely devoid of physicians, making it incredibly difficult for the administration to **UNDERSTAND** or **COMMUNICATE** with its med staff."

"As a contracted physician, we are more afraid to have a **DISAGREEMENT** with leadership and be terminated than to stand up for what is right and what makes the most sense."

"I feel a complete **DISCONNECT** with the leadership here. Because of my frustration with leadership, I no longer have the energy or time to expend any effort on anything but my own practice."

"We need to increase **INFORMATION GATHERING** from doctors and employees about ways to improve quality and patient safety. Many opportunities to improve processes are lost because of the mechanisms currently in place ('has to go through committee,' 'add it to next month's agenda, etc.)."

"I would like for there to be more **DIRECT COMMUNICATION** between the admitting physician and the consults, including the hospitalist, so that proper and complete care is given to the patient. That way efficiency is being met and patients are well taken care of and sent home in a timely manner."

CATEGORY	MY QUESTIONS
Work Environment (Organization) • Day in the life of a physician • Turnover rate • Leadership, administration and employee relationships, teamwork • Payor mix • Work environment (pace, number of patients) • Quality of care, patient safety • Hospital technology and equipment • Advancement opportunities Sample Questions: *I am sure there are times when things don't go as planned, or we may have a difference of opinion. When these types of encounters occur, how do you work through them with your physicians?* *What is the role of your physicians when it comes to making decisions? Do you ask for their opinion? What happens when physicians and administration disagree on how to move forward?* *With the current state of healthcare, how is your hospital preparing for and adapting to these changes?*	
Work (Job Responsibilities, Expectations) • Clinical work • Patient mix • Support staff • Schedule (hours, on-call, part-time/full-time) • Pace of work (fast, medium, slow) • Number of patients per day • Call, jeopardy call schedule • Role of hospitalist • CME • Electronic medical records Sample Questions: *Can you walk me through how you schedule patients?* *What's the work schedule for physicians?* *Describe a typical day in terms of activity, types of patients, etc.*	

FINISHING UP THE INTERVIEW

Don't forget to ask, "**WHAT ARE THE NEXT STEPS?**" You can also ask them where you stand amongst the other candidates, how you fit in with the organization, and when to expect a decision to be made.

Finally, make sure to ask the interviewers for their business cards.

POST-INTERVIEW FOLLOW-UP

After the interview, write down important information while it's fresh in your mind, including:

- Your impressions
- Facts covered
- Additional questions you have
- Personal information about the people you met (about their family, vacations, etc.) so you can refer to it and add a personal touch in subsequent conversations

It's **YOUR RESPONSIBILITY** to initiate follow-up after the interview by sending a **THANK-YOU NOTE.** Write a personal thank-you note by hand, not over e-mail, to the people who interviewed you. Thank them for their time and the information about their practice you gained in the interview and also confirm your interest in the position.

If you want to learn more about the practice and continue as a candidate, say so. This also helps them in remembering your name and demonstrates professionalism as well as your written communication skills.

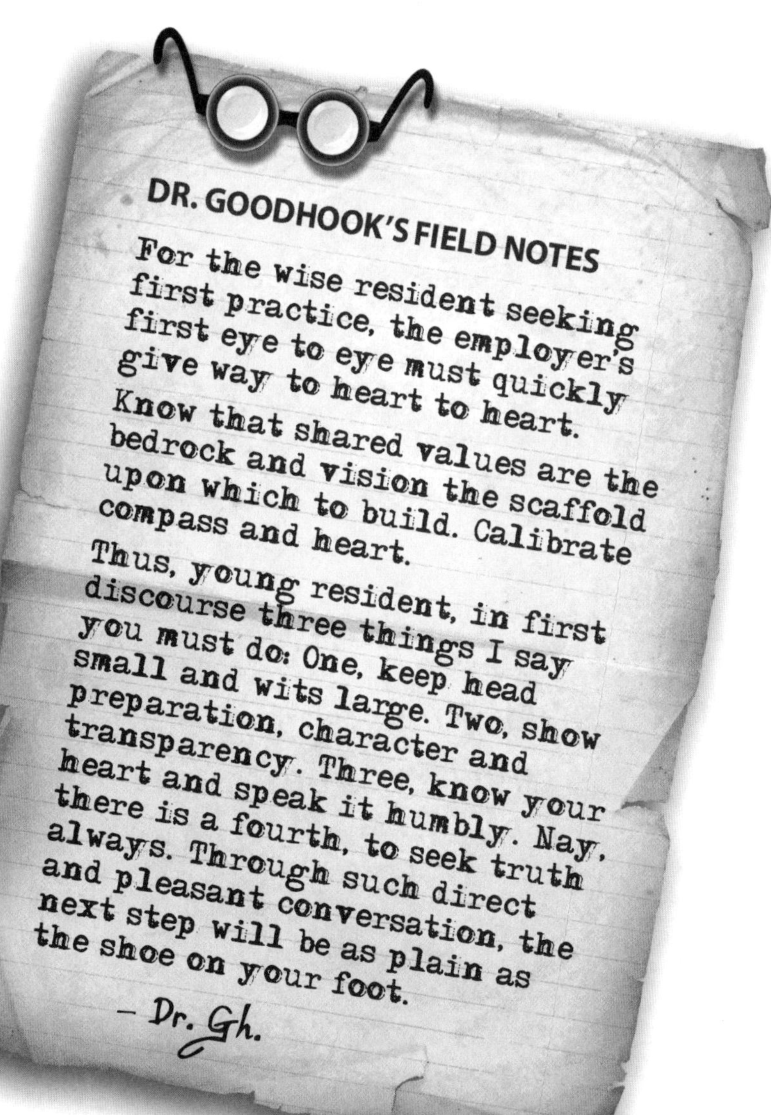

DR. GOODHOOK'S FIELD NOTES
For the wise resident seeking first practice, the employer's first eye to eye must quickly give way to heart to heart.
Know that shared values are the bedrock and vision the scaffold upon which to build. Calibrate compass and heart.
Thus, young resident, in first discourse three things I say you must do: One, keep head small and wits large. Two, show preparation, character and transparency. Three, know your heart and speak it humbly. Nay, there is a fourth, to seek truth always. Through such direct and pleasant conversation, the next step will be as plain as the shoe on your foot.
– Dr. Gh.

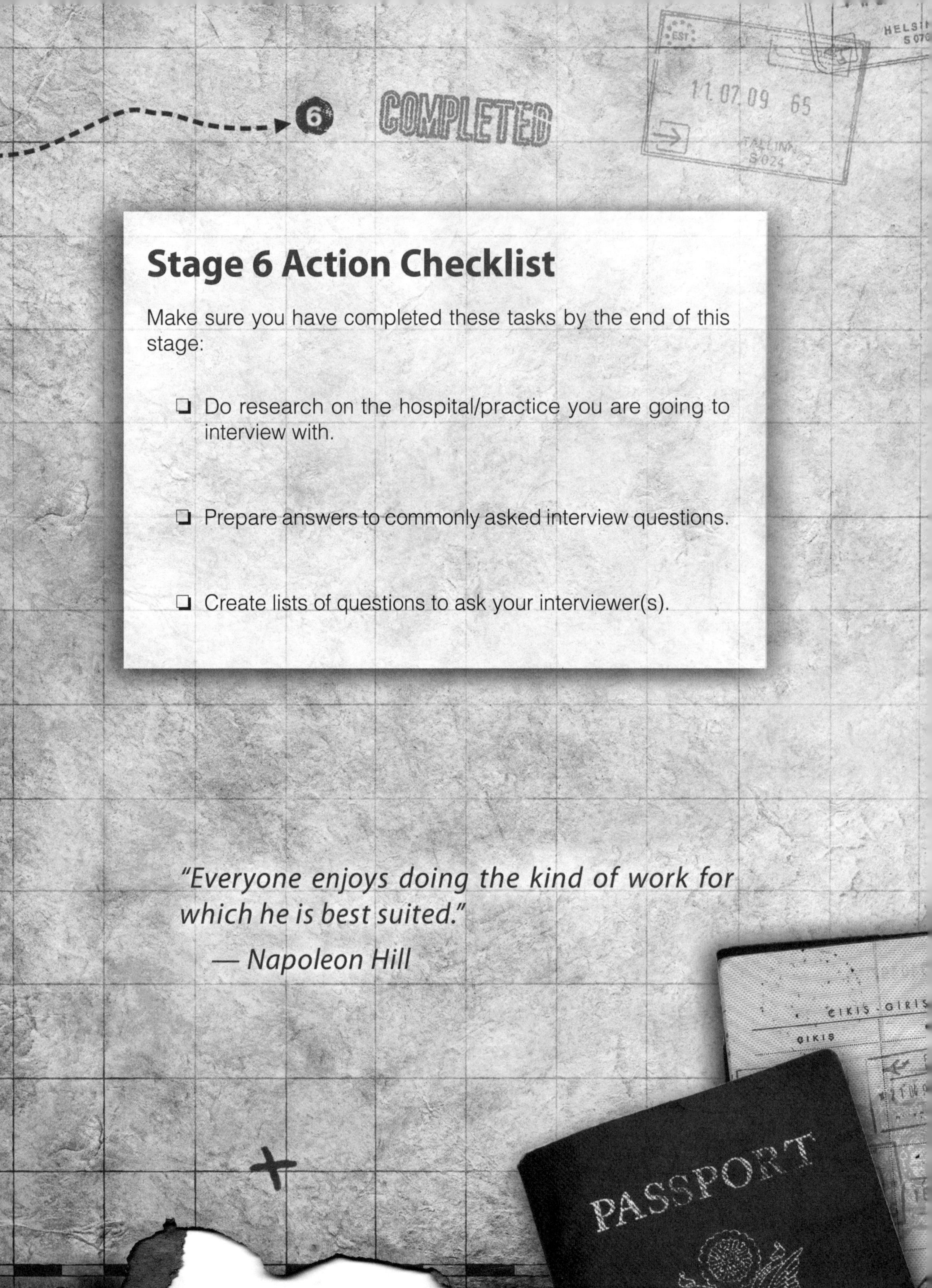

Stage 6 Action Checklist

Make sure you have completed these tasks by the end of this stage:

- ❑ Do research on the hospital/practice you are going to interview with.
- ❑ Prepare answers to commonly asked interview questions.
- ❑ Create lists of questions to ask your interviewer(s).

"Everyone enjoys doing the kind of work for which he is best suited."

— Napoleon Hill

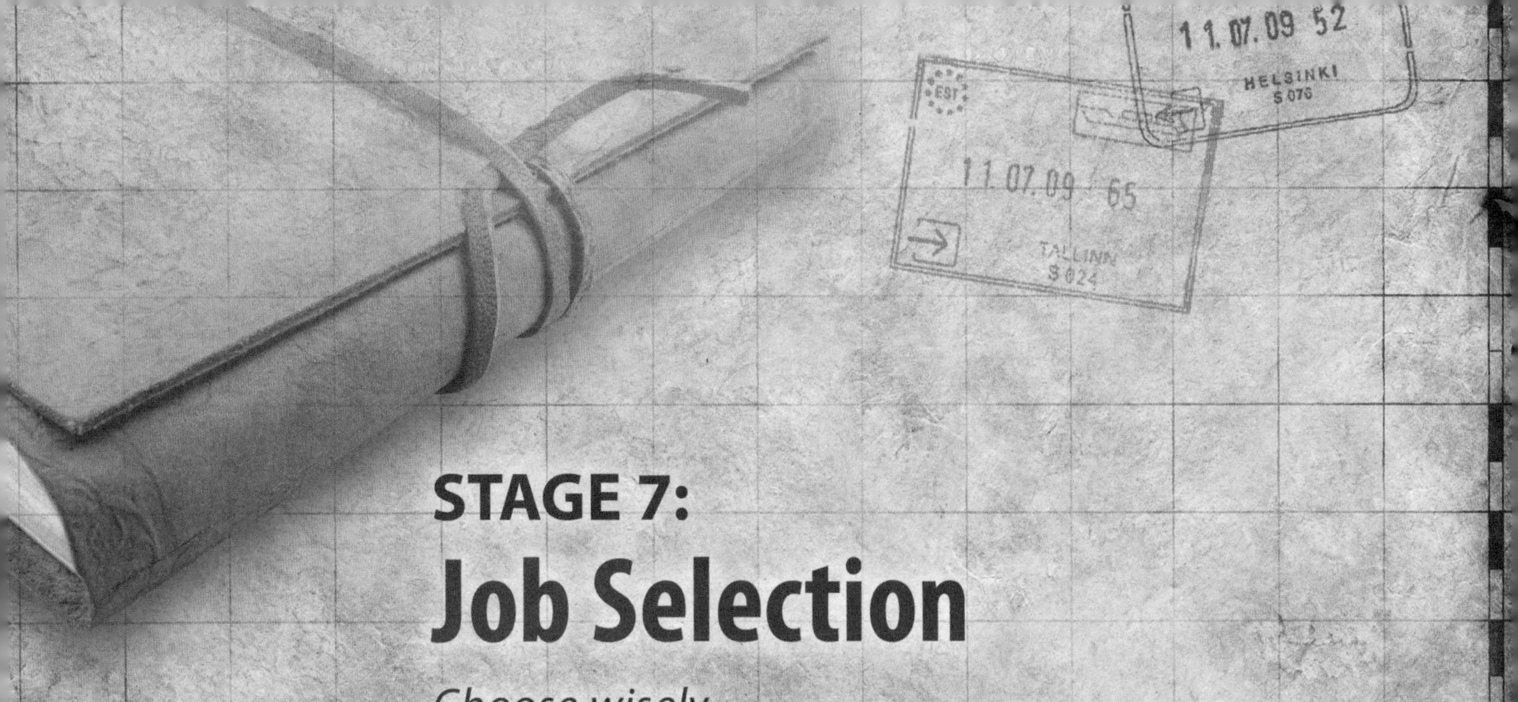

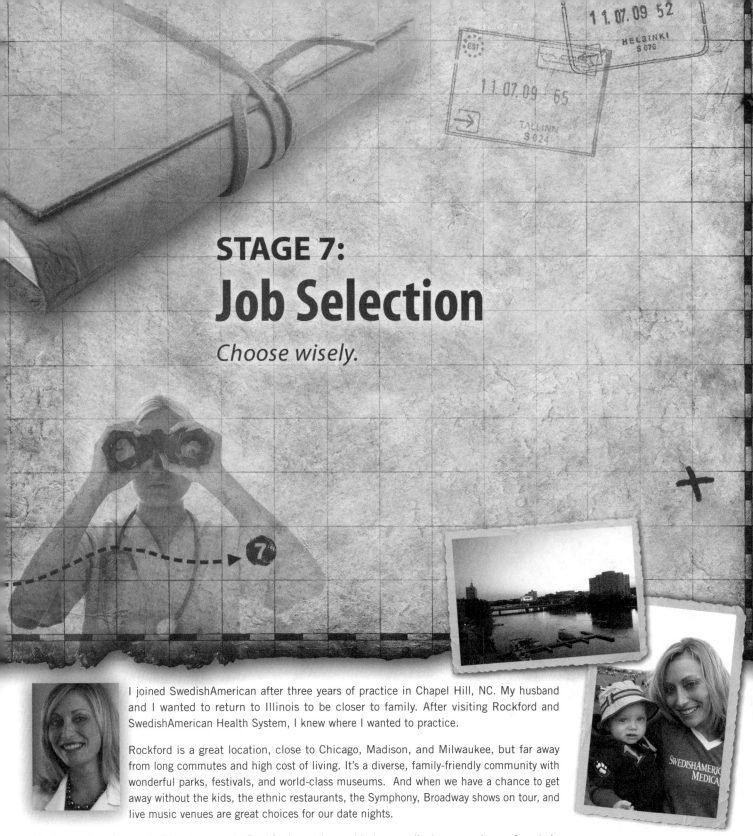

Your Job Offer Guide:

John Dawes, FACHE

President & Chief Executive Officer
Bothwell Regional Health Center

BS, Wichita State University;
Master of Health Administration,
Washington University School of Medicine

A healthcare executive for over 30 years, John Dawes has held leadership roles in health systems in four states, which together comprise more than 500 physicians, 3,500 employees and volunteers, 85,000 patient admissions, and $500 million in revenues. He serves on the Board of the Missouri Hospital Association and the Missouri Regents Advisory Council of the American College of Healthcare Executives. Earlier he was President and CEO of Mercy Hospital Clermont near Cincinnati. Previous posts in nationally known health systems included Vice President of Operations and Vice President of Medicine/Outpatient Service Centers. He is passionate about raising his three daughters, traveling, and college football and basketball.

Todd Skertich

Chief Executive Officer, Arlington HealthCare

B.A., Indiana University Northwest

Todd Skertich has directly overseen more than 2,000 permanent physician placements and negotiated a combined $400 million in starting salaries. His impact on the top-line revenue of his hospital and medical group clients is estimated at $1.8 billion.

Currently, Todd consults and educates senior leadership on best practices for hiring physicians. He has given more than 100 keynote speeches at residency programs on employment contracts, malpractice, interview tips, markets and trends. In addition, he has presented more than 750 workshops to recruiting consultants on the entire physician recruitment process.

Todd created, produced, and co-authored *Adventures in Medicine: The Resident's Guide to Life and Practice* to help physicians discover their path to success. To do so, Todd assembled a top-notch team of program directors, residents, fellows, practicing physicians, subject matter experts, and thought leaders in life balance and personal mission, vision and values.

Todd's own vision is to create a platform for physicians and their families to discover — or rediscover — their mission and vision beyond being a physician and to align their values with their future employer. His vision also encompasses providing physicians with the tools to become part of the solution to the many challenges facing our healthcare system today.

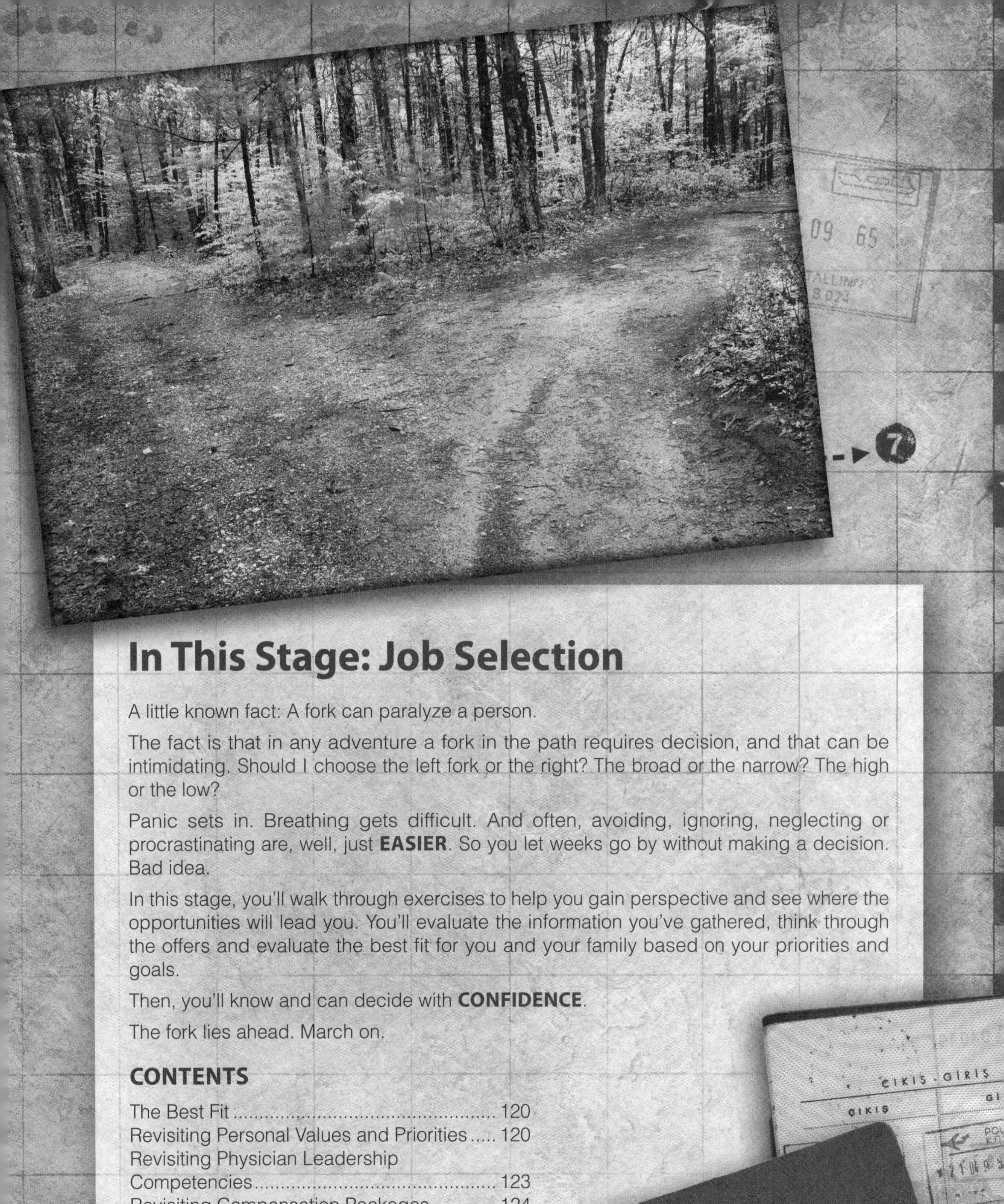

In This Stage: Job Selection

A little known fact: A fork can paralyze a person.

The fact is that in any adventure a fork in the path requires decision, and that can be intimidating. Should I choose the left fork or the right? The broad or the narrow? The high or the low?

Panic sets in. Breathing gets difficult. And often, avoiding, ignoring, neglecting or procrastinating are, well, just **EASIER**. So you let weeks go by without making a decision. Bad idea.

In this stage, you'll walk through exercises to help you gain perspective and see where the opportunities will lead you. You'll evaluate the information you've gathered, think through the offers and evaluate the best fit for you and your family based on your priorities and goals.

Then, you'll know and can decide with **CONFIDENCE**.

The fork lies ahead. March on.

CONTENTS

The Best Fit

Throughout this guidebook, the concept of "**BEST FIT**" has been mentioned several times. When it comes to making the decision of which job offer you will accept, keep in mind the best fit for both parties: you and the hospital/group you will be working with.

Job offers for physicians tend to be more complex than in many other professions because of the nature of the work and the high risk associated with compensation, malpractice, etc. In this stage, we will review three areas you need to evaluate in order to make a decision that you can feel confident about, and that meets your best-fit criteria: personal values and priorities, "must have" physician leadership competencies (non-clinical), and compensation packages.

Revisiting Personal Values and Priorities

The time and effort you invested in completing the exercises and assessments in Stage 4 now comes full circle. In case you haven't completed Stage 4, we recommend that you do so before proceeding. At a minimum, complete the priority worksheets. Gaining insight from your responses will help you tremendously during the decision-making process.

Keep an open mind when comparing offers, and make sure that money doesn't drive the overall decision. Compensation is important, but ignoring values and priorities can result in **DISCONTENTMENT**, **FRUSTRATION** and **RESENTMENT**. As a result, you may be miserable and feel trapped in a position, or you may decide to quit after a year or two and look for a new job — which causes stress as well.

As you compare offers, consider these life and career questions:

- Life Buckets: How do these offers support my needs, wants and dreams?
- Core Values: Which offer(s) allow me to fulfill my core values?
- Life Purpose: Which offer(s) support my life purpose and enable me to fulfill it?
- Priorities: Which offer(s) match my highest priority items (location, quality of life, etc.)?

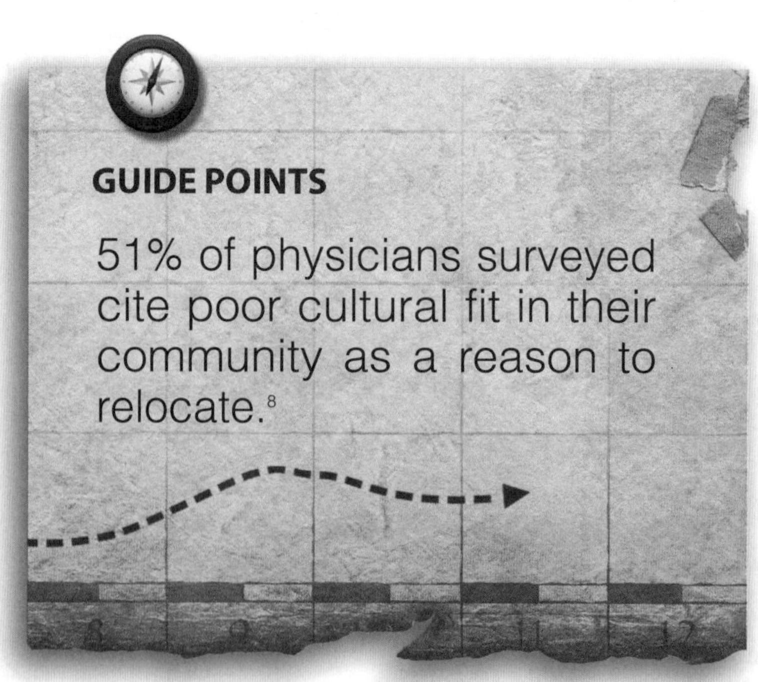

GUIDE POINTS
51% of physicians surveyed cite poor cultural fit in their community as a reason to relocate.[8]

Assuming you've received offers through letters of intent or you've identified top contenders based on interviews, you're now ready to step back and conduct a side-by-side comparison of each opportunity.

On the following pages, there are three worksheets. One allows you to compare offers as they relate to your personal values and priorities. Another will help you determine which ones offer the opportunity to continue to develop your professional competencies. The last allows you to compare compensation packages. Separating compensation from the other areas of comparison enables you to more objectively evaluate the importance and impact of life and money decisions.

PERSONAL VALUES AND PRIORITIES WORKSHEET INSTRUCTIONS

Follow these steps in completing the personal values and priorities worksheet on the following page.

STEP	INSTRUCTIONS
1. Job offers and possibilities	At the top of the worksheet, list the hospital or group name for up to three job offers or possibilities you are considering. If you have more than three, then pick the top three contenders or expand the worksheet.
2. Values and priorities	In the left-hand column, list up to 10 important values or priorities that will impact your decision. Use the suggestions provided beneath the chart or refer to the Stage 4 worksheets to decide on what to include.
3. Importance	In the importance column, rate the level of importance for each value or priority on a scale from 1 to 5 (1 = not very important; 5 = absolutely critical).
4. Probability	In the probability column, rate the likelihood that each offer or possibility will fulfill each value or priority on a scale of 1 to 5 (1 = very little chance the value or priority will be fulfilled; 5 = no doubt the value or priority will be fulfilled).
5. Quantify each value and priority	For each value and priority, multiply the importance number by the probability number and enter the result in the subtotal column for each hospital/group. For example, if you ranked location as a "5" in importance and a "3" in probability, its quantifiable value is 15.
6. Totals	Add the subtotals for each hospital/group, and enter the sums at the bottom of the chart.
7. Compare totals	Compare the totals of each hospital/group. Note which one has the highest total. **IMPORTANT:** This does not mean that you should accept the position with the highest number. Complete the other two worksheets and evaluate all aspects before making the final decision.

PERSONAL VALUES & PRIORITIES WORKSHEET

Values & Priorities *	Importance (1-5)	Hospital/Group #1 Probability (1-5)	Hospital/Group #1 Subtotal	Hospital/Group #2 Probability (1-5)	Hospital/Group #2 Subtotal	Hospital/Group #3 Probability (1-5)	Hospital/Group #3 Subtotal
Example: Geographic location	*5*	*3*	*15*	*2*	*10*	*4*	*20*
1.							
2.							
3.							
4.							
5.							
6.							
7.							
8.							
9.							
10.							
	Totals	**#1:**		**#2:**		**#3:**	

* Consider your Life Buckets (needs, wants, dreams), core values, life-purpose statement, and priorities (geographic location, quality of life, practice setting, work environment, and daily work).

Revisiting Physician Leadership Competencies

As discussed in Stage 2, there are competencies that every physician must possess and continue to develop throughout his or her career. In the worksheet below, rate the degree to which you believe each offer or possibility will allow you to both demonstrate as well as develop each of the five competencies (1 = no opportunity; 5 = significant opportunity). When you finish, add up the totals for each hospital/group.

PHYSICIAN LEADERSHIP COMPETENCIES WORKSHEET	Hospital/Group #1	Hospital/Group #2	Hospital/Group #3
Physician Competencies	Opportunity to Demonstrate & Develop (1-5)	Opportunity to Demonstrate & Develop (1-5)	Opportunity to Demonstrate & Develop (1-5)
Patient Centric: Focus on the patient; understand and effectively communicate the impact on the patient for every decision			
Business Acumen: Have working knowledge of the world of medicine from a business perspective; understand cost drivers, financial implications			
Team Focus: Collaborate, build cohesion, communicate effectively to non-physician leaders			
Facilitator of Change: Seek out differing points of view; encourage active discourse; bring out the best in the team			
Systems/Strategic Thinking: Understand roles inside a complex system; develop a strategic mindset and methodology for leading complex organizational systems			
Totals	#1:	#2:	#3:

Revisiting Compensation Packages

Follow these steps to complete the compensation package worksheet that begins on the following page:

STEP	INSTRUCTIONS
1. Importance	In the importance column, rate the level of importance for each compensation and benefits element on a scale from 1 to 5 (1 = not very important; 5 = absolutely critical).
2. Offer	Fill in the base salary, signing bonus (if applicable), loan repayment plan (if applicable), and productivity compensation for each hospital/group. For each benefits element, record the dollar value of the offer for each hospital/group. For example, for paid time off, calculate one week's pay, and then multiply the amount by the number of weeks of paid time off offered. Although you will need to do some calculations to quantify this way, doing so allows you to compare offers more easily. If both you and the employer contribute an amount in a particular area, such as health insurance, record both numbers, and then subtract your contribution from the employer's for the total monetary value.
3. Satisfaction	On a scale from 1 to 5 (1 = not acceptable; 5 = very satisfied), rate each compensation and benefits item offered by each hospital/group. By assessing the satisfaction level, you will be able to identify items that you would like to negotiate. (Remember that not all items are negotiable, depending on the hospital/group and their employment policies.)
4. Subtotal	Now multiply the importance number by the satisfaction number for each element and enter the result in the subtotal column for each hospital/group. For example, if you ranked base salary as a "5" in importance and a "3" in satisfaction with a particular offer, its quantifiable value is 15.
5. Totals	At the bottom of the table, add the subtotals from compensation and benefits to calculate a monetary and satisfaction total for each offer.

COMPENSATION PACKAGE WORKSHEET

		Hospital/Group #1			Hospital/Group #2			Hospital/Group #3		
Compensation	Importance (1-5)	Offer	Satisfaction (1-5)	Subtotal	Offer	Satisfaction (1-5)	Subtotal	Offer	Satisfaction (1-5)	Subtotal
Base salary (first-year wages)										
Signing bonus										
Loan repayment										
Productivity compensation (gross charges, net collections, RVUs)										
Compensation Subtotal										
Benefits	Importance (1-5)	Offer	Satisfaction (1-5)	Subtotal	Offer	Satisfaction (1-5)	Subtotal	Offer	Satisfaction (1-5)	Subtotal
Paid time off										
Relocation package										
Temporary housing										
Pension/retirement plan/401(k)										
Health insurance										
Dental insurance										
Life insurance										
Benefits Page 1 Subtotal										

COMPENSATION PACKAGE WORKSHEET *continued*		**Hospital/Group #1**			**Hospital/Group #2**			**Hospital/Group #3**		
Benefits	**Importance (1-5)**	**Offer**	**Satisfaction (1-5)**	**Subtotal**	**Offer**	**Satisfaction (1-5)**	**Subtotal**	**Offer**	**Satisfaction (1-5)**	**Subtotal**
Disability insurance										
Continuing medical education (CMEs)										
Reimbursement of dues, memberships and licenses										
Malpractice insurance										
Automobile allowance										
Cell phone allowance										
Other business expenses										
Payroll taxes (Social Security, Medicare)										
Other (e.g., on-boarding, coaching)										
Benefits Page 2 Subtotal										
Benefits Page 1 Subtotal										
Compensation Subtotal										
Totals										

Prioritizing Offers

It's decision-making time. Write the totals from the three preceding worksheets in the space below. Then, for each offer, record pros and cons based on what you like and don't like about that offer or hospital/group. Remember to consider things that may not have been accounted for on the worksheets, like the start date and term of employment. Do any cons represent deal breakers? Why or why not?

	Hospital/Group #1	Hospital/Group #2	Hospital/Group #3
Personal Values & Priorities Worksheet Total			
Physician Leadership Competencies Worksheet Total			
Compensation Package Worksheet Compensation Total			
Pros			
Cons			

GUIDE POINTS

Choosing the Best Offer

- Ask yourself these questions:
  - Does this offer represent the best fit overall?
  - Based on what I know, will I be **HAPPY** there?
  - Will I be able to contribute to the overall success of the hospital/group?
  - Does my spouse or significant other and children, if applicable, support the decision?
  - Will I be able to grow and develop professionally?
  - Will I be able to achieve an acceptable level of work-life balance?
- Do not accept more than one offer at a time.
- Once you decide, **WAIT 24-48 HOURS**, or at least one night's sleep, before communicating your decision.

Based on the information that you have in front of you after weighing the pros and cons, prioritize your offers.

CHOICE	NAME OF HOSPITAL/GROUP
First	
Second	
Third	

IMPORTANT: The offer that scored the highest points overall may **NOT** be the offer that becomes your first choice, and that's OK. Those exercises are meant to give you a point of reference from which to compare the offers, not to make the decision for you.

Communicating Your Decision

Accepting a job is relatively easy once verbal acceptance and letter of intent are complete. Communicating your acceptance to the hospital/group is a matter of a phone call, face-to-face meeting or written communication via e-mail or letter. It's important to be **POSITIVE** and communicate your level of **ENTHUSIASM** and **APPRECIATION** for the offer.

For offers you choose to decline, give the hospital/group the courtesy of an expedient response. Don't keep them waiting for an answer. Remember, they need to move forward with the hiring process as well. Be prepared for them to ask about the specific reasons you have declined

their offer, as they may want to learn from you about your experience with their interviewing process and/or negotiating. Keep the communication **SHORT** and **CONCISE**. A phone call is probably the most courteous option for informing the organization of your decision. Try to speak to the internal coordinator of the interview process or hiring director directly as opposed to leaving a voicemail or sending an e-mail. You may also work through the external recruiter to coordinate the communication process. Keep the explanation short and concise like:

"I appreciate the opportunity to interview for the open position. After careful consideration, I decided to accept another offer with another hospital. Thank you for your time and effort. I enjoyed meeting everyone and I wish you the best in finding a physician to meet your needs."

Moving Toward Employment

Once you've accepted a position, the credentialing and background check process begins. There are many elements associated with this process, which may be confusing and time-consuming, but the hospital or group will help coordinate it. This process must be completed before you start working.

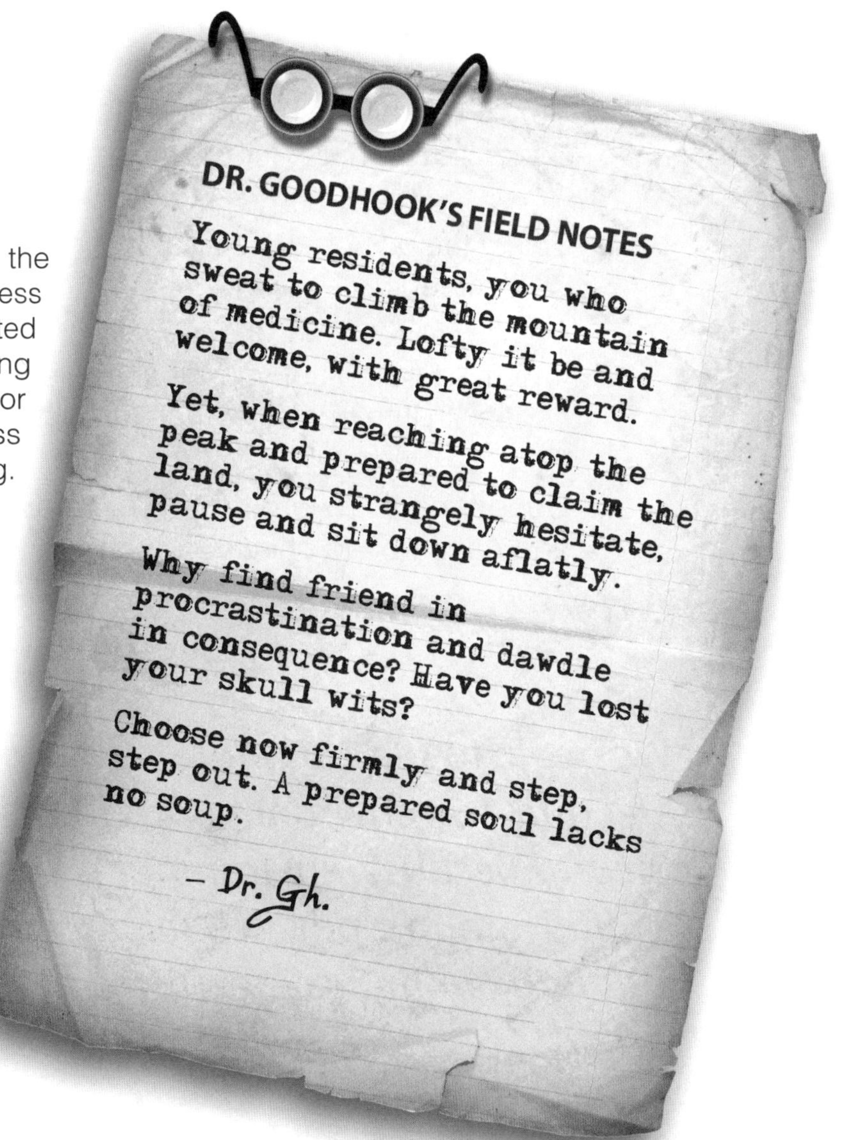

DR. GOODHOOK'S FIELD NOTES
Young residents, you who sweat to climb the mountain of medicine. Lofty it be and welcome, with great reward.
Yet, when reaching atop the peak and prepared to claim the land, you strangely hesitate, pause and sit down aflatly.
Why find friend in procrastination and dawdle in consequence? Have you lost your skull wits?
Choose now firmly and step, step out. A prepared soul lacks no soup.
– Dr. Gh.

7 COMPLETED

Stage 7 Action Checklist

Make sure you have completed these tasks by the end of this stage:

- ❑ Evaluate each offer based on personal values and priorities, physician leadership competencies and compensation.
- ❑ Based on various criteria (location, specialty, population), understand what's negotiable and what's not.
- ❑ Select the offer that provides the best overall fit for your life and career.
- ❑ Inform all parties of your final decision in a timely fashion, especially the positions that you turn down.
- ❑ Cooperate with your employer through the credentialing and background check process.

"We begin to see, therefore, the importance of selecting our environment with the greatest of care, because environment is the mental feeding ground out of which the food that goes into our minds is extracted."

— Napoleon Hill

STAGE 8:

Contract Negotiation

Do's and Don'ts

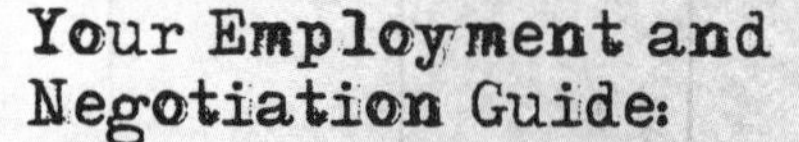

Thomas R. Palmer, Esq.

Partner, Meltzer, Purtill & Stelle LLC
J.D., B.A., DePaul University

Tom Palmer heads the employment group in a law firm representing more than 1,000 companies, professional practices and entrepreneurs. Recognized by the Leading Lawyers Network as a top attorney in the areas of employment law and closely-held business law, he has practiced law for more than 30 years, addressing such medical practice issues as non-compete agreements, shareholder disputes, practice acquisitions and sales, financing, and estate and succession planning. He endeavors to help parties find common ground in complex matters involving competing interests. He also has served on the board and quality councils of several hospitals. An avid sports fan and music lover, he regularly attends concerts and professional sporting events.

Your Employment and Negotiation Guide:

Mark Raymond, Esq.

Partner, Meltzer, Purtill & Stelle LLC

B.S., Northern Michigan University;
J.D., Loyola Chicago School of Law

Mark Raymond has practiced law for 12 years, providing counsel to closely held businesses and their owners, including physicians, for such issues as practice transitions, joint venture arrangements, employment agreements, special compensation arrangements, and shareholder agreements. He devises and implements ownership transitions and advises physicians and others on the efficient preservation and disposition of their assets. Before becoming an attorney, he gained extensive experience in estate, trust, tax, retirement, and other financial matters while at the Northern Trust Company, First National Bank of Chicago, and Deloitte and Touche. Mark and his family enjoy sports year round, but particularly relish their summer fun in Green Lake, Wisconsin.

8

In This Stage: Contract Negotiation

Is riding an elephant in your contract?

An important task for any expeditionary team is to negotiate a deal with a benefactor. Benefactors set the goals and guarantee funding to make sure the team has what they need, (like elephants, airplanes, Sherpas or pack burros). With a good benefactor, like a good employer, everyone gets paid.

While you won't have a benefactor or necessarily need to ride an elephant to work, you will negotiate a contract with your employer.

How do you negotiate a contract? Can you mess up getting that perfect job in your negotiation?

YES, many have and with great **REGRET**.

In this stage we'll discuss negotiating your contract, the terms and compensation structures.

Don't make a dumb mistake.

Get help. Get smart. Get ready to negotiate.

CONTENTS

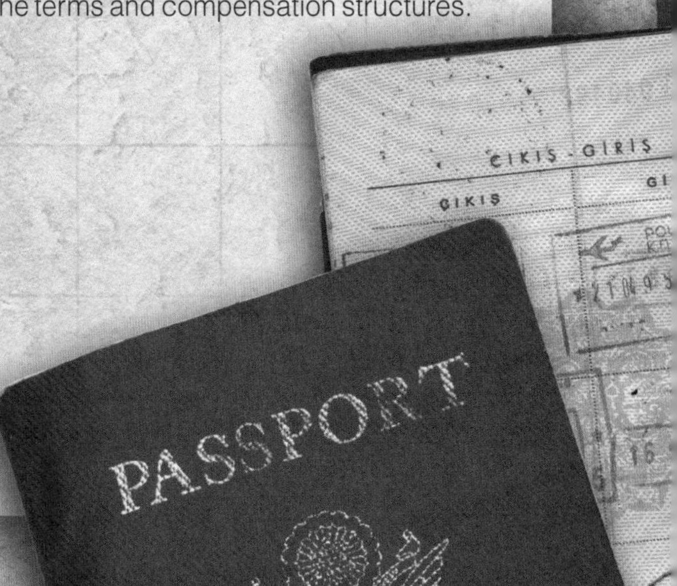

GUIDE POINTS

Negotiation Etiquette

- Move on to the contract negotiation stage only if you are prepared and confident to accept the position!
- Do not burn bridges by indicating to the employer that you will accept the job offer when in reality you are unsure. This hurts you, the employer and other candidates vying for a potential position with the employer.
- The time to negotiate the essential business terms of the offer letter is when you receive the offer letter, not after the formal contract is sent to you to be finalized.
- The verbal acceptance or offer letter acceptance is pending a successful review of the contract agreement.
- Keep in mind that you should not try to negotiate all the material terms of employment during the contract review stage.
- Remember that the manner and timing of accepting an opportunity is as important as whether to accept it at all.

Getting Started on the Right Path

Residents who are pursuing their first job are typically unfamiliar with the contract negotiation process, and they are also unlikely to know who to trust, especially when each hospital and group has its own persuasive "**SPIN**." As a result, you can become defensive, stressed and frustrated with the process. In extreme cases, there is a temptation to overstep your bounds, leading to a rescission of your "**DREAM OFFER**" and causing you to walk away with nothing.

Certainly, there is an opportunity to negotiate an employment agreement offered by a potential employer; however, it's important to have an appropriate perspective of the content and purpose of the agreement provisions so that the negotiation can be done in an **AMICABLE** and **EFFICIENT** manner. Employment contracts are legally binding documents that reflect work arrangements, including rights, compensation, benefits, process for termination, and post-employment obligations. Once signed, contracts require **MUTUAL AGREEMENT** to change, so they should be understood and revised, if needed, before signing.

Negotiating to Win: A Two-Way Street

One of the most **EXCITING** and perhaps **NERVE-WRACKING** times in a physician's life is being offered your first position and negotiating your first employment contract. Rightfully so, you deserve to enjoy being pursued as you've trained most of your adult life to become a physician. However, the excitement can turn into stress, which can lead to poor decisions. Gaining perspective on employment agreements and the risk-benefit provisions they contain for each of the parties can go far to keep the first offer and employment agreement negotiation a very positive experience.

Graduates entering the market may be pursued by several hospitals or physician practices because of the shortage of physicians. It is not uncommon for a resident to have many opportunities to choose from. Residents talk among themselves and it's easy for them to be influenced by all of the comments that **APPEAR** to place them in the driver's seat of employment negotiations.

Take a look at four residents and what really happened in each scenario.

RESIDENT	ONE SIDE OF THE STORY	THE OTHER SIDE
A	Received $50,000	Documented in contract as a loan forgiven over five years with payback provision for early termination.
B	Negotiated non-compete clause out of agreement	Traded income guarantee. Working in a less desirable area.
C	Her attorney rewrote the hospital's entire agreement.	Hospital rescinded offer.
D	Received four offers.	Four potential employers expressed interest. Only one extended an offer, which was way less than what the physician had hoped for.

Remember, there are two sides to every story.

OFFER LETTER

An offer letter lists the material terms (such as compensation, insurance, paid time off, etc.) of the employment relationship. While acceptance of an offer letter can serve as a binding contract, when a formal contract is anticipated, the offer letter typically states that it is non-binding and subject to the execution of a formal contract.

WHEN A CONTRACT IS DRAFTED

A draft contract is typically provided when the

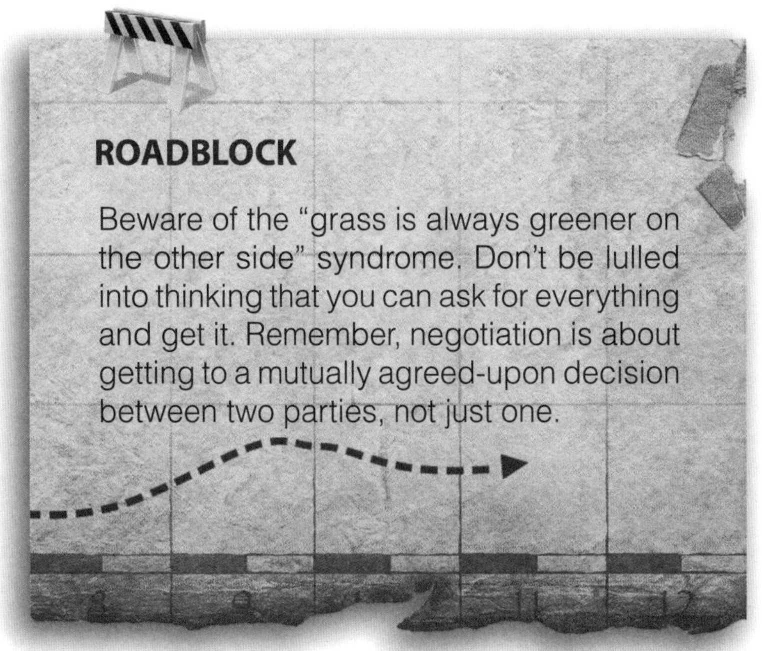

ROADBLOCK
Beware of the "grass is always greener on the other side" syndrome. Don't be lulled into thinking that you can ask for everything and get it. Remember, negotiation is about getting to a mutually agreed-upon decision between two parties, not just one.

candidate is ready to accept a position. At that point, the terms of the offer have been verbally accepted and the parties are ready to execute an agreement in writing. An offer letter may first outline the material terms that have been verbally accepted. Then, a formal contract is drawn up and becomes effective upon execution by the parties.

MOVING FORWARD WITH A CONTRACT

The employer will generate the proposed contract. An employer will generally not move to the contract stage unless you have indicated a willingness to accept the offer. From the employer's perspective, when a candidate agrees to move to the contract stage, the position may be considered filled, causing the employer to stop interviewing. The goal of some candidates is to collect a number of agreements before deciding which one to take. While this approach may be rewarding to the ego, collecting contracts may provide a **FALSE** sense of security and control over a negotiation. If the employer finds out later that you have accepted another position, a bridge is almost certainly burned for any future opportunities. In addition, undecided candidates have less bargaining power than candidates who are fully prepared to accept an opportunity. The former may lose the chance to obtain key accommodations during the negotiation phase since they cannot create a sense of urgency for the employer to accept their terms.

Seeking Legal Counsel

Whether or not to seek legal counsel for the contract-negotiation process is an individual choice. Most people presented with an employment contract seek legal counsel, while some may feel comfortable talking through the clarifications and negotiations on their own. Each person must weigh the cost versus the benefit and then determine what is right for them.

An attorney helps interpret and translate the language of the agreement. More specifically, an attorney helps the physician address needs and interests in the contract, understand risks and responsibilities, identify key points for negotiation, and determine how to advance such negotiations. Generally, the attorney does not negotiate the agreement. Instead, you or your physician recruiter are responsible for this activity.

Being **CLEAR** and **PRECISE** with an attorney regarding your needs and expectations is the best way to avoid inefficiency or misunderstandings. For example, identify clearly whether the attorney, after reviewing the contract, will make recommended changes to the contract or merely provide comments for consideration. Sometimes an agreement is sent to the attorney with no instructions, and the attorney proceeds to mark it up or substantially rewrite it. As a result, the cost might be higher than anticipated and valuable time can be wasted.

In addition, many organizations have standard contracts that only permit changes to names and financial terms of the contract. In such cases, an attorney should not attempt to rewrite the agreement but should educate the physician as to its content and prepare the physician for the discussions that will occur before the contract is signed.

When communicating expectations to an attorney, consider saying something like the following:

"Please briefly review this agreement and contact me to discuss your initial comments and how best to proceed. I would certainly like to know about things that may stand out as unusual or may need further clarification or explanation."

SELECTING AN ATTORNEY: TIME IS MONEY

The amount of time an attorney spends on a matter depends on such things as the length of the contract and whether the attorney is reviewing and commenting or rewriting the agreement. Before you commit to an attorney, you might ask them to estimate the time involved to complete the work requested.

There are three primary criteria for selecting an attorney:

1. **Expertise**
   At a minimum, the attorney should be a specialist in employment law. Experience should also include dealing with physician employment contracts.

2. **Hourly Rates**
   Legal fees can range from $200 to $600 an hour or even higher. It is far better to have effective representation from an attorney experienced in employment and healthcare law for four hours at $500 per hour than less-effective representation from a less-experienced attorney for 12 hours at $250 per hour.

3. **Accessibility**
   The attorney should be available to meet with you and respond to your questions promptly.

When you send an agreement to your attorney, it's helpful to provide the following information, if available.

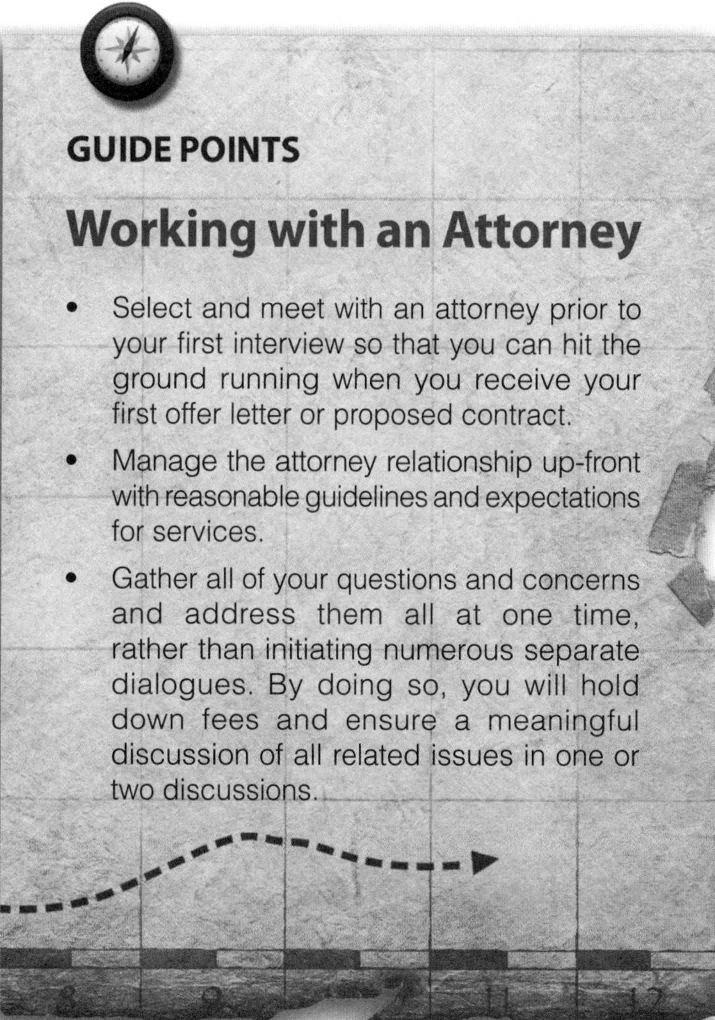

GUIDE POINTS

Working with an Attorney

- Select and meet with an attorney prior to your first interview so that you can hit the ground running when you receive your first offer letter or proposed contract.
- Manage the attorney relationship up-front with reasonable guidelines and expectations for services.
- Gather all of your questions and concerns and address them all at one time, rather than initiating numerous separate dialogues. By doing so, you will hold down fees and ensure a meaningful discussion of all related issues in one or two discussions.

- Whether the agreement is the same essential document other individuals in the same department have signed.

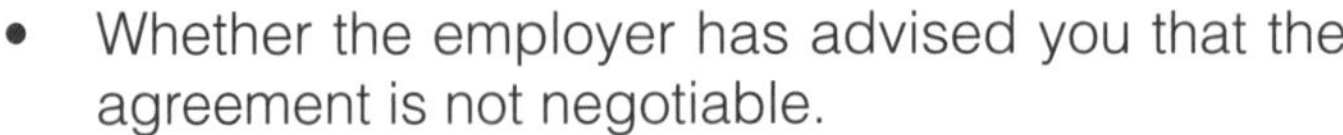

TRAILBLAZERS

"I found my dream job. I was excited, and so was my family. My wife placed a bid on a home that overlooked a lake. The community had a hockey field house, perfect for my six- and eight-year-old boys. I called my parents and told them I was finally starting my life. Then, the bottom fell out.

I got cocky and started negotiating terms that my colleagues had done with other hospitals. Inexperienced, I took the sign-on bonus my buddy negotiated, the starting salary of another one of my friends, the loan repayment with another, and tried to negotiate the non-compete (I thought of that one on my own).

What happened in the end was no counter offer was given. I was shocked and disappointed. My ideal employer called and shared with me, "We decided to go in a different direction." I immediately backtracked but the decision was already made. I had gotten caught up in the moment and I lost my way. I accepted a position with my third-choice employer after the second offer went to another candidate when I was negotiating the first."

- Whether the employer has advised you that the agreement is not negotiable.

- A deadline for the agreement review, comment and/or rewriting assignment. In general, agreements should be reviewed and signed within seven to ten days of being tendered. This means that the agreement should be reviewed with the attorney within a couple of days of receipt in case there are questions, clarifications or other concerns.

Negotiating a Contract

Effective communication is extremely important during the negotiation process because it is very difficult to go back and renegotiate terms once they have been agreed upon. In the event terms are not agreeable, you need to decide if you are **WILLING TO WALK** from the opportunity. It is important to be realistic in identifying deal-breaker points. Being willing to walk away is ultimately the best leverage available to a physician, but it is very difficult to wield and should be asserted very carefully. If compensation is most important and location is secondary, you should decline unacceptable offers in preferred markets and consider looking in secondary markets where there is much more flexibility in compensation.

WHAT'S NEGOTIABLE VERSUS WHAT'S NOT

In some agreements, none of the terms are negotiable, and in other agreements, some of the terms may be negotiable, including salary, signing bonus and start date. Other terms that may be negotiable are paid time off, relocation package and type of compensation structure.

As with so many matters, the market usually dictates whether terms of the agreement are negotiable. The more limited the supply of physicians in relation to the demand in a position, the more flexibility there is in negotiation.

Additionally, the geographic market may also play a significant role in whether there is room for negotiation. Opportunities in the Midwest tend to be more negotiable than opportunities in the Northeast, and rural markets tend to be more negotiable than metro markets in order to attract solid candidates. Mainly, negotiations depend on supply and demand — the higher the demand, the more likely that the opportunity is negotiable.

Learn from the employer which items are negotiable and which ones are not. Once you learn this information, select the items that you choose to negotiate very carefully. It's important not to appear over zealous or selfish. Both parties need to walk away from the negotiating table feeling like a **WINNER**, not a loser, disappointed in the results.

TIMEFRAME FOR NEGOTIATIONS

After you provide the terms that you would accept, the employer should be able to provide you with an answer quickly. If the employer comes back with a counter offer, you may have one more opportunity to go back and work out the details. The negotiations should not take longer than a few days if the negotiations are positioned the right way.

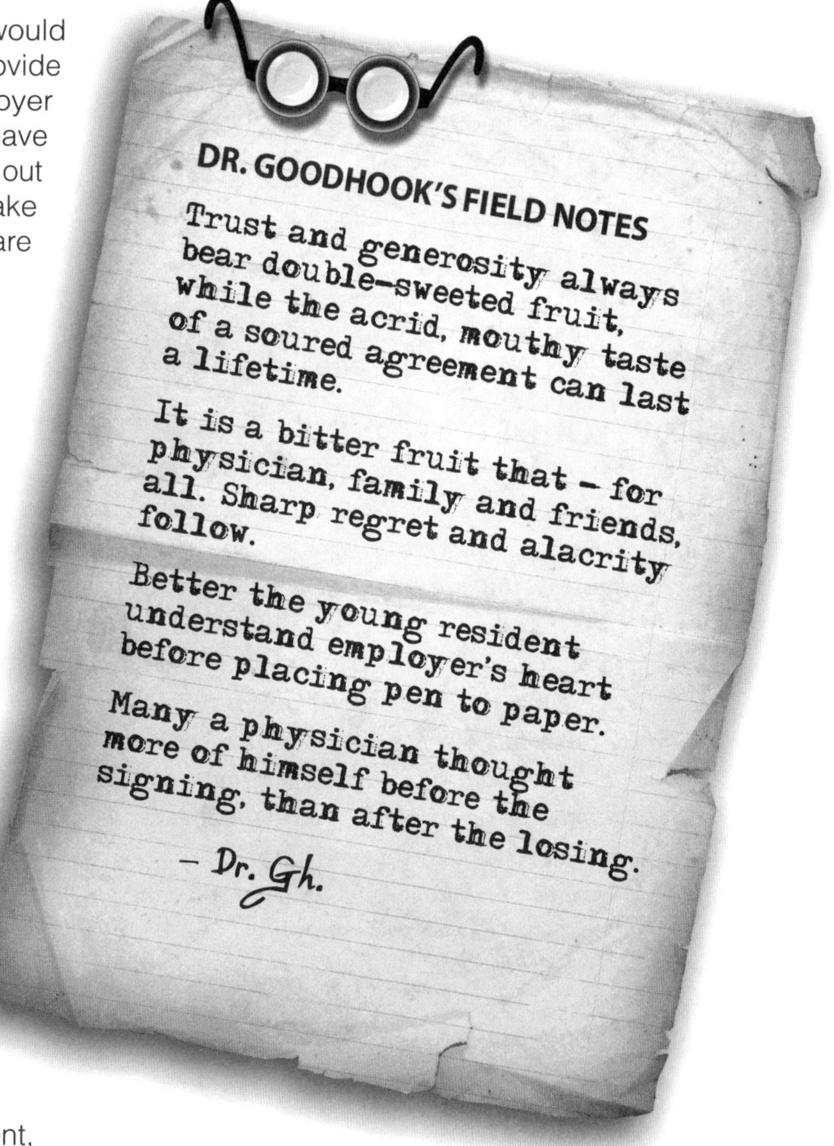

DR. GOODHOOK'S FIELD NOTES
Trust and generosity always bear double-sweeted fruit, while the acrid, mouthy taste of a soured agreement can last a lifetime.
It is a bitter fruit that - for physician, family and friends, all. Sharp regret and alacrity follow.
Better the young resident understand employer's heart before placing pen to paper.
Many a physician thought more of himself before the signing, than after the losing.
- Dr. Gh.

EMPLOYER NEGOTIATOR

Depending on the organization, you may negotiate with the CEO (generally in rural communities and small- to medium-size organizations), CFO, director, manager, in-house recruiter, or the recruiting firm that represents the employer.

END OF NEGOTIATIONS

If the terms are reasonable, you should hear back soon, and the employer should be able to advise you whether or not they can meet those terms.

If the terms are not reasonable, or if you are asking for something that is not customary, like negotiating a non-compete clause out of the agreement,

GUIDE POINTS

Feeling inadequate, uncomfortable and/or nervous about the negotiation process? Recruiting firms can be very helpful in negotiating agreements; however, you are ultimately the one responsible for determining the ideal position for your life and career priorities. Below are some tips:

KNOW YOUR MARKET

- Is your specialty or area of experience in demand?
- Is your region in demand?
- Is your community in demand?
- What are similar opportunities in similar communities paying? (Make sure to compare apples with apples.)

KNOW WHEN YOU'RE READY

- Under what circumstances would you accept the opportunity? (If you cannot answer this question, you're not ready to negotiate!)
- If you proceed with negotiation, make sure you are prepared to accept the opportunity if the organization agrees to your terms.

KNOW YOUR LIMITS

- Are the terms you're trying to negotiate reasonable, or are your demands likely to be viewed as tactless overreacting?

KNOW YOUR POSITIONING

Below is an example of physician responding to an offer letter that she received.

"I have trained for more than 12 years and am ready to start my medical career. The interview process has been both exciting and overwhelming. During the past six months, I have interviewed at five different organizations and this is by far the opportunity that feels right and where I can make a strong contribution to your hospital and community. My husband and daughter are very excited about the possibility of us moving forward. The last thing that I want is to come across as money hungry or self-serving. I want to make sure that you know that I'm looking at this opportunity long-term and the bottom-line is working toward the productivity bonus where I will be justifying my higher compensation by greater contribution to the organization. Although I have offers that are higher, this is the place that my family and I want to be and I'm trying to get comfortable with the terms so we can move forward. After finishing up residency and having debt of $200,000, along with buying our first home, and the unknown of how long it's going to take to get up and running, I am looking for "X amount" and "X benefits." I am prepared to execute an agreement with you within five days of receiving a mutually acceptable agreement."

there are times when the employer will not respond back. This is because those non-customary terms lead them to conclude there is not a match.

As long as you are forthright, present yourself well and communicate effectively, there is no reason that there should be any concerns. Know what you want, but evaluate the situation from the employer's perspective as well. If you make it too hard for the employer to work with you, you may **JEOPARDIZE** a good deal.

ROADBLOCK

Comparing Offers

Your career is a big part of your life and you should feel good about going into a new opportunity.

It may be difficult to avoid comparing your offers with the offers your colleagues are getting; however, remember that each region is very different, as is each market within each region.

There are different opportunities, so when a colleague is getting one offer, it may or may not be comparable to yours, and your colleagues' goals may be very different than yours.

Remember not to take anything personally. Most of the negotiations have to do with organizational standards and objectives and the market and are less about your individual needs.

If you're reasonable, the market and the contract negotiation process should take care of you.

Understanding Employment Contracts

It's a good idea to familiarize yourself with common terminology found in an employment contract. Knowledge of employment contracts enables you to:

- Become familiar with the different sections of a contract
- Interact with a potential employer as well as an attorney with more knowledge
- Focus on matters most important to you
- Minimize the time to review and sign a contract
- Be more self-assured and confident (not arrogant) when interacting with a potential employer and your attorney
- Be more professional and business-savvy

Both parties benefit from solidifying employment contracts because they are able to clearly set forth material rights and obligations, thereby managing risk of the matters addressed.

CONTRACT TERMS

The following is a list of common contract terms and their meanings. Please note that these definitions are for informational purposes only and are not intended to be legal advice. Consult an attorney if you have questions about your particular situation.

TERM	DEFINITION
Term	The specified beginning and ending dates of the contract along with any provisions describing the renewal or extension of the contract term.
Employment	The hiring of a person for a salary, fee or other payment to perform work for an employer.
Responsibilities	Duties and performance expectations, qualifications, licensing requirements, certifications and staffing privileges.
Compensation	Payment for work performed by salary, fees or otherwise.
Benefits	All perquisites provided or made available to employees by employers, including paid time off, group health and dental insurance, life insurance, sick leave, disability insurance and retirement plans.
Expenses	Defines the business-related expenses that will be paid on behalf of the physician such as licensing fees, CMEs, medical journal, association dues and the like.
Facilities	Addresses basic practice needs such as office space, examination rooms, equipment and support staff.
Loyalty	Generally prohibits the physician from providing similar services to another employer without the current employer's consent.
Supervision	Provides the structure for supervision and evaluation by someone familiar with the employee's role and responsibilities.
Compliance	Requires the physician to adhere to the employer's policies and procedures as well as all applicable licenses, laws, rules and regulations.
Acceptance of Patients	Specifies protocols for accepting patients.
Vacation and Meetings	Defines the amount of time, usually expressed in terms of days or weeks for which the physician will be given leave from job duties for vacation or to attend CME programs, with or without pay.
Disability	Describes the circumstances in which an employee not able to perform job duties due to illness or injury may continue to receive compensation (or a percentage of compensation) for some pre-determined period of time.

TERM	DEFINITION
Termination	Discusses specific circumstances under which employment may be terminated either with or without cause, with cause being carefully and clearly defined.
Records and Files	Defines who patient records belong to and the continuing access a physician will have to the records, including post-employment access and/or duty to turn over files and records.
Internal Revenue Code References	Refers to specific sections of tax laws that may be relevant to either the employer or physician, particularly with respect to compensation and benefit issues.
Non-Compete Covenants	A restrictive agreement whereby the physician agrees to refrain from practicing within a specified geographic area or at certain hospitals for a specified period of time after the physician's employment ends.
Non-Solicitation Covenants	A restrictive agreement whereby the physician agrees to refrain from soliciting patients and/or employees of the employer for a specified period of time after the physician's employment ends.
Confidentiality Covenants	A restrictive agreement whereby the physician agrees to refrain from divulging or using the employer's proprietary and confidential information after the physician's employment ends.
Track to Partnership (if applicable)	Defines the conditions that must be met in order for the physician to be eligible for an ownership position with the employer.
Buy-In (if applicable)	Specifies the fixed dollar amount or formula used to determine the cost of purchasing an ownership interest in the medical practice.
Productivity Formula	Defines the formula used to divide income among practice owners, typically based on RVUs or relative collections.
Indemnity and Malpractice Insurance	Employers may provide insurance or agree to defend a physician named as a defendant in a lawsuit. It is important to know who is paying the premiums and what the coverage limits are. Additionally, continuing coverage after employment has ended (tail coverage) should be addressed in this section.
Applicable Law; Venue	Determines by agreement of the parties the particular state law that will apply in the event that a dispute arises involving the terms of the contract. In addition, this section of the contract may define the location where a lawsuit involving the contract will be heard.
Modifications	Generally provides that the written contract contains the entire agreement between the parties and further provides that the contract can only be modified in writing and signed by both parties.
Severability and Judicial Construction	This provision allows a judge to make a determination as to the meaning and intention of a provision in the event of a legal dispute over its meaning. It further allows any contract provision that is deemed to be illegal to be removed from the contract without the entire contract becoming null and void.

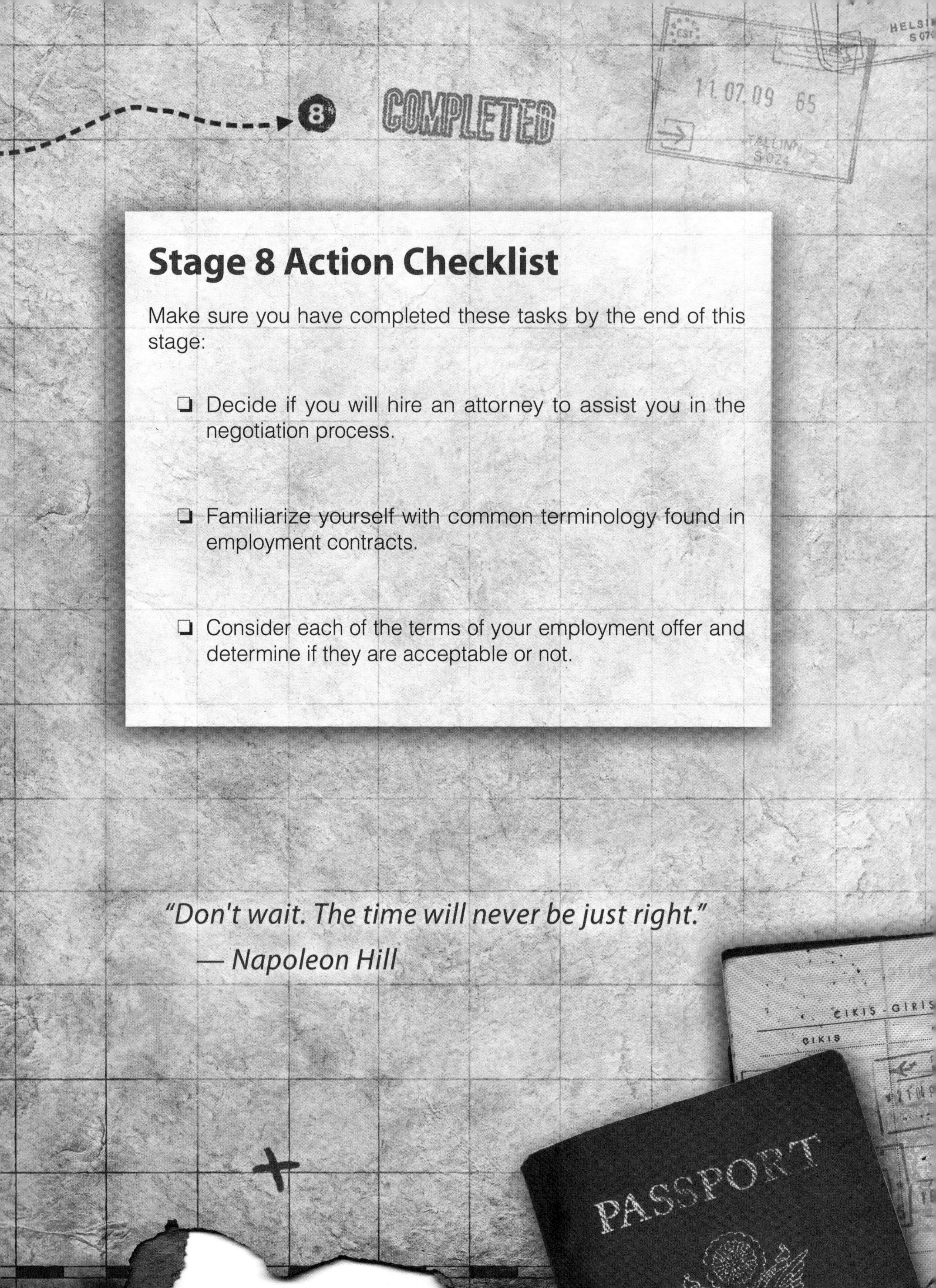

Stage 8 Action Checklist

Make sure you have completed these tasks by the end of this stage:

- ❑ Decide if you will hire an attorney to assist you in the negotiation process.
- ❑ Familiarize yourself with common terminology found in employment contracts.
- ❑ Consider each of the terms of your employment offer and determine if they are acceptable or not.

"Don't wait. The time will never be just right."

— Napoleon Hill

STAGE 9:

Finance Basics

Be wise in spending, saving and investing NOW!

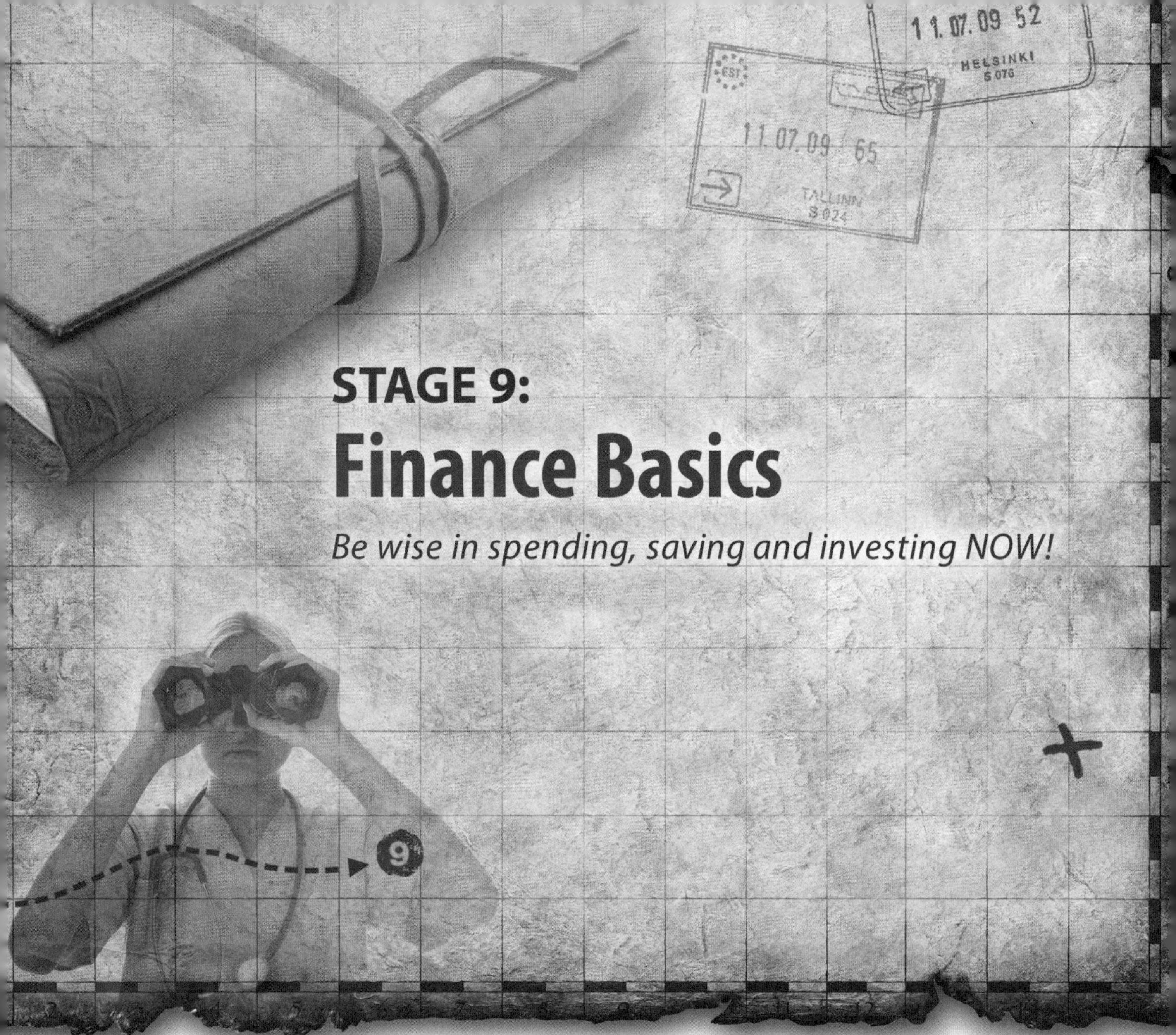

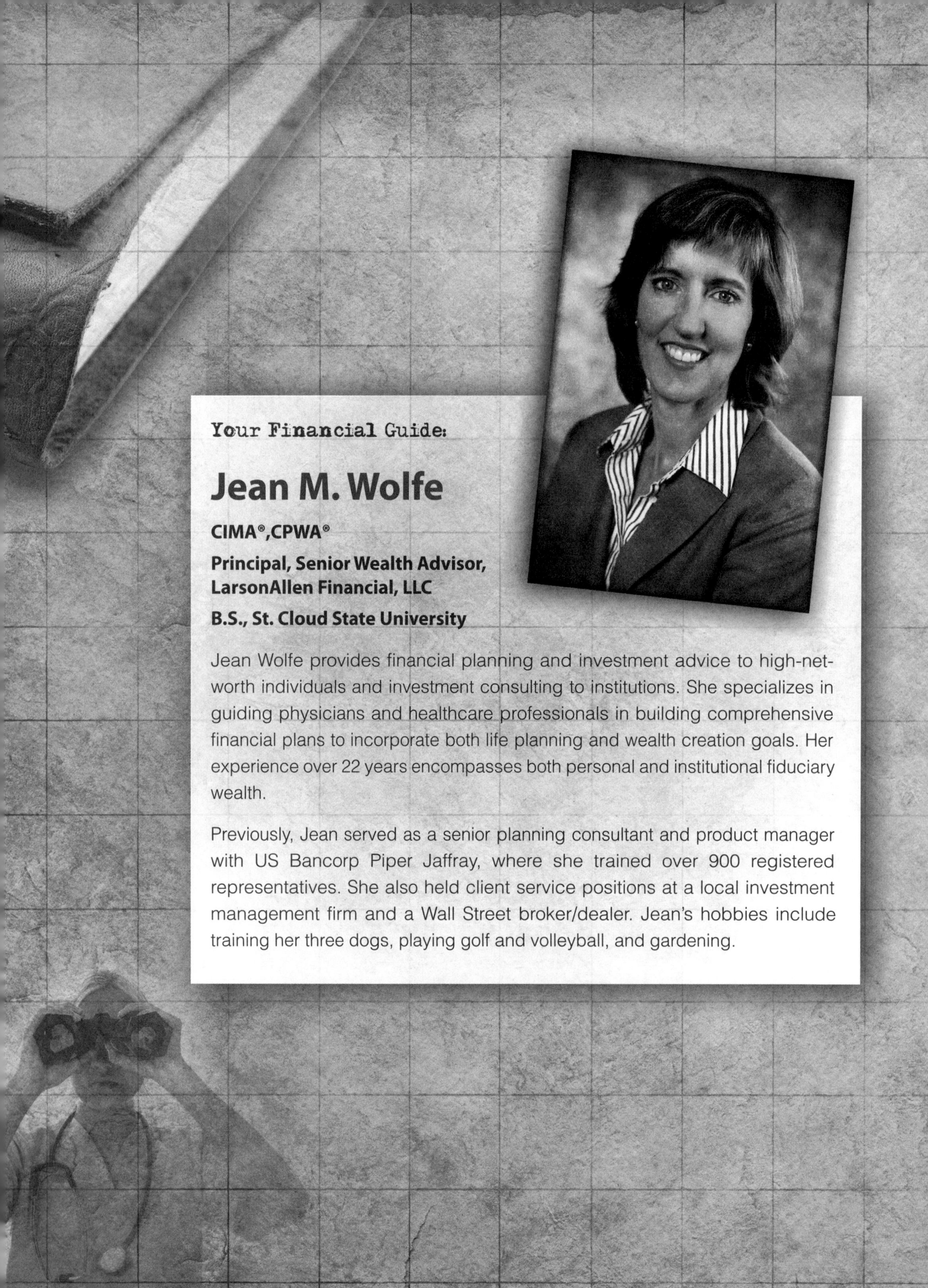

Your Financial Guide:

Jean M. Wolfe

CIMA®,CPWA®

Principal, Senior Wealth Advisor, LarsonAllen Financial, LLC

B.S., St. Cloud State University

Jean Wolfe provides financial planning and investment advice to high-net-worth individuals and investment consulting to institutions. She specializes in guiding physicians and healthcare professionals in building comprehensive financial plans to incorporate both life planning and wealth creation goals. Her experience over 22 years encompasses both personal and institutional fiduciary wealth.

Previously, Jean served as a senior planning consultant and product manager with US Bancorp Piper Jaffray, where she trained over 900 registered representatives. She also held client service positions at a local investment management firm and a Wall Street broker/dealer. Jean's hobbies include training her three dogs, playing golf and volleyball, and gardening.

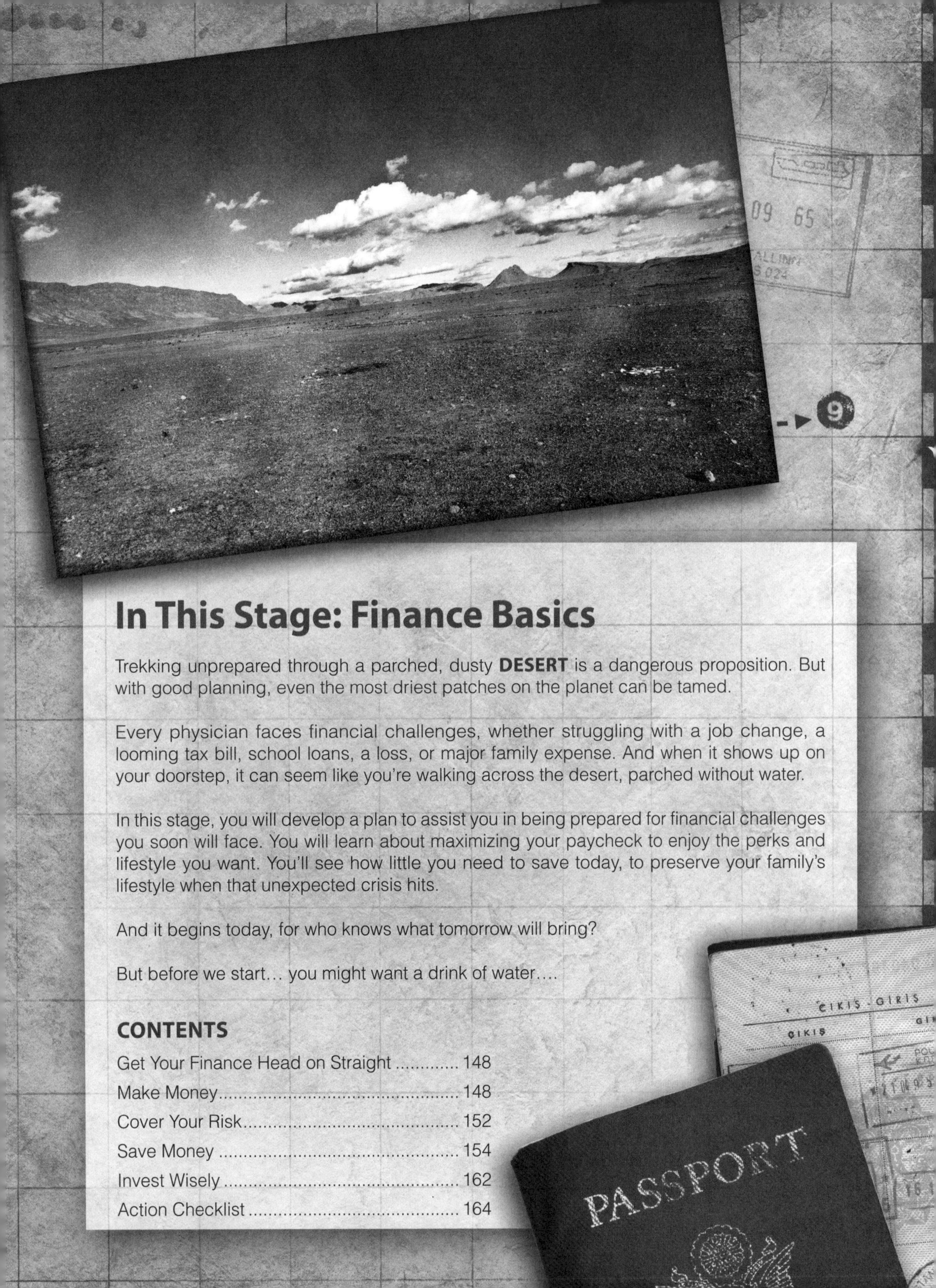

In This Stage: Finance Basics

Trekking unprepared through a parched, dusty **DESERT** is a dangerous proposition. But with good planning, even the most driest patches on the planet can be tamed.

Every physician faces financial challenges, whether struggling with a job change, a looming tax bill, school loans, a loss, or major family expense. And when it shows up on your doorstep, it can seem like you're walking across the desert, parched without water.

In this stage, you will develop a plan to assist you in being prepared for financial challenges you soon will face. You will learn about maximizing your paycheck to enjoy the perks and lifestyle you want. You'll see how little you need to save today, to preserve your family's lifestyle when that unexpected crisis hits.

And it begins today, for who knows what tomorrow will bring?

But before we start… you might want a drink of water….

CONTENTS

Get Your Finance Head On Straight

If you talk to physicians who graduated before you — whether it is five, 20 or 30 years — most will say they have **REGRETS** about choices they've made when it comes to personal finances. Decisions like buying a big house and luxury car resulted in a huge amount of debt, or high-risk investments have left them with little money or assets to show for all their hard work. Now they face situations where they are forced to work longer hours and more years before they can enjoy the life that they truly wanted in the first place.

Be wise and make prudent decisions now so you can look back without regret and achieve the goals you have set for yourself.

Keep in mind that financial matters and decisions can be complicated, confusing, and overwhelming. A high-level overview of finance basics is provided in this stage, but for information that relates more specifically to your particular situation, we advise you to speak with a financial-planning professional.

Make Money

In order to spend money, you must make it first! By now, you've accepted the job, negotiated the contract and know your salary and compensation package. Based on your salary, which is framed by your specialty, geographic location and demographics, it's important to calculate **NET INCOME** (after **TAXES** and **DEBT**) and develop a simple budget taking into account the three life buckets: Needs, Wants and Dreams.

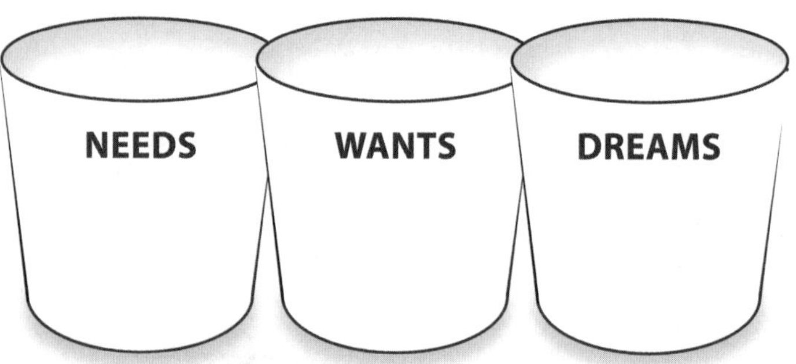

Reflecting on the exercises and assessments completed in Stage 4, you should have a good understanding of your values, life purpose and priorities. As you work through this segment, financial decisions tied to needs, wants and dreams should become clearer once you understand how much money you make and what you can afford to spend now and in the future.

SPEND MONEY WISELY

How much money will you take home each month? Financial success relates to decisions regarding expenses, spending habits and savings goals, and understanding taxation on your income.

Discretionary income represents money left over after supporting basic financial needs. In many cases, new physicians overestimate this amount due to a lack of understanding of the impact of taxes, additional insurance costs or ultimately the amount of spending they can afford. Make sure you review large discretionary purchases with a keen eye toward "**CARRYING COSTS**." For example, you purchase a luxury vehicle without examining the cost to insure and maintain it. Clearly understanding the sunk cost (cost to purchase) and carrying cost (cost to own) will help you to make wise decisions based on affordability now, later or never.

GUIDE POINTS

Facts & Figures

- The average total debt for a physician graduating from medical school in 2009 was roughly $158,000.[9]
- Right now, most physicians are men, age 42 and older; however, women made up half of medical school graduates for the first time in history in 2007.[8]
- In light of these trends, you may also have to manage:
  - Family issues such as childcare, if both spouses work
  - Intermittent career disruptions (e.g., maternity/paternity leave) as well as sabbaticals and training enhancement gaps to work around
  - Relocation or dislocation due to the impact of the latest government changes impacting the U.S. healthcare industry

EXAMPLE

To provide a good working example of income, saving and spending decisions, let's review this case.

Facts of the Case

- An internal medicine physician
- $210,000 annual income
- Five years into the practice
- Has two children
- Spouse doesn't work outside the home

1. Calculate income tax impact.

One of the largest impact single items decreasing take-home pay is federal income tax. The table on the following page lists the federal income tax rates for 2010 for married filing jointly.[10] (In addition to federal taxes, remember to consider all state and local taxes as well.) Let's see what this physician's federal income tax is.

2010 TAXABLE INCOME	YOUR TAX IS:
Over $0 but not over $16,750	10% of taxable income
Over $16,750 but not over $68,000	$1,675 + 15% of the amount over $16,750
Over $68,000 but not over $137,300	$9,362.50 + 25% of the amount over $68,000
Over $137,300 but not over $209,250	$26,687.50 + 28% of the amount over $137,300
Over $209,250 but not over $373,650	$46,833.50 + 33% of the amount over $209,250 **= $47,081**
Over $373,650	$101,085.50 +35% of the amount over $373,650

2. **Calculate expenses.**

Identify monthly and annual expenditures. For this example, this physician's insurance costs were covered through the practice but he added a supplemental disability policy (under living expenses).

EXPENSE ITEM	2010 AMOUNT Annual	2010 AMOUNT Monthly	EST. 2015 AMOUNT *(3% inflation adjusted)*
Living expenses (food, utilities, clothing, cell phones, entertainment, cable, disability insurance)	$48,000	$4,000	$55,645
Kids' activities, sports, college savings	$7,500	$625	$8,695
Vacations	$7,500	$625	$8,695
Home mortgage ($300,000; 30-year fixed, 5.5% interest rate)	$20,000	$1,666.67	$20,000
Debt servicing: medical school, credit card, car	$16,000	$1,333.34	$16,000
Real estate taxes	$4,020	$335	$4,660
Auto/home insurance	$3,000	$250	$3,478
Life insurance	$5,000	$416.67	$5,000
Charitable contributions	$2,000	$166.67	$2,319
TOTAL	**$113,020**	$9,418.35	**$124,492**

3. **Determine discretionary income including savings.**

Study the chart that follows. At the end of a year, for this physician making $210,000 gross income, his discretionary income remaining after debt and retirement deferral savings is about $8,000. It doesn't seem like a lot of money for someone who draws a six-figure income.

ITEM	AMOUNT
Salary	$200,000
LP (practice)	$10,000
Gross income	**$210,000**
Less 401(k) contribution	($16,000)
Less intermediate savings (next car)	($5,000)
Less income tax ($47,081 federal income tax calculated previously, assuming with other taxes totalling approximately 32% of gross income)	($68,000)
Less spending (calculated previously)	($113,020)
TOTAL ANNUAL DISCRETIONARY INCOME	**$7,980** $665/month

This physician's desire is to save 10 % of his income for the unexpected (e.g., emergencies) which equals $20,000. Where will these savings come from? Our doctor must reconsider things like:

- Reduce spending on debt service.
- Reduce spending on vacations.
- Increase deferrals to additional retirement savings. (Can he? Is there the opportunity to do this?)
- Less education savings for his kids.

As you can see, it won't be easy. These important decisions will have **LONG-TERM RAMIFICATIONS**.

We've discussed the effort you have taken to secure a position in the type of practice that fits you perfectly. Now let's make sure you keep the income you need for obligations such as a mortgage and school debt.

ROADBLOCK

Avoiding the Spending Frenzy

Your needs, wants and dreams can get tangled in the rush and frenzy when making your first real paycheck. You survived on crackers and water for a decade or so, and now you deserve to indulge in as much chocolate and champagne as your heart and stomach desires. Your spending appetite feels huge since you've lived in delayed gratification mode for so long.

Before making any large purchases, step back and do your research! Consider the cost of living in your town. Check out the local, state and municipal taxes. Consider the cost of housing, as well as the cost of utilities and maintenance. Research the schools (even if you are single) and consider whether you will utilize public or private schools for your future family. All of this homework will enable you to understand what your life and lifestyle will be.

Cover Your Risk

Risk is a vague term that up to this point has possibly been more about liability in your career than any other component. Risk may equate to making **RISKY** decisions with your career track, but in this area we will explore risk related to disability or death, additional liability risk, health costs (out-of-pocket expenses), and investment risk or loss of investment principal. Managing and controlling risk associated with these items can primarily be covered through insurance options. The following is a brief overview of common types of insurance.

DISABILITY INSURANCE

Disability insurance is very important. As you know, sometimes health issues are outside of your control. Let's review how disability insurance works. If you are covered under a group plan, there are usual limits based on the policy and coverage. Identifying your income needs and suitably covering 60 to 80% or more will be your goal. When securing a policy, we recommend that you:

- Make sure your coverage is suited to your profession. This is truly important when comparing costs. Conducting a fine-line review of coverage is very important.

- Review the economic and tax impact of payout from your group policy and supplemental policies. Typically group policies have a maximum benefit of $5,000 per month, and if you pay with pre-tax dollars, your benefit after tax is notably less. Consider that if you pay with after-tax dollars, your benefit can be received free from income tax. The rationale for 60% coverage is that if you receive benefits equaling 60% of your income, and your combined federal and state taxes equal the other 40%, your net benefit will be 100% of your net pay.

- Make sure the company is reputable and well rated (for example, AM Best A+).

- Consider an inflation rider, and consider a 90-day waiting period to lower costs. Cost is typically 1 to 4% of compensation.

- Review other sources of income with your disability; short-term disability income, workmen's compensation insurance and Social Security will be considered.

- Use a specialist or possibly a broker instead of a company representative.

LIFE INSURANCE

Simple rules of thumb typically don't apply with physicians. Based on specialty and student loan debt, your life insurance needs may be more **COMPLEX**. Many physicians consider complex insurance strategies that combine benefits of cash accumulation in universal life insurance policies rather than basic level term insurance. We would advise caution in your review of insurance due to its cost and variances; consider your debt, your personal obligations (e.g., dependents, spouse) and your desire to at least cover the bare minimum. We suggest a thorough life insurance review periodically due to changing products, rules and mortality tables.

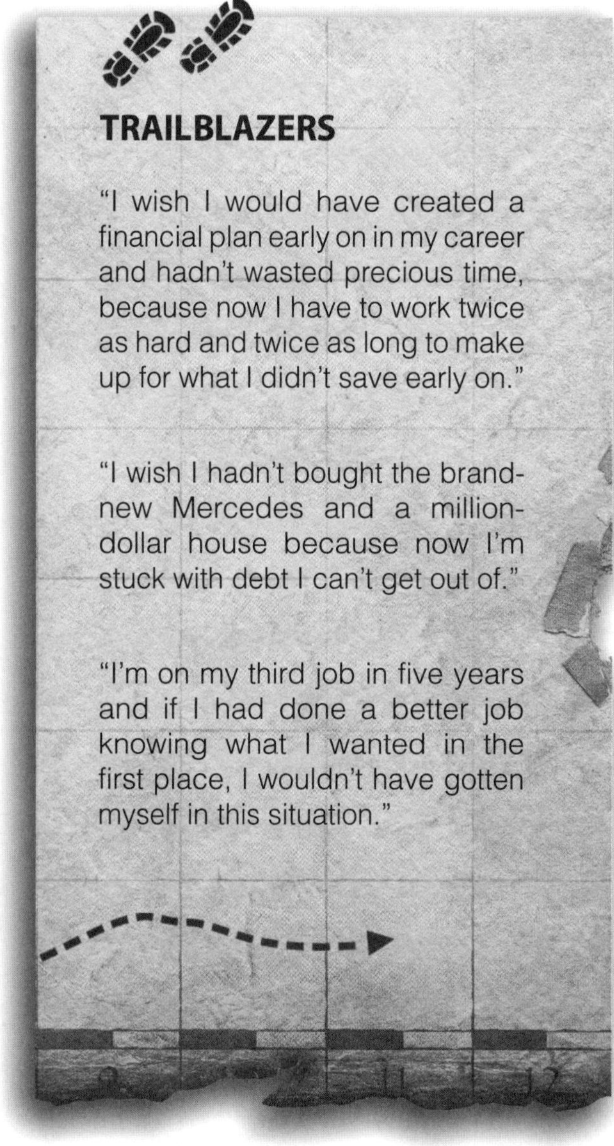

TRAILBLAZERS

"I wish I would have created a financial plan early on in my career and hadn't wasted precious time, because now I have to work twice as hard and twice as long to make up for what I didn't save early on."

"I wish I hadn't bought the brand-new Mercedes and a million-dollar house because now I'm stuck with debt I can't get out of."

"I'm on my third job in five years and if I had done a better job knowing what I wanted in the first place, I wouldn't have gotten myself in this situation."

LIABILITY INSURANCE

This is simply making sure you have adequate liability insurance in all other areas of your life. It is wise to have adequate liability coverage on vehicles and homes. You may also want to consider an umbrella policy that provides additional coverage. Note that with the "doctor" title, unscrupulous individuals may target you for additional nuisance lawsuits.

HEALTH INSURANCE

Generally the trend for practices large and small has been the increased use of Health Savings Accounts (HSA) combined with a High Deductible Health Plan (HDHP). This combination has continued to replace the traditional HMO/PPO type of program that many companies used to offer. The pros and cons of these programs will not be addressed here but will have noted impact on your coverage needs. We would recommend thorough review of the plans and the administrative design of whatever program you access. Consider other insurance areas for additional needs.

Typically with the HSA/HDHP option, spending management and review of out-of-pocket expenses will require more thoughtful review of your program. Some clients can be better served net out of pocket with an HMO versus this option. If you are able to access a spouse's employer benefit, we encourage a fine-line review of all programs and the realistic goals of your health insurance needs. Consider possible family needs in this as your own personal health may not be of significance, but the need for increased healthcare by your spouse and family may change your insurance needs dramatically from one year to the next.

INVESTMENT RISK

As your income grows, so do investment risks. Some simple rules of thumb to keep in mind:

- **DON'T** invest savings that are set aside for emergency or intermediate needs in investments that are highly concentrated, themed or leveraged (e.g., mortgage, college loans). This isn't the money you need to attempt huge returns with.
- Invest in strategies you can understand. If you can't explain the strategy to your mother or, even better, your grandmother, you're probably in over your head.
- Risk is price volatility or standard deviation or loss of principal — make sure to review these when investing for long-term purposes.

Save Money

Spending and saving should go hand in hand with your life buckets. It's important to put aside money for emergencies (i.e., needs that surface), short-term savings for wants, and long-term savings for dreams. This is based on the premise of paying for things with cash versus taking on debt, and what constitutes good versus bad debt.

"Cash is king" is a common phrase, often times used to describe a company or investor's fiscal responsibility. In simple terms, money that's readily available — whether it's deposited in a checking, money market, savings or CD (certificate of deposit) account — will keep you out of debt and in a positive cash flow situation.

Consider saving money to serve three goals:

- Emergency funds — used for unexpected, unplanned expenses; keeps you from using credit or incurring more debt to cover these expenses.
- Intermediate spending goals — saving for larger purchases in the next one to 10 years.
- Long-term savings (investment vehicles) — money saved for 10+ years, such as education funds for young children (under age 10), retirement funds, or mid-career changes.

EMERGENCY FUNDS

"Save for a rainy day" is a common saying, as is "hope for the best, plan for the worst." Many individuals unfortunately fall into the credit card debt trap by not planning and saving for emergencies. We suggest three months spending reserve as a general rule of thumb, but in some cases we may recommend higher reserves. These funds should be invested with low-risk, liquid investment tools. One popular, low-risk, short-term option for saving and having access to "liquid" funds is through Certificate of Deposits (CDs).

Dr. Smith is investing $24,000 into a bank-sponsored CD. He invests in a five-year or 60-month CD, which is the total number of months for his CD to mature. His bank credits his interest annually. The Interest rate is posted as 5%. For this example, we will assume this rate is the effective annual interest rate earned and compounded annually for this CD. A CD's annual percentage yield (APY) depends on the frequency of compounding and the interest rate. For this purpose we will assume the APY is the same at 5%. For the first year, Dr. Smith wants to calculate his net annual return after taxes. Dr. Smith's federal marginal (highest) income tax is 33%; his state income tax rate is 9%. His first year's annual interest rate credit is $1,200 (5% of the $24,000). He files this income on his tax return and is given a 1099 from the bank notifying the IRS of the interest credit to Dr. Smith. He files his income tax return and pays $396 in federal income tax and $108 in state income tax. His net income after tax impact is now $696. Based on the original investment of $24,000, he has made 2.9% net of tax return. If he also concerned about the current annual rate of 2% inflation – his real rate of return, net of inflation and tax, is now a small 0.9% return on his investment. This final number is the real net rate of return. With all investment strategies – costs to invest, tax impact, and inflation impact should be reviewed.

INTERMEDIATE SPENDING GOALS

Intermediate goals can represent items on the wants and dreams lists. These goals would typically take less than 10 years to fulfill. They might include, for example:

- Replacement items such as vehicles
- Purchasing a particular larger item like a boat, specialty car or collectible
- Remodeling
- Significant travel plans
- Funding 100 % of your kids' college costs
- Vacation home or second home where you'll retire

Use caution as it relates to investment risks on these items. Many investors were dramatically impacted by bear markets by maintaining overly aggressive investment strategies for planned spending in these areas.

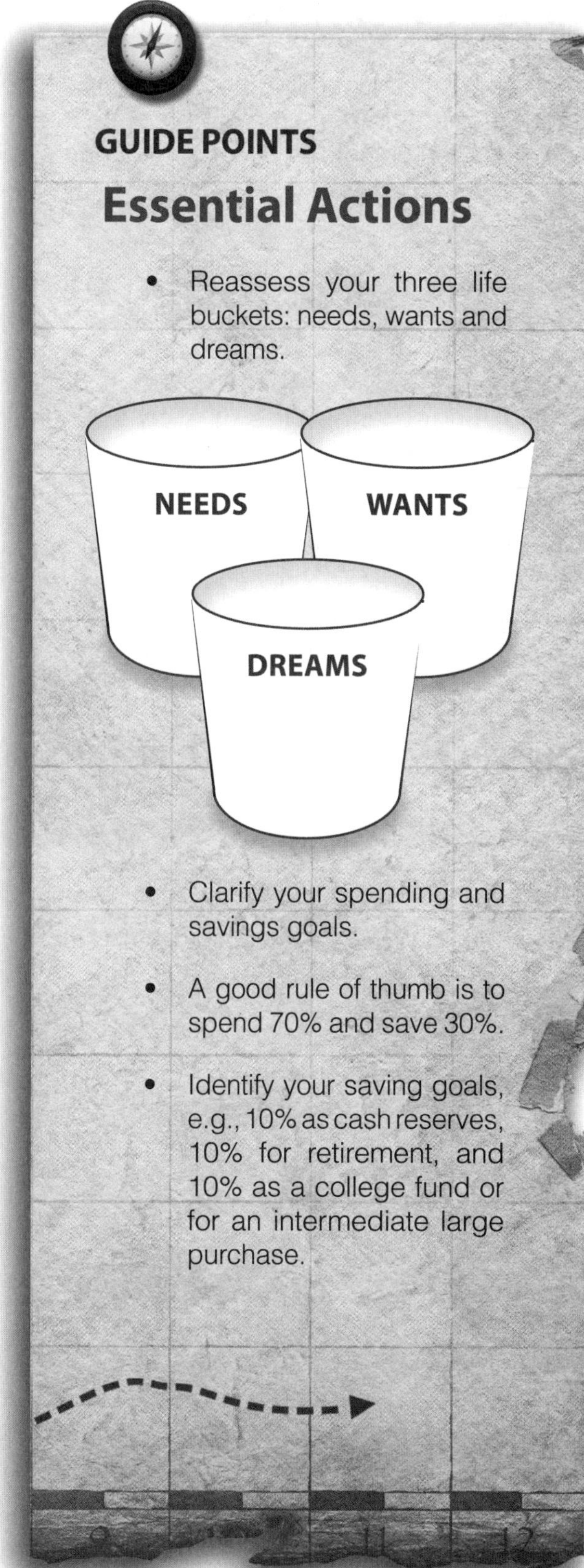

GUIDE POINTS
Essential Actions
• Reassess your three life buckets: needs, wants and dreams.
NEEDS
WANTS
DREAMS
• Clarify your spending and savings goals.
• A good rule of thumb is to spend 70% and save 30%.
• Identify your saving goals, e.g., 10% as cash reserves, 10% for retirement, and 10% as a college fund or for an intermediate large purchase.

LONG-TERM SAVINGS

Long-term savings are for spending that is 10 to 20+ years away. This usually represents retirement funding through appropriate retirement plans such as a 401(k), profit sharing, or SEP IRAs. When thinking about saving for retirement, it's important to understand some concepts that will help you get the most out of your hard-earned money. The online Farlex Financial Dictionary provides the following definitions.

Compounding: "The process of earning interest on a loan or other fixed-income instrument where the interest can itself earn interest. That is, interest previously calculated is included in the calculation of future interest. For example, suppose someone had the same certificate of deposit for $1,000 that pays 3%, compounding each month. The interest paid is $30 in the first month (3% of $1,000), $30.90 in the second month (3% of $1,030), and so forth. In this situation, the more frequently interest is compounded, the higher the yield will be on the instrument."[11]

Time Value of Money: "A fundamental idea in finance is that money that one has now is worth more than money one will receive in the future. Because money can earn interest or be invested, it is worth more ... if it is available immediately. ... This concept may be thought of as a financial application of the saying, 'A bird in the hand is worth two in the bush.'"[12]

EXAMPLE: COMPARE TWO PHYSICIANS

	DR. A	DR. B.
Amount invested	$2,000 per month	$2,000 per month
When	Immediately after residency	After 10 years of practicing medicine
Investment time	30 years	20 years
Total out-of-pocket expense	$720,000	$480,000

The two scenarios are very realistic as most young professionals rarely consider retirement savings as an important component of their spending plan.

When saving for retirement, we consider various approaches. For this example, we took a very simple approach to show the impact of compounding using real market investment scenarios. The example has several components worth noting:

1. **SIMPLE:** A consistent dollar figure added annually. $24,000 is not a large sum annually but can grow to a large balance due to the impact of compounding.

2. **TAX-DEFERRED:** When these dollars are added to a qualified retirement account, the investor would pay no tax on the gains or income/dividends of their investment until they distribute these from the account in retirement.

3. **REAL:** We also used "real" capital market proxies or indexes to represent a basket of investments. This demonstrates the impact of several large global bear market environments and various interest rate environments. The impact on a long-term rate of return and volatility is also measured (worst case scenarios). The data used is based on the market of January 1990 through March 2010 producing returns of 8.04 % and volatility of return based on a standard deviation of 11.15 %.

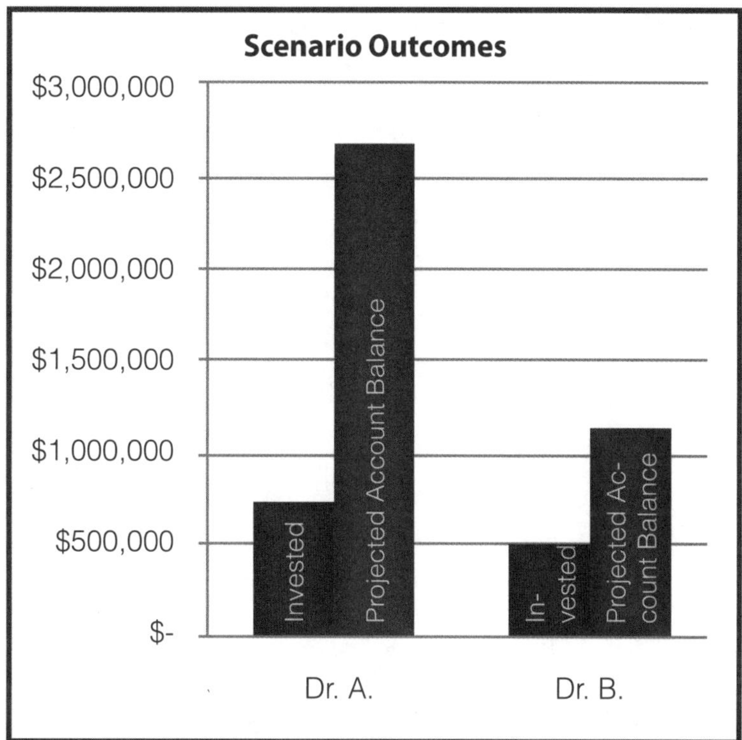

Supposing this investment contains a mix of stocks and bonds, and both doctors add $24,000 annually at year's end, the impact on the size of this account can be remarkable. With the returns and volatility previously noted, the average balance (50th percentile) of **DR. A'S ACCOUNT WOULD BE $2,683,505** (after 30 years of investing) and **DR. B'S ACCOUNT WOULD BE $1,131,137** (after 20 years of investing). See the difference 10 years makes!

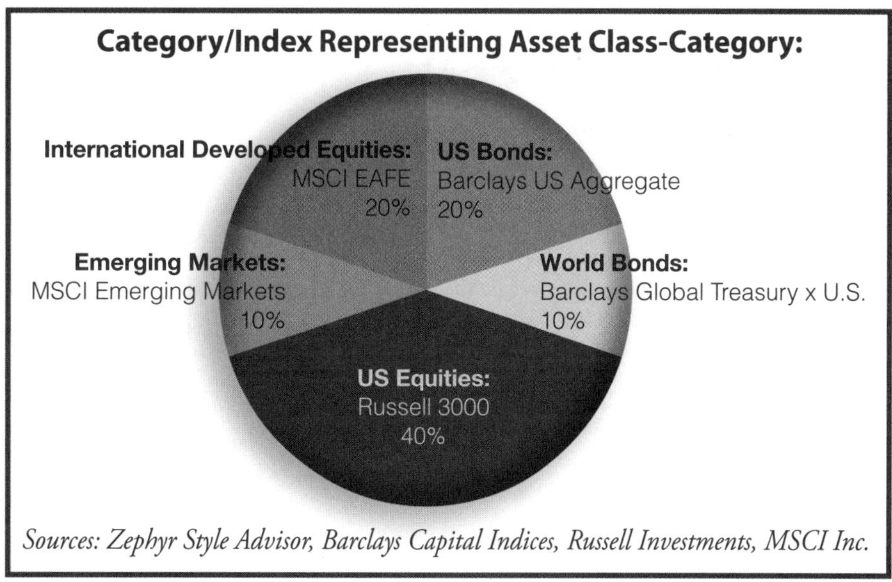

Sources: Zephyr Style Advisor, Barclays Capital Indices, Russell Investments, MSCI Inc.

Note: This reflects an IRA that is non-deductible with no taxes and no inflation rate increases. Keep in mind that past history is no guarantee of future events, and that these illustrations are based on a simple use of index returns, which do not reflect taxes, costs of trading or management. The outcome illustrates the best use of the rule of compounding combined with diversified investments and rebalancing to target weight allocations annually.

EXERCISE: CREATE A SPENDING AND SAVINGS PLAN

Now that you've had a chance to learn more about spending, risk and savings, it's your turn to create a spending and savings plan. The following is a worksheet to create a budget and estimate discretionary income. By this time, you may know your starting salary; however, you may not have the actual amounts of some of the expenses listed. Do your best to estimate based on what you would like to or plan to spend. (If you're in a rush, use the express budget method.)

Go back and look at your life buckets. You may need to move some of these items from one bucket to another based on the outcomes of this exercise.

Once you've filled out the chart, you'll see what discretionary income you have left, and you can then adjust your assumptions as needed. By completing this exercise, this information provides a more realistic picture of what you can afford before you make large purchases such as a home or car.

Spending

EXPENSE ITEM	AMOUNT	DESCRIPTION
Living expenses		Food, utilities, clothing, cell phones, entertainment, cable
Kids' activities/daycare		
Vacations		Discretionary?
Home mortgage		Consider fixed or variable.
Debt servicing: education, credit card, car		Review all schedules to plan when increased amounts are due.
Real estate taxes		
Medical insurance		
Auto/home insurance		
Life insurance		
Charitable contributions		
TOTAL		

Income, Savings and Discretionary

ITEM	AMOUNT	DESCRIPTION
Salary		
Bonus/additional income (e.g., Limited Partnership)		
Gross income		
Less 401(k) contribution		
Less education savings		
Less income tax (federal and state)		Review IRS tables and state tax rates.
Less spending		Calculated previously
TOTAL ANNUAL DISCRETIONARY INCOME		Divide by 12 to calculate per month:

Express Budget Method

Combined net income (take-home)	
Minus monthly savings	
Equals monthly expenses	

KEY QUESTION: How much money do you plan to save every month?

In liquid assets: savings account, money market, CD	
In a deferred retirement account: IRA or 401(k)	

A WORD OF WARNING

Note: This story is hypothetical and does not represent an actual client; however, it is realistic and portrays doctors we work with.

Dr. X was hardworking and motivated with a passion to make a difference in his patients' lives, and was excited to begin his medical career after graduation. As his first day approached, Dr. X created a financial and investment wish list. Although he earned an income that put him the top 2 % in the nation for wages, he looks back now and states, "It is very easy to spend as much money as you bring home, regardless of whether it's $150,000, $200,000 or $300,000."

Dr. X continues: "My intention after residency was to start investing right away with my first job. I remember saying to myself, 'Right after orientation I will start.' But I didn't. Then I said, 'Once I get a few months into my practice, I will sit down and initiate the process.' But it didn't happen. A few months came and went, and then I said, 'Once my first kid is born, I will knock out my investment plan as well as savings for my child's college education.' Ten years later, I have nothing to show for my hard work. As I see it, over the next ten years I have to buckle down and invest so I can be in a position to slow down and perhaps one day retire. Looking back, it would have been easy to put away a good portion of my monthly income. It's very frustrating that I spent money on things that I could have done without!"

DR. GOODHOOK'S FIELD NOTES

Beware the unexpected. The young physician cannot know what snake pit, river and ravine lie in the practice of medicine ahead. What seemed as the most solid of ground in my own practice has, at the most inopportune times and most unexpectedly, crumbled beneath my feet. It is not pleasant, but panic that overtakes. Take heed, physician. There are scrapes in medicine you cannot foresee, yet you will nonetheless their taskmaster be with wee bit of planning, preparation and frugality. Prepare. Prepare. Prepare. You then, my young friend, will prevail.

– Dr. Gh.

Is this story unique? Sadly, no. As with any activity, the attention you give to setting up and managing your financial affairs will be rewarded. Intentions are not actions.

GUIDE POINTS

Creating a Spending and Savings Plan

- Compile all income sources; this is an important part of your budget process and will be necessary to establish base compensation with supplemental income sources that may be established in your first years in practice.
- Review employer benefits and any additional costs to your budget beyond employer-covered costs (health, disability, life and liability).
- Review costs of basic needs (housing, transportation costs, food).
- Do a plan even if it's a simple budget with a goal of saving 3% of adjusted gross income.
- Make the budget real and, if appropriate, do this with a spouse/significant partner and keep track of your expenses.
- Review the budget on your birthday or if you get a raise – or on both dates. (You'll possibly think about the speed of your life moving forward at the former and consider saving more of your pay raise at the latter).
- Review debt servicing (med school debt, consumer credit card debt, mortgage/rent and real estate tax/insurance).
- Calculate remainder income for additional debt servicing, discretionary savings or purchases.
- Review your immediate goals of any discretionary savings to the benefit of utilizing any retirement savings programs you can participate.

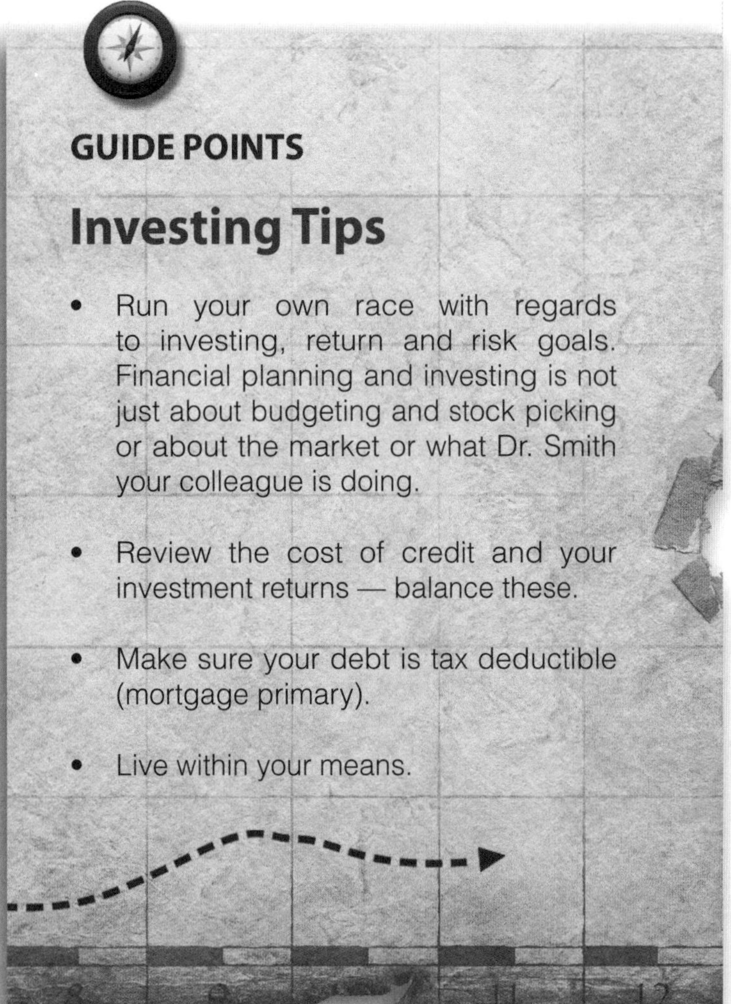

GUIDE POINTS

Investing Tips

- Run your own race with regards to investing, return and risk goals. Financial planning and investing is not just about budgeting and stock picking or about the market or what Dr. Smith your colleague is doing.
- Review the cost of credit and your investment returns — balance these.
- Make sure your debt is tax deductible (mortgage primary).
- Live within your means.

Invest Wisely

Investment management for growth, for tax and investment efficiency, and for different funding needs with your discretionary savings is very important to consider.

Understanding how and what to invest in both **NON-QUALIFIED** (taxable) accounts versus **QUALIFIED** (non-taxable) accounts is also vital.

Consider the 33 % federal tax level if you and your spouse make combined income of $210,000, plus a state tax of 9 %, to take a base estimate of 42 % of any interest into account. With tax rates in most states approaching 10 %, many physicians can be in the **HIGHEST MARGINAL TAX RATE** within a few years of practicing medicine.

There are many factors that impact your ability to grow financial assets:

- Risk and return goals for the assets are dependent on purpose and timeline
- Tax-qualified (tax-deferred) status and impact of taxes eroding the returns of stocks and bonds
- Costs of the investment strategies: management costs, trading costs, etc.
- Incorporating a timing decision with investment strategies (buying "high" prices and selling "low")
- Cost of monitoring your investment assets equated to rebalancing (transaction cost) or lack of creating a modification of your allocation without rebalancing

YEARLY CHECK-UPS

The last part of your financial plan is monitoring the plan to make sure you stay on track or adjust to changes in your career, family, tax or health.

Similar to advice given to patients, we suggest an annual check-up. This will help keep your financial life **HEALTHY** and may solve painful issues that surface that need to be treated.

Disclosure: The content of this chapter has been provided by LarsonAllen Financial, LLC, Member FINRA & SIPC and is for information and illustrative purposes only. One should not rely on this information for the primary basis of investment, tax or financial planning. General market information does not take into account such factors as an individual's goals, objectives, risk tolerance, tax situation, age, or time frame. We believe the information obtained from third-party sources to be reliable, but neither LarsonAllen Financial, LLC nor its affiliates guarantee its accuracy, timeliness, or completeness. The views, opinions, and estimates herein are subject to change without notice at any time in reaction to shifting market conditions. Tax laws change and investments in the stock market entail risk and potential loss of principal. Note that one cannot invest directly into an index and diversification cannot assure a profit or guarantee against a loss. Past performance is no guarantee of future results. This material may not be republished in any format without prior consent.

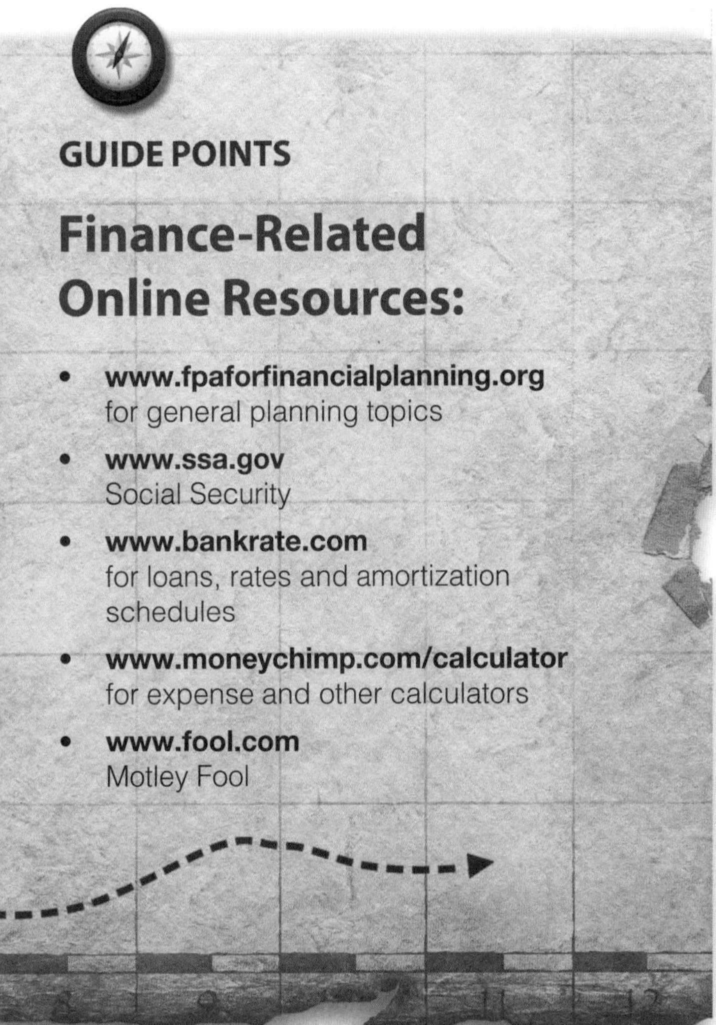

GUIDE POINTS

Finance-Related Online Resources:

- **www.fpaforfinancialplanning.org**
  for general planning topics
- **www.ssa.gov**
  Social Security
- **www.bankrate.com**
  for loans, rates and amortization schedules
- **www.moneychimp.com/calculator**
  for expense and other calculators
- **www.fool.com**
  Motley Fool

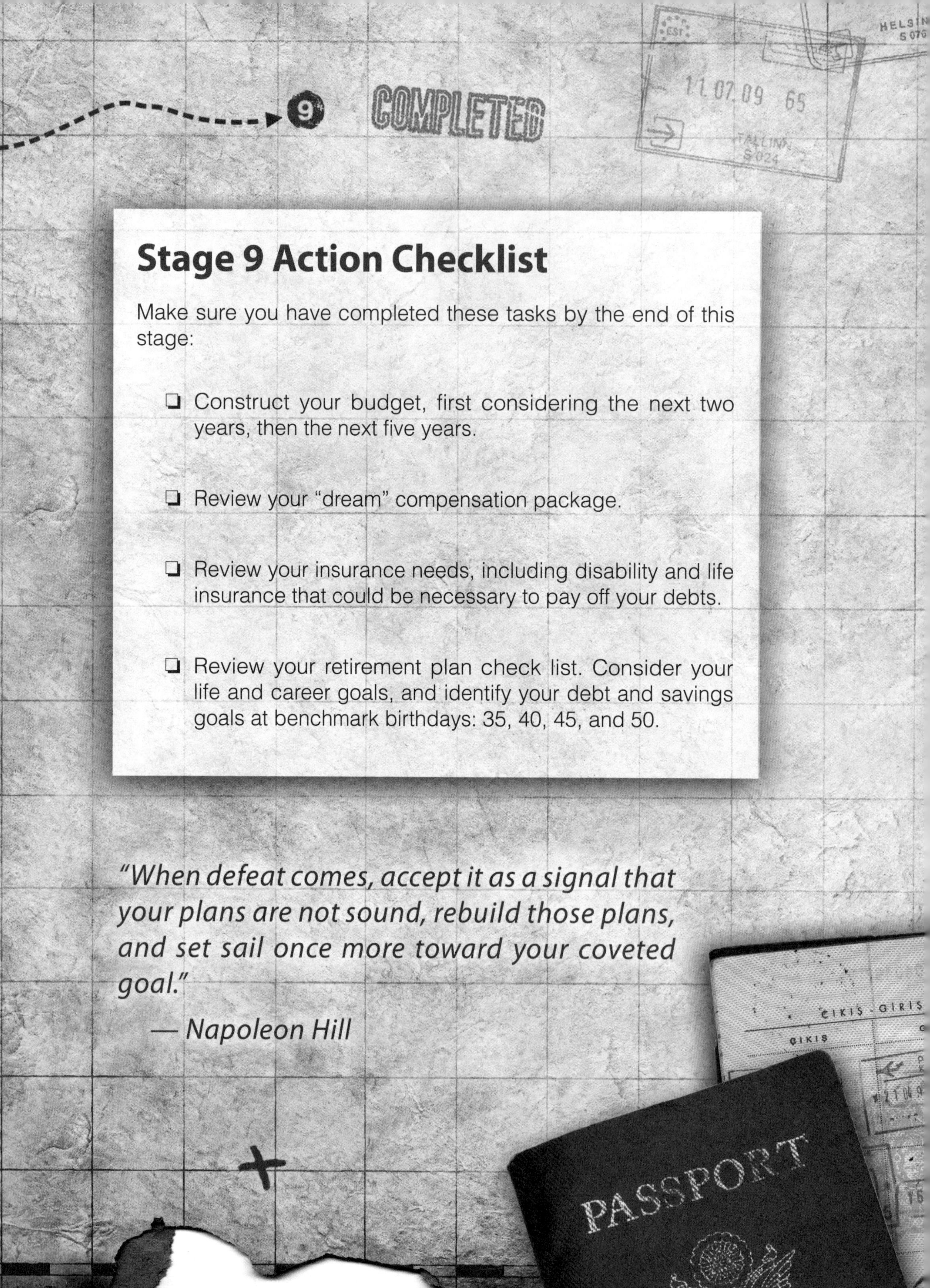

Stage 9 Action Checklist

Make sure you have completed these tasks by the end of this stage:

- ❑ Construct your budget, first considering the next two years, then the next five years.
- ❑ Review your "dream" compensation package.
- ❑ Review your insurance needs, including disability and life insurance that could be necessary to pay off your debts.
- ❑ Review your retirement plan check list. Consider your life and career goals, and identify your debt and savings goals at benchmark birthdays: 35, 40, 45, and 50.

"When defeat comes, accept it as a signal that your plans are not sound, rebuild those plans, and set sail once more toward your coveted goal."

— Napoleon Hill

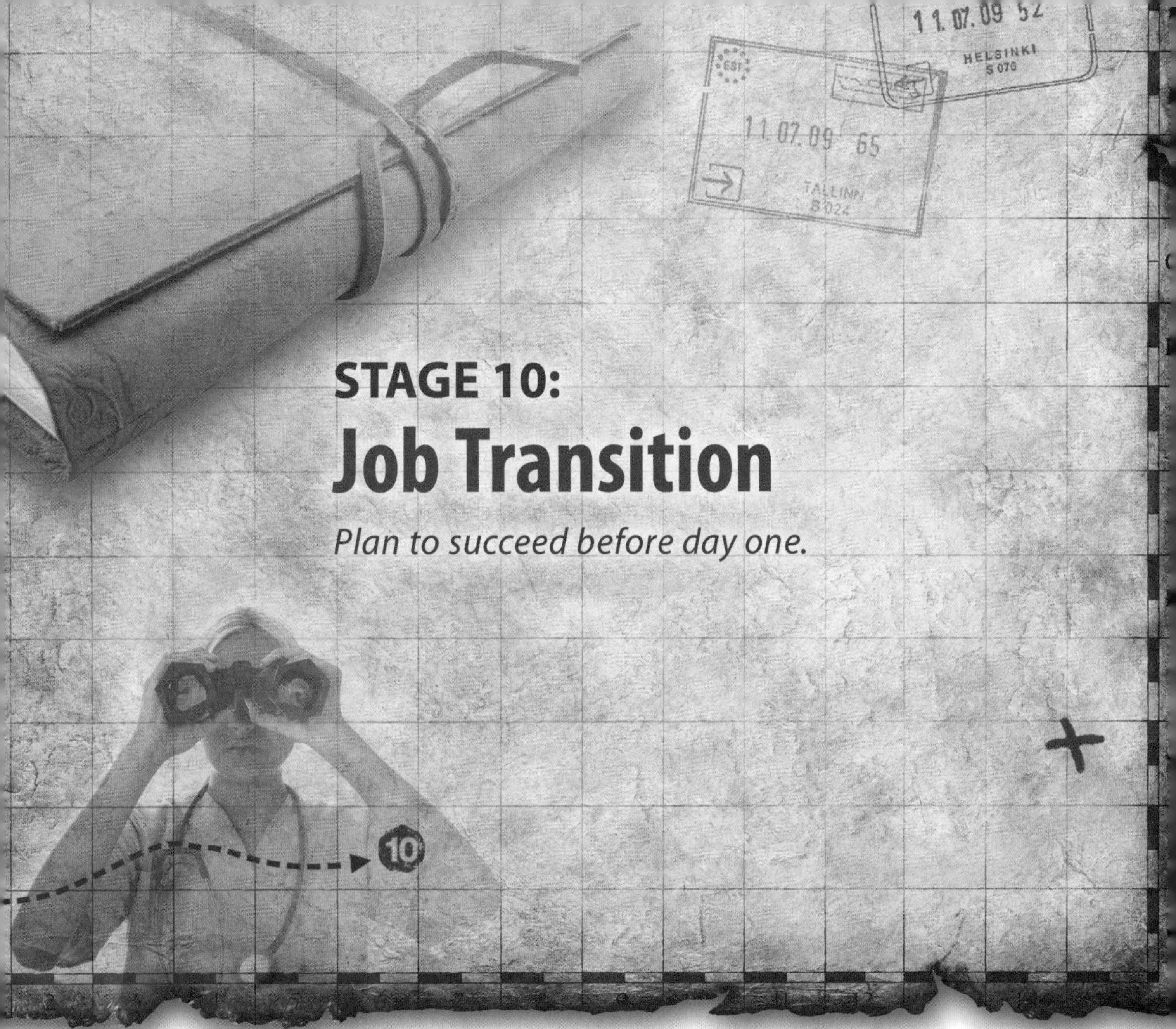

Where everybody knows your name

Growing up in Davenport – one of the four Quad-Cities on the eastern Iowa/western Illinois border – Dr. Nathan Fierce loved the hometown feel of "everybody knowing everybody." So it was only natural that the area's family-friendly charm drew him back home from Detroit to build his surgery practice.

The active father of four enjoys riding his bike on one of the many riverfront trails and visiting the beautiful city parks with his kids. Having great schools where his children would get one-on-one attention is just another reason why he chose to come back to a community that wasn't just where he was raised. It's truly a place a family can call home.

So if you run into Dr. Fierce ordering a chocolate Oreo shake at the local Whitey's ice cream shop, and he greets you by name, don't be surprised. It's just what people do here in the Quad-Cities.

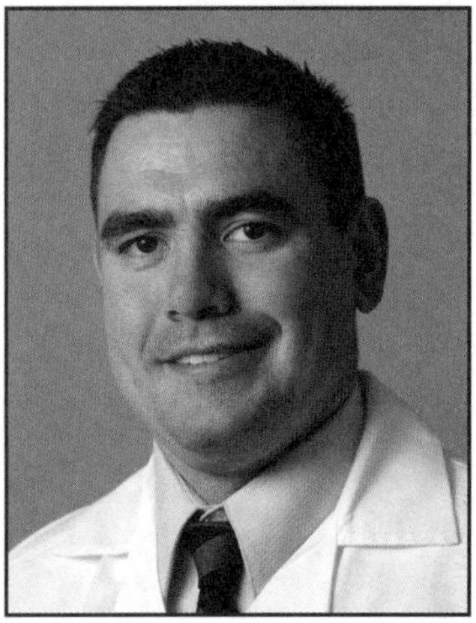

Dr. Nathan Fierce Trinity Physician

TRINITY

IOWA HEALTH SYSTEM

Moline • Rock Island • Bettendorf • Muscatine

To learn more about Trinity:
Marcia Youngvorst, MS, BSN
(309) 779-3701 or youngvorstm@ihs.org

www.trinityqc.com
or www.trinitymuscatine.com

Your Work-Life Balance Guide:

Iris Grimm

Owner/Coach, Balanced Physician

B.S., Mainz (Germany) University of Applied Science

Raised in a family of physicians, Iris Grimm understands the difficulties of balancing a personal life while maintaining the dedication and hard work needed to build a thriving medical practice. Her personal experience, along with degrees in business management, communication, corporate and personal coaching, led her to create The Balanced Physician Program.

She provides individual and group coaching programs, as well as workshops and presentations to thousands of physicians on topics such as work-life balance, leadership, effective communication and physician wellness. Her advice has appeared in numerous medical publications including *American Medical News*. When not training people, she trains dogs and enjoys hiking in the mountains with her own dogs.

10

In This Stage: Job Transition

Adventurers know that keeping your balance is critical. Without balance, reaching the goal could be impossible.

Is your life in balance? **MOST LIKELY NOT.**

These years of training have been intense. While this has been necessary to learn important clinical skills, many physicians can't sustain that sleep-deprived, 24/7/365 lifestyle without becoming anti-social, obsessive, and, well, rude. While you could be a great clinician, people won't like you. Not pretty.

But a new day dawns. Within a few months your job will be under contract, your new home and community set, and your transition into practice beginning.

Recapture **BALANCE**.

You can't just flip a switch. You need to define your work-life balance, then learn ways to set good habits and protect your priorities. Some say the next 24 months will set the tone for the rest of your life.

It's time to get a life again.

CONTENTS

Welcome to the Other Side (Almost)

Congratulations! You made it! You are about to embark on the next monumental phase of your medical journey — the actual, real-world experience as a certified and credentialed practicing physician.

At this point, one of the biggest **MISTAKES** practicing physicians make is to keep moving full speed ahead. Oftentimes, their goal is to become a successful and affluent physician: build a practice, pay off debt and provide financial security for their family. And of course, they want a better work-life balance, but many don't know yet what that could look like. Does this sound familiar?

Getting ready for your first job is a big deal. You are transitioning from a follower position into a leader position. You will have your own team that you manage and lead. You will be responsible for bringing in patients and for delivering treatments. You want to make sure you are building strong relationships with the hospital administration, staff and other physicians while balancing all that with your desire to lead a happy life, build a family, buy a house, have a social life, so on and so on.

The question becomes: How do you **MENTALLY**, **EMOTIONALLY** and **PHYSICALLY** get ready for your first job as a practicing physician? This stage answers this question by helping you define work-life balance for yourself, teaching you how to achieve and maintain it, and giving you the opportunity to create a networking strategy and build an advisory team to help you navigate through business, professional and personal aspects of your new life.

Work-Life Balance: Why Should I Care?

Many people think that work-life balance is a 50/50 split of their time devoted for work and for personal life. Actually, it has less to do with time but more to do with **ENERGY**. Burnout and fatigue can adversely affect one's ability to practice medicine, especially with respect to errors and level of patient care. In light of these elements, it's important to make proactive decisions about work-life balance.

Work-life balance represents contentment with one's personal and professional life. It is that place where you find middle ground, where work feeds your personal life and personal life feeds your professional life. It is something you must pay attention to every day, because work-life balance is based on your values, priorities and everyday choices.

MISCONCEPTIONS THAT LEAD TO BURNOUT AND DISSATISFACTION

Hard work will get me where I want to go. Working hard and long hours may lead you down a path of financial success and professional recognition, but it can also lead you towards personal destruction. To achieve a well-balanced life, the focus should be on working smart versus hard. Working smart includes

taking time out to reflect on your life and career priorities and goals. In addition, it's imperative that you take care of yourself which represents the most expensive instrument in your medical practice: **YOU.**

Work-life balance and career advancement cannot co-exist. Many people think that they have to give up their sense of balance to achieve success. We know that success without work-life balance is not sustainable long term and is very expensive. The price for that kind of success can be divorce, strained relationships with children, health issues, burnout, premature end to your medical practice.

My clinical skills are the only skills I need to be successful. Clinical skills are the foundation of your medical career, but they are not the only determinant of your success. Like any other professional, your success is determined by a combination of your interpersonal and self-management skills and your clinical skills. This doesn't mean that clinical training and education can be neglected, but the best clinical skills cannot be truly leveraged without appropriate interpersonal and self-management skills.

PRINCIPLES FOR A BALANCED LIFE

Work-life balance is personal and ever changing. Work-life balance is a state of living that is very personal and changes with personal preferences, circumstances and ambitions. It is closely connected with one's values. For example, for a single person in their twenties with little financial obligations, the definition of work-life balance is most likely different compared to a thirty-something who is married with children. What works well for one person might not work so well for someone else.

Don't let the first year become the norm without evaluating work-life balance overall. During the first year as a practicing physician, your definition of work-life balance might be completely different compared to someone who's been practicing for 10 years. There are things that you will encounter throughout the first year

TRAILBLAZERS

"I wished I would have attended a program on work-life balance 25 years ago. I had to go through all the drama — divorce with three young children, burnout, medical malpractice lawsuit — before I realized that I needed to focus more on my personal well-being and life balance."

"I never paid any attention to work-life balance until I turned 49 years old. I rarely made it to 7 p.m. family dinners and missed many of my children's school activities.

At age 49, I was at the point of burnout, and I had to make drastic changes. Now I'm more content with my life. I triage my work, I take at least two vacations a year, and I always make it home for dinner with my wife.

The children left for college a year ago and I regret that I didn't make family life a bigger priority early in my life."

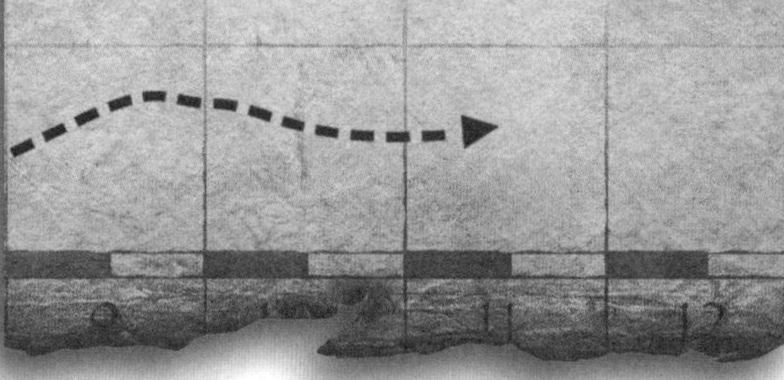

ROADBLOCK

Fatigue and Burnout Can Cause Poor Decision-Making

Burnout is a syndrome of emotional exhaustion combined with a sense of low personal accomplishment. At this point, there are few studies about burnout in residents or its relationship to patient care. A cross-sectional study[13] using an anonymous mailed survey to internal medicine residents (n=115) at a university-based residency program determined that 87 of the 115 (76%) met the criteria for burnout. Compared with non-burned-out residents, residents who reported burnout were more likely to self-report providing at least one type of **SUB-OPTIMAL PATIENT CARE** at least monthly (53% versus 21%).

Young physicians who sacrifice their personal lives during training, believing they will reap the rewards of a balanced life after graduation, often find themselves without skills to clarify and prioritize values or to develop a personal philosophy that integrates professional, personal and spiritual domains.

that may cause you to go outside your comfort zone (e.g., learning new procedures and protocols, building a patient base, getting to know your peers and staff members, becoming familiar with the politics in the organization), so you may need to invest more time and energy until you have the confidence and knowledge of the new job, responsibilities, procedures, etc.

Our goal in this stage is to increase your **AWARENESS** of work-life balance and encourage you to define what it means to you so that you have a target to work for. The first year or two as a practicing physician might be a bit off-target, but you still want to make sure that you are juggling all the balls that are necessary for your personal well-being and professional performance. They may be not as high as you want them to be, but you definitely want to keep them in the air. And make sure you are regularly reflecting on your satisfaction in work and life so that you won't get off-target too much.

Every prize has its price. It's commonly said that anything worth having is worth sacrificing for. Everything we do or choose comes with a cost, whether it's opportunity, time, effort, happiness or money. All too often when we make decisions, we don't weigh the costs. Be sure you consider what you are willing to sacrifice to experience a balanced life with healthy success.

Avoid the comparison game — you'll lose every time. Everyone suffers in their own way with regards to achieving work-life balance. Spending energy wondering what you are doing wrong or why someone has it better than you is an energy zapper. Manufacturing all sorts of stories around why you have it so bad, and how everyone else is to blame, drains even more energy. All of us suffer, whether you are rich or poor, powerful or weak, beautiful or ugly.

EXERCISE: WORK-LIFE BALANCE

1. Write down two areas to focus on over the next one or two years that bring you happiness or satisfaction and would create a more balanced life compared to your present situation as a resident. For example, you might consider family, friends, hobbies, recreation, fitness, spiritual activities, or your spouse or significant other.

2. For each area, circle the number that represents the current level of contentment you feel towards that element.

3. For each area, list action items that you would like to work on or incorporate into your life that would increase your level of contentment and work-life balance.

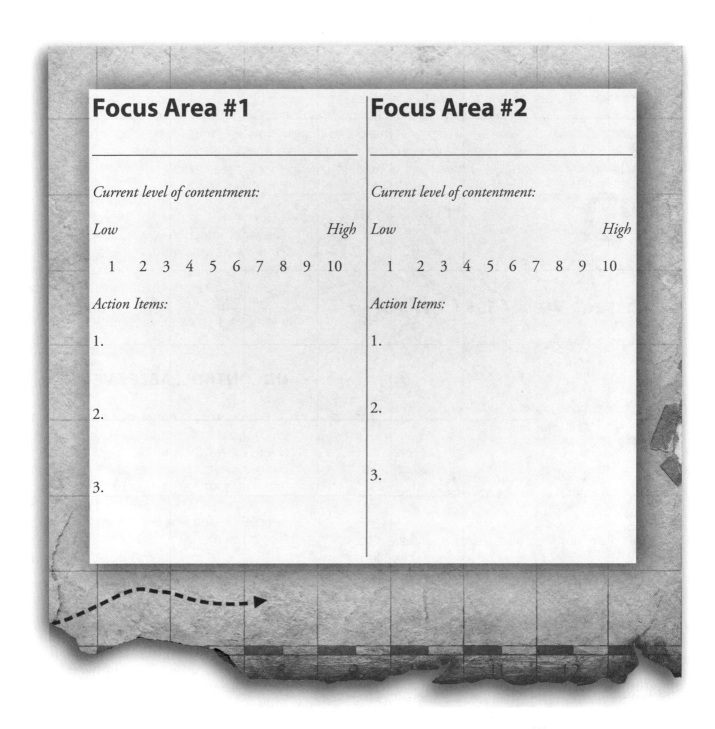

Focus Area #1	**Focus Area #2**
_______________	_______________
Current level of contentment:	*Current level of contentment:*
Low *High*	*Low* *High*
1 2 3 4 5 6 7 8 9 10	1 2 3 4 5 6 7 8 9 10
Action Items:	*Action Items:*
1.	1.
2.	2.
3.	3.

There are several techniques that you can implement to achieve satisfied levels of work-life balance. We will highlight four of them: stress control, setting boundaries, simplifying your life, and developing a healthy attitude.

Stress Control

The key to balancing your personal life with your desire to achieve, perform and earn a living is in controlling the stress in your life. It is impossible to completely eliminate stress, and truthfully, you wouldn't want to. The key is not to avoid stress altogether, but to control stress by avoiding its negative consequences. Stress can be anything — positive or negative — at any time and any place that creates pressure and takes you out of your comfort zone or routine — things that make you uptight. It is a mental illusion, an interpretation and a perception. What is stressful to one person is blissful to another. Most people only notice stress when the pressure becomes unbearable. Others have become so numb to the stress around us that they walk around like stress zombies.

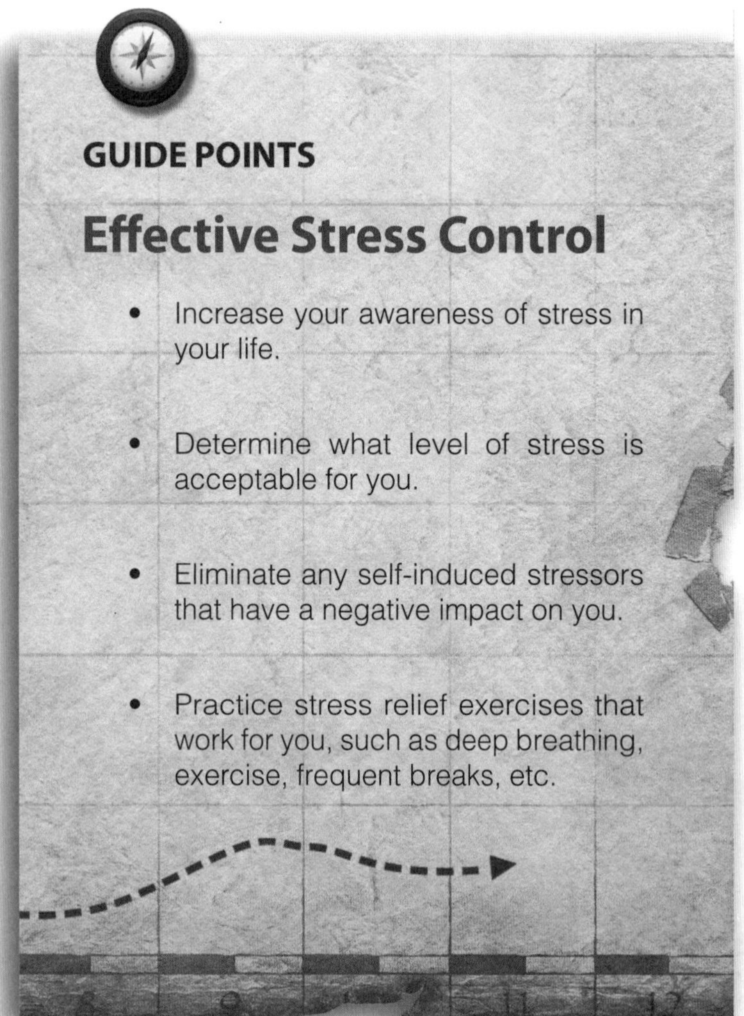

GUIDE POINTS

Effective Stress Control

- Increase your awareness of stress in your life.
- Determine what level of stress is acceptable for you.
- Eliminate any self-induced stressors that have a negative impact on you.
- Practice stress relief exercises that work for you, such as deep breathing, exercise, frequent breaks, etc.

The first step in controlling stress is to identify the causes of stress, which fall into two main categories: external and internal. External stressors result from uncontrollable or unpredictable events in our lives, while internal stressors are self-induced.

UNCONTROLLABLE EVENTS

Physicians face numerous events that they cannot control. Although you may not have control over the situation, you have control over how you respond to the situation with your attitude and perspective. Examples of uncontrollable events include other people's rude behavior, decreased insurance reimbursements, outside pressure to keep targets, changes in the healthcare industry and family demands.

UNPREDICTABLE EVENTS

Many times, unpredictable events may be even more stressful than uncontrollable events since they are so-called "**SNEAK ATTACKS**."

When it comes to uncontrollable events, at least we know they are coming and we can plan for them. Unpredictable events hit us when we least expect them. Suddenly they smack us, take away all our mental energy and make us shift mental gears. Examples of unpredictable events include a medical malpractice claim against you, sudden loss of a family member, IRS or RAC (Recovery Act Compliance) audit and unexpected complications or sudden death of a patient.

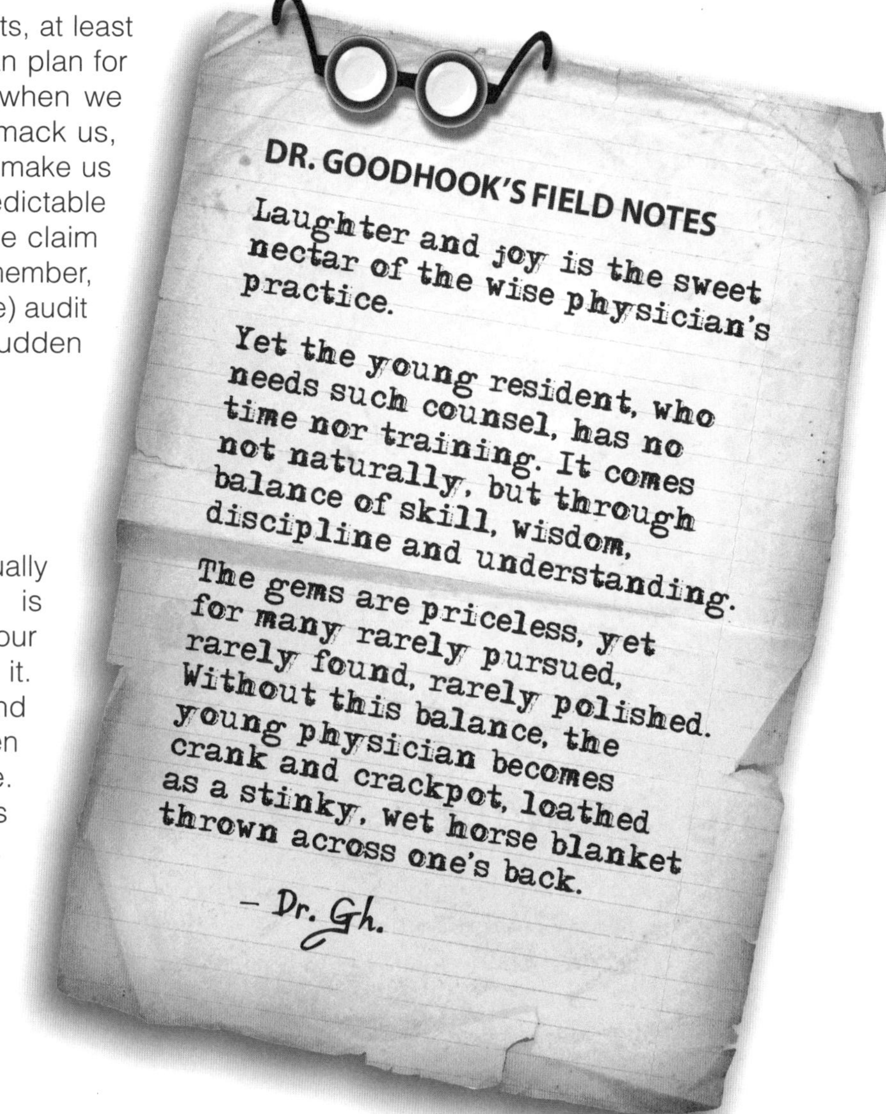

DR. GOODHOOK'S FIELD NOTES
Laughter and joy is the sweet nectar of the wise physician's practice.
Yet the young resident, who needs such counsel, has no time nor training. It comes not naturally, but through balance of skill, wisdom, discipline and understanding.
The gems are priceless, yet for many rarely pursued, rarely found, rarely polished. Without this balance, the young physician becomes crank and crackpot, loathed as a stinky, wet horse blanket thrown across one's back.
– Dr. Gh.

SELF-INDUCED STRESSORS

Most stress that we experience is actually **SELF-INDUCED**. The good news is that since we create the majority of our upsets, we can do something about it. This gives us a measure of choice and control that we do not always have when outside forces enter into the picture. Examples of self-induced stressors are neglect of relationships or family, workaholic behavior, perfectionism and unrealistic expectations.

EXERCISE: WHAT'S MAKING YOU UPTIGHT THESE DAYS?

Review the list of uncontrollable, unpredictable, and self-induced stressors. In the space below, list situations, events, thought patterns and behaviors that cause you to feel uptight.

Uncontrollable Events	Unpredictable Events	Self-Induced Stressors

Reflection

- What impact do the listed stressors have on your personal and professional life?
- Is your stress getting out of control? Describe the feelings or emotions you're experiencing.
- What can you change about your situation, especially for items listed under self-induced?
- What action will you take to make this change happen?

Setting Boundaries

Boundaries represent the way we allow other people to treat us. Boundaries indicate the level of conviction, respect and honor we show for our own needs. Inherent in this, of course, is that we know what our needs are and how to communicate them honestly to the people around us.

It is necessary to say no sometimes. You are the only person who can set boundaries, and you are the only one who can let others invade them. Managing commitments, requests, expectations, priorities, and decisions involves being willing to say no. Saying no isn't easy, especially for physicians, because they didn't go into this profession to turn down people who ask for help. Research shows that the overwhelming reason medical students chose medicine was the desire to serve others. They are anxious to serve and feel guilty if they aren't so that the word "no" often sticks in their throats.

Here are some tips to help you say "no" or "not now."

- Recognize that a desire to please often prevents us from saying no.
- Stick to your plan. If you have a written set of goals and priorities, this gives you a reason to stick to your course. ("Thanks, but I already have …")
- Make sure you understand exactly what is being asked of you before you respond.

GUIDE POINTS

Stress in Marriages & Relationships

An article[14] in *American Medical News* indicates that one of the most prevalent areas of stress faced by many physicians is personal relationships. Today's diverse physician population has pretty much the same problems that everyone else does.

But they are different in one significant way: Physicians tend to deny that they have problems — physical, mental or marital. Medical training inculcates an "us vs. them" mentality, says Michael F. Myers, M.D., a psychiatrist and author of the book *Doctors' Marriages: A Look at the Problems and Their Solutions*, in which only patients are allowed to have problems. "We forget that physicians are human, too."

Due to the stresses of medical training and the early years of practice, physician marriages can face trouble early on. "The most common problems in the marriages of young physicians are not enough time together and not enough money. The two seem to go hand in hand, because the couple may be working extra hours to pay off educational debts. Male physicians are more prone to neglect their relationships and ignore warning signals of emerging problems.

"It's very common for men to not worry about their marriages unless the messages are coming pretty strongly from the partner or wife that there's a problem. They tend to rationalize: 'That's what it's like being married to a doctor.' Or 'You can't have it both ways. You can't have all this money and a happy marriage too.'"

Female physicians' marital problems are in some ways the reverse of those of male physicians, said Dr. Myers. Women in general are likely to see themselves as the caretakers of their marriages, and women physicians are no exception. Thus the problems of married women physicians tend to stem not from neglecting the relationship but rather from trying to stretch themselves too thin.

Setting Boundaries, continued

- Excel at a few things, rather than being average at many. Don't try to do everything.
- You have a right to say no. Remember that others may take you for granted and even lose respect for you if you don't.
- Be polite but firm in saying no. You only build false hopes with wishy-washy responses.

REFLECTION

As you face your first year as a practicing physician, what career and personal life boundaries will you set in order to experience a healthy, realistic dose of work-life balance?

Simplifying Your Life

Starting out in your career takes a lot of energy and focus; therefore, you should allow for **SPACE** and **SIMPLICITY** in the other areas of your life. If possible, it's a good idea to take two or three weeks off before you start your new position as a practicing physician in order to regain energy and settle your personal situation.

Simplification is the process of purging responsibilities, outdated goals, physical clutter, draining relationships and boring tasks. Doing so allows you to free up mental space and to create room for new opportunities. The following are 10 steps for helping you simplify your life in anticipation of your new role.

10 STEPS TO SIMPLIFYING YOUR LIFE

1. Take some time to evaluate your current life honestly. Where is the "**CLUTTER**," and what is eating up your time, your peace of mind and your energy? Make a list, be specific and judge the negative value of these things, as well as the positive.

2. You have most likely gained a great deal from your frenzied pursuits over the past years. This includes both material things (like books, furniture and other possessions) and immaterial (like routines and pet peeves). Make a list of both. What are you willing to let go of? What are you not willing to part with?

3. Make a list of how much of your "busy-ness" is composed of "shoulds." Who or what is making you feel that you "should" do these things? How would you feel if you let them go?

4. Make a list of all of your current commitments: business, family, personal, financial, etc. What's your reaction to seeing them all in one place?

5. Make a list of your habits. Which of these drain you and add to the craziness? Which add value? Distinguish them well.

6. Refer back to your list of self-induced stressors. What could you do to eliminate them all?

7. Reorganize your schedule to increase efficiency, even if you don't eliminate anything. (Of course, deleting things is usually the best way.)

8. Analyze your current financial situation.

9. Armed with this information, make a solid plan to simplify.

10. Identify tasks or responsibilities that can be automated or delegated (e.g., automatic bill payment) to give you more mental space.

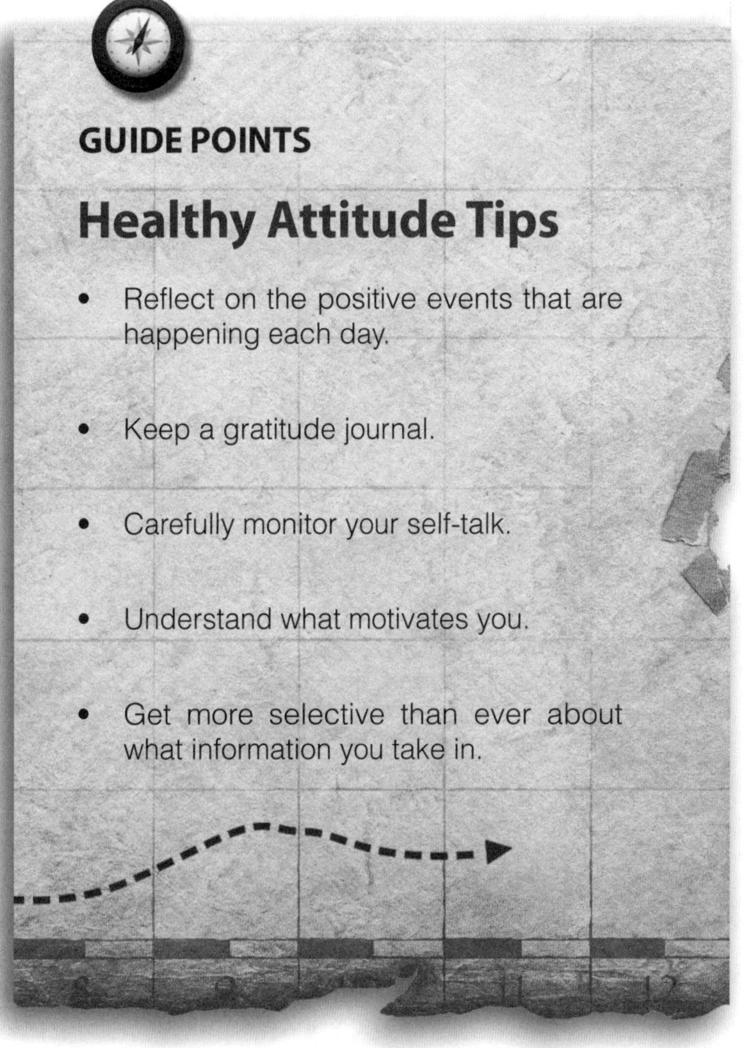

GUIDE POINTS

Healthy Attitude Tips

- Reflect on the positive events that are happening each day.
- Keep a gratitude journal.
- Carefully monitor your self-talk.
- Understand what motivates you.
- Get more selective than ever about what information you take in.

Develop and Maintain a Positive Attitude

As a physician starting your career, you have big career goals, immense responsibilities and high expectations of yourself and of the people you work with. Additionally, your staff looks to you for leadership and guidance. The one thing that determines the level of your potential, that influences the fellowship, collaboration and performance of your staff, and that predicts the quality outputs with patients is your attitude.

Your **ATTITUDE** determines the level of achievement for your goals. It determines the size of your dreams and influences your determination and response when you are faced with new challenges. Nobody but you has control over your attitude. People can affect your attitude by misinforming you or making repetitive mistakes, but no one can control your attitude unless you voluntarily surrender that control.

No one else "makes you angry." You make yourself angry when you surrender control of your attitude. What someone else may have done is irrelevant. **YOU CHOOSE**, not they. They merely put your attitude to a test. If you select a volatile attitude by becoming hostile, angry, or disruptive, then you have failed the test.

Maintaining a healthy and positive attitude is one of the basics that success requires. The combination of a sound personal mission, personal philosophy and a positive attitude about yourself and the people you work with gives you an inner strength and a firm resolve that influences all the other areas of your existence.

Here are a few strategies to follow when you find your attitude declining:

- Recognize when you are having a **BAD DAY**. Everyone can have a bad day, even a doctor. If you feel you are about to lose yourself or explode, leave the situation and step into your office for a few minutes. Let your nurse or assistant cover for you until you return. Be kind to yourself.

- Recognize before you are **BURNING THE CANDLE ON BOTH ENDS**. Attitude and behavior typically decline when your personal needs are unfulfilled, (i.e., rest) or when the level of commitments and problems exceed available energy, time and resources. Taking time off, putting work in perspective and ensuring that you have a fulfilled personal life will boost your attitude.

- Recognize that there are several solutions to a situation. Many physicians can be high-strung and dominant personalities that sometimes can be difficult to handle. They become overpowering with their opinions, attitude and aggressiveness. Remind yourself that teamwork requires **TEAM EFFORT** and **TEAM INPUT**. It is hard to encourage staff's buy-in if the need to be in charge dominates.

- Recognize that your practice is a **TEAM**. You are a member and leader of a team with integrated systems to ensure that everyone can accomplish their job smoothly. You rely on your staff to keep the practice going, so that you can deliver quality patient care. Hold yourself to the same standards that you require of your staff.

Networking

One common denominator that coincides with achieving success in life and career is one's ability to cultivate, build and maintain relationships. This requires that you start off on the right foot by planning and implementing a networking strategy. In stage 5, the topic of networking was covered within the context of finding a job. Here, networking pertains to building a **STRONG REFERRAL NETWORK**, building **RAPPORT** with patients and **ACTIVELY PURSUING** contacts and relationships over time.

To build a referral network, start by introducing yourself to referring physicians and develop strong relationships with them. Introduce your services to the community. Most patients are referred by word of mouth, other physicians or insurer networks; however, they won't refer you when they don't know you.

Next, you need to build a strong patient base. Getting to know your patients once they walk in the door is easy. Allowing potential patients to get to know you is another matter altogether. Think about what other services you have to offer to the community. For example, oncologists could offer support services, and cardiologists could give talks on avoiding heart attacks. Volunteering to give a talk on immunization may be a great way to introduce yourself to parents at a local school. You could also take advantage of health-related days of the year — like Child Health Day (June 6) or Diabetes Day (November 14) — to host an evening open house at your practice. Community members can learn more about the topic and pick up literature on your services.

FIND A STRONG MENTOR

As a new physician, you have significant clinical knowledge, but you may not understand procedural issues such as using the hospital's EHR/EMR system or how the practice schedules procedures. The best way to learn is to ask a senior physician to become your mentor and take time with you to discuss patient interactions, problems and questions. You may want to include nursing and administrative staff as well. Staff members can be a rich source of practice information and can help transition you into practice operations.

BUILD AN ADVISORY TEAM

In the introduction to this guidebook, we discussed the importance of building an advisory team to assist you in the job search process. This also holds true as you continue your career. Finding and maintaining a group of people whom you respect and trust to give you career and life advice is critical to your success. Potential advisory team members include your spouse, significant other or a good friend, a physician mentor, and professionals such as a coach, attorney, insurance agent, financial planner and accountant.

EXERCISE: ADVISORY TEAM WISH LIST

To help you establish your advisory team, first determine areas where you could benefit from the support of others, and note them in the space provided. Next, identify the qualities that are important to you for members of your advisory team. Finally, record some ideas for potential team members. If you know their names, write them down; if not, you can note something like "physician who's been with the practice for 5+ years."

Areas where you could benefit from the support of others	**Important qualities for advisory team members**	**Ideas for potential advisory team members**
Examples: work-life balance, clinical skills, leadership skills, legal issues	*Examples: experienced, trustworthy, reputable, knowledgeable, successful*	

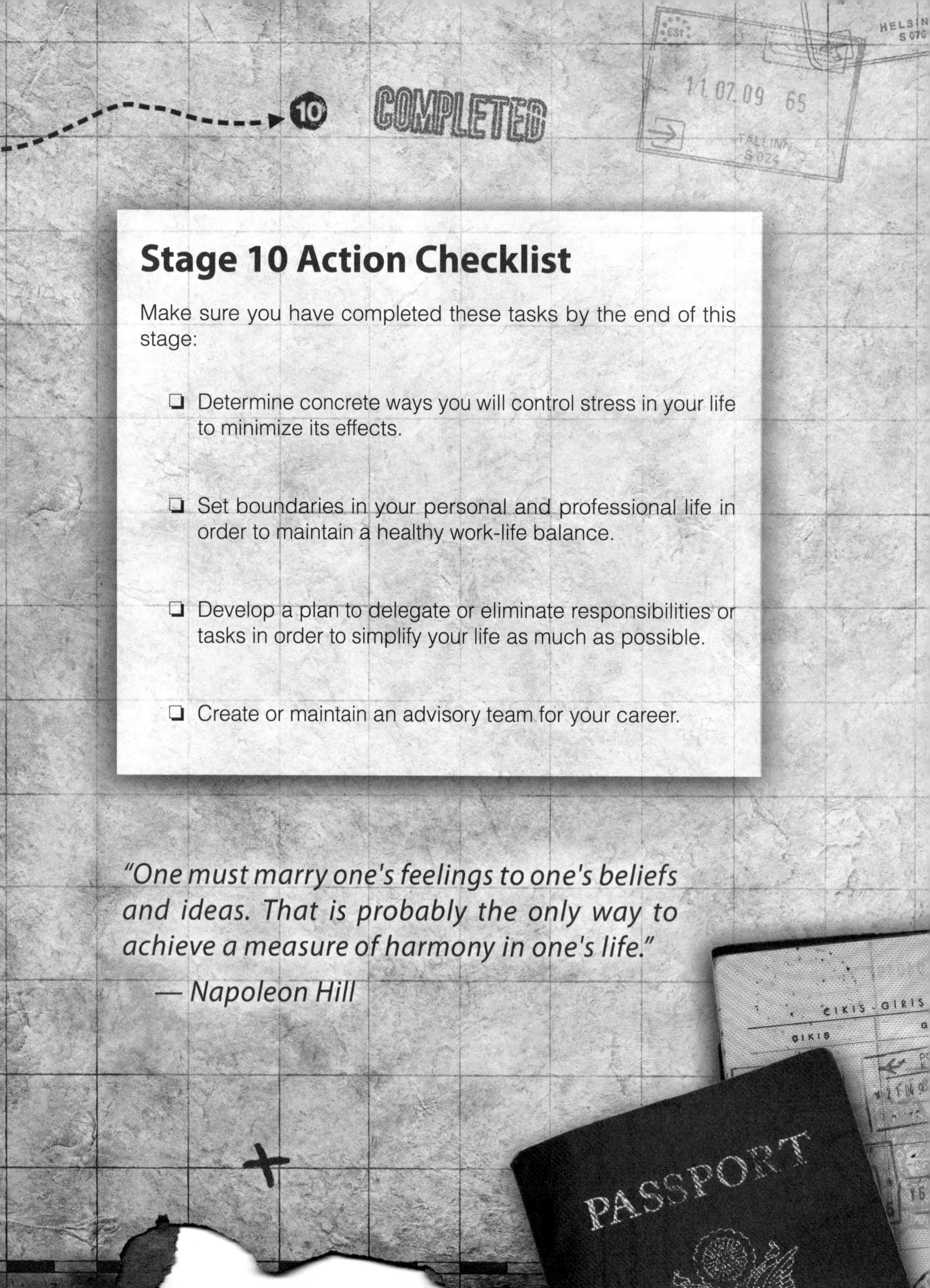

Stage 10 Action Checklist

Make sure you have completed these tasks by the end of this stage:

- ❑ Determine concrete ways you will control stress in your life to minimize its effects.
- ❑ Set boundaries in your personal and professional life in order to maintain a healthy work-life balance.
- ❑ Develop a plan to delegate or eliminate responsibilities or tasks in order to simplify your life as much as possible.
- ❑ Create or maintain an advisory team for your career.

"One must marry one's feelings to one's beliefs and ideas. That is probably the only way to achieve a measure of harmony in one's life."

— Napoleon Hill

NOTES

IT'S AN AWESOME SIGHT.

There's nothing quite like standing at the top of the peak, looking back at the footsteps of the assent that led you to reach this goal.

YOU ARE TO BE COMMENDED.

You have walked through this guide, penciled in the margins, highlighted the quotes and key facts, and filled out the blanks. Thumb through the book and look at your accomplishment. You've mapped your path, completed your search, negotiated your contract, and taken important first steps into the transition! Congratulations!

WHAT'S NEXT?

As you begin the next phase of the adventure, there are three things to keep in mind.

1. **Medicine is a journey, not a destination.**
   - The fallacy is the belief that there is some "end point", some point in the future at which you will be done, complete, successful and you can relax, have a lot of money, do what you want to do. Listen carefully: Not true!
   - And as you continue to walk into the adventure, there will be constantly emerging opportunities, surprises, obstacles and victories. And with these opportunities and challenges come the freedom to choose, adjust, decide and act. You may not know your final destination as things, people, hospitals, medicine and, well, life changes. It is an Adventure, be flexible!
2. **Enjoy the moment.**
   - If you're obsessing on the future, you'll miss the enjoyment of the present. Your flexibility and transparency during your Adventure in Medicine will bring opportunity, excitement, friendship and success.
   - Stay alert and aware of the dynamics around you.
   - Laugh, pause, poke and ponder with the people, friends and family around you. These are rich treasures.
3. **Seek counsel.**
   - We began this book recommending that you put together an "advisory team". This is a group of experts, wise counselors, mentors who will listen to your questions, provide feedback, and help you map out your decisions wisely.
   - There is much you do not know and don't have the time to learn. Find experts you trust, and listen to their counsel
   - Meet regularly, treat them with respect, and be generous in thanking them. They'll keep you safe and headache free (mostly) for years to come.

THIS ADVENTURE IS CHALLENGING, STIMULATING, REWARDING, EXCITING!

We hope you've been challenged to think differently about your career in medicine. The few minutes you've spent in this book will serve you well as you take your next step in The Adventure.

What a great career and journey lies before you.

Get your boots on. Let's tackle the adventure!

EDITORS NOTE: We're embarrassed to say that we did not intend to include a final field note from Dr. Goodhook, but after receiving a rather irate call from the good doctor, felt compelled to include his musing of advice here.

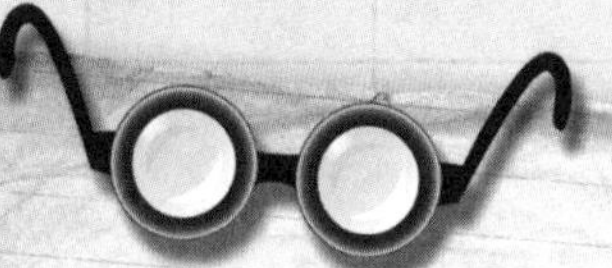

DR. GOODHOOK'S FIELD NOTES

Whatever befall, remember thy course, stay true and squinty for the horizon where landfall lies and fruit is plenty. Come wind or rain, blow and bluster, a course set to True North of the heart never fails. Seek, young resident, to find the greatest treasures in medicine the healing of the sick, the love of family, and the laughter of friends.

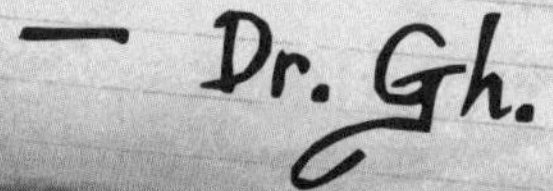

WWW.ADVENTURESINMEDICINE.NET

Did you know?

www.adventuresinmedicine.net is another great resource? The interactive online version of *Adventures in Medicine, The Resident's Guide* is the complete guide, plus more advice, information, learning exercises, charts, links and resources.

Online you can...

- Connect with others like you. Become a part of our Adventures in Medicine community. Membership is free for your first year giving you access to the online guide plus additional resources.
- Get smarter. Attend a webinar, live presentation, eLearning program, workshop. These are available to you as an Alumni of AHC's Adventures In Medicine! Simply sign up for the alerts!
- Seek counsel. Start a discussion with our Experts and Guides, seek their counsel and see how they can advise you online, over the phone or in person. Need some coaching, someone to listen and advise? That's available, too.
- Help out your fellow residents. Contribute to the next edition of the guide. We want to hear from you, what worked and what you found difficult. What advice would you offer other graduating residents? Tell us your story and you may even see it in the next edition!
- Read Dr. Goodhook's Window. While it doesn't really suit his cantankerous personality, he has informed us that he's up for the adventure of blogging. Frankly, we're surprised, curious, and even a bit apprehensive. Watch for his blog at AdventuresinMedicine.net and sign up for it soon.
- Let us get in your face. We know you're busy. And often if important information and deadlines aren't in your face, well, often they're forgotten or overlooked. Use our eNewsletter as a reminder to stay engaged in the process. Keep your job search in front of your face. Sign up for our Adventures In Medicine eNewsletter. Soon to be blasted across mobile devices, iPads, and pdas…

Visit www.adventuresinmedicine.net and sign up. Now! We would like to hear your comments about the guide, email us comments@adventuresinmedicine.net

References

1. Noonan, D. Doctors who kill themselves. [*Newsweek* Web site]. April 28, 2008;151(17):16. Available at: http://www.newsweek.com/id/132887. Accessed July 31, 2010.

2. Balch C., Freischlag J., Shanafelt T. Stress and burnout among surgeons: Understanding and managing the syndrome and avoiding the adverse consequences. *Arch Surg*. 2009;144(4):371-376.

3. Gundersen L. Physician burnout. *Ann Intern Med*. 2001 Jul 17;135(2):145-148.

4. MomMD. Women in medicine survey results: Demographics and characteristics. Available at: http://www.mommd.com/surveydemog.shtml. Accessed July 31, 2010.

5. University of Nevada School of Medicine. University of Nevada School of Medicine Exiting Medical Residents 2007 Annual Survey. Available at: http://www.medicine.nevada.edu/cehso/Pubs/res_exit_07.pdf. Accessed on July 31, 2010.

6. Paul Schyve, M.D. Leadership in Healthcare Organizations: A Guide to Joint Commission Leadership Standards (white paper). *The Governance Institute*, 2009.

7. Medical Group Management Association. *Physician Placement Starting Salary Survey: 2009 Report Based on 2008 Data*. Englewood, CO: Medical Group Management Association; 2009.

8. Cejka Search. Physician demographics evident in turnover rates; "fit and family" are driving forces: AMGA and Cejka Search 2006 Physician Retention Survey identifies trends. Available at: http://www.cejkasearch.com/Physician-Retention-Survey/2006RetentionSurvey/default.htm. Accessed on July 29, 2010.

9. Association of American Medical Colleges. 2009 GQ Medical School Graduation Questionnaire: All Schools Summary Report. Available at: http://www.aamc.org/data/gq/allschoolsreports/gqfinalreport_2009.pdf. Accessed on July 31, 2010.

10. Internal Revenue Sercvice. www.irs.gov. Accessed on July 15, 2010.

11. Farlex Financial Dictionary. Compounding. Available at: http://financial-dictionary.thefreedictionary.com/Compounding. Accessed on July 31, 2010.

12. Farlex Financial Dictionary. Time Value of Money. Available at: http://financial-dictionary.thefreedictionary.com/time+value+of+money. Accessed on July 31, 2010.

13. Thomas NK. Resident burnout. JAMA. 2004;292:2880-2889.

14. Skelly, F. Physician marriages. Am Med News. April 11, 1994.

Finding Your Unique Opportunity

Connecting with great organizations

We want to introduce you to unique organizations that have shown by their sponsorship of this guide that they are invested in your personal and career success. You want to know **WHO** they are and **WHAT** drives them forward.

So study these presentations carefully. Discern the **VALUES** and **VISION** that drive them. Who knows, you might just find your future employer here.

Introducing our Sponsors

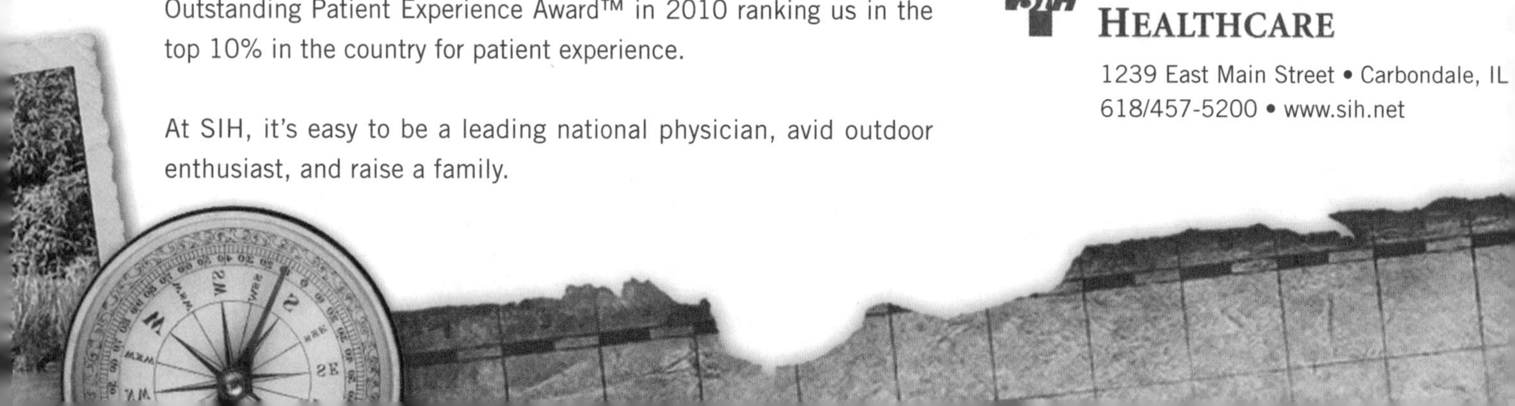

Understanding Leadership

An interview with **Rex Budde**, President and CEO of SIH Healthcare

What obstacles have your faced that have equipped you to lead SIH into the future?
When I was just out of college I started working in public accounting, auditing healthcare organizations. I enjoyed the work from an intellectual standpoint. During the period I lost both my grandmothers within three months. It was my first real experience with hospitals from the patient/family perspective. For the first time it really registered with me about the good work people in those settings perform. It was at that moment I decided that I wanted to be involved in helping others. Since that time, I have also had some very difficult experiences with family members' care at other institutions. I know how that made me feel and that drives me to make SIH a safe and caring organization for every patient and family member who comes through our doors.

When you think of SIH in ten years, how will SIH better serve the community?
What I picture in my mind is SIH being the hub for healthcare in the region. By that I mean we are really connected with our communities and other providers. I would like SIH to be the force that drives integration so that the patient's care is seamless and well coordinated. Across the country, patient care is too chopped up into distinct events or interactions between different physicians, providers and agencies. We have to develop a mindset across the care continuum that doesn't treat these interactions as distinct occurrences but rather an ongoing coordinated experience of personal care for the patient.

What do you want the doctor/patient experience to look like at SIH?
Our focus has been to drive quality and satisfaction for our patients and physicians. I want SIH to be as integrated as possible with our physicians so that we can provide very efficient and effective care. I want the physicians to have a very high level of satisfaction with the care rendered to their patients. I also want processes in place that lets our physicians maximize the use of their time while caring for patients. Patients should be able to really sense that they are in a safe and caring environment while at our facilities.

For many residents, it's difficult to really understand what makes one hospital better than another. So many words, so little meaning. What would you say makes SIH a unique place to work for a resident beginning their new job search?
I have worked at several large institutions in my career. While they were technologically advanced they were not necessarily very "touch" oriented. I believe that SIH has developed a great balance between technology and touch. We are a progressive organization that has a good view of the future. We don't rest and are always trying to anticipate and prepare for the next challenge. We have modern facilities and seek out the best equipment and techniques to care for our patients. We strive to create an environment that allows physicians to practice in a efficient manner and to be confident their patients are safe. I believe we do all of the above well without losing sight of the fact that we are interacting with our patients and families at a time when they are very vulnerable. It is critical that we never lose sight of the need to balance both the technology we use to care for our patients and the caring manner with which we interact with patients and their families.

"Building trust requires understanding the values and vision of leadership."

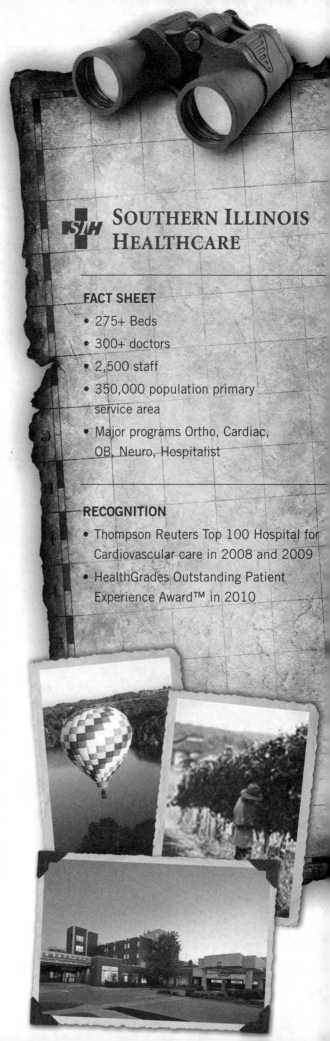

SOUTHERN ILLINOIS HEALTHCARE

FACT SHEET

- 275+ Beds
- 300+ doctors
- 2,500 staff
- 350,000 population primary service area
- Major programs Ortho, Cardiac, OB, Neuro, Hospitalist

RECOGNITION

- Thompson Reuters Top 100 Hospital for Cardiovascular care in 2008 and 2009
- HealthGrades Outstanding Patient Experience Award™ in 2010

Maximize your possibilities

Whether your life's plan is carefully calculated or guided by a flair for recognizing opportunity, Trinity presents an intriguing prospect. Trinity Regional Health System is one of two acute care providers serving a population of more than 500,000. In most cities that size, you'd find as many as six hospitals. If you're looking to establish a stable practice, that's a distinct advantage.

We're full of surprises

While statistics favor us with an unusually strong base, our size and commitment provide opportunities to excel. Trinity receives strong support from the community and has the resources to make strong contributions to research in several areas. Along with opportunities that arise within the system, that makes Trinity a great place to build a career.

Our community is special, too

When it comes to lifestyle, it's hard to beat the Quad-Cities area for a family friendly atmosphere. We have all the amenities you'd expect in a community this size and much more – cultural, recreational and intellectual. The cost of living is appealing, too, both in terms of daily expenses and the cost of housing.

But one of the best things about living here is the way it opens up the world. Whether you're talking about driving around town or traveling the world, it's always easy to get there from here. It takes less than 30 minutes to drive across town and air travel from the local airport is convenient and affordable.

Now recruiting for:

Family Practice, Internal Medicine, Ob/Gyn, Pediatrics, Dermatology, Emergency Medicine, Endocrinology, Hematology/Oncology, Orthopedic Surgery, Otolaryngology, General Surgery, Urology, Pulmonary/Critical Care

To learn more about Trinity or the Quad-Cities area, contact:

Marcia Youngvorst, MS, BSN
Director, Physician Recruitment/Clinic Development
500 John Deere Rd., Suite 300
Moline, IL 61265
309-779-3701
youngvorstm@ihs.org

Bruce Bailey
Physician Recruiter
500 John Deere Rd., Suite 300
Moline. IL 61265
309-779-3706
baileybm@ihs.org

Moline • Rock Island • Bettendorf • Muscatine

www.trinityqc.com
www.trinitymuscatine.com

A Culture of Collaboration

By **Rick Seidler**, President and CEO
Trinity Regional Health System

One thing I've learned throughout my more than 30 years of executive health-care experience: hire great people, give them resources, and stay out of the way. By doing so, it allows for ideas to germinate and take root. And in such a dynamic and ever-changing field as health care, fresh ideas are our lifeblood.

At Trinity, we strive to provide the "best outcome for every patient, every time." We do that by working together. That ensures we provide the best care for our patients, as well as a positive work environment for both medical and hospital staff.

While it's easy to spout rhetoric about the importance of two-way dialogue and collaboration though, here at Trinity it's more than just words. It's our culture.

A few years ago we overhauled our heart attack response process. Cardiologists can tell you that time is heart muscle; just a few minutes can mean the difference between life and death. Physicians sat side-by-side with clinical and support staff across multiple disciplines to help determine the best way to shave off that precious time. A free exchange of ideas led to this improvement, meaning there's a 63-year-old still able to read stories to his granddaughter as we speak.

More recently a pulmonologist approached us about the development of an asthma clinic. Because we welcome fresh ideas, we are currently putting together a pro-forma to identify the needs of our community and how it would benefit from such a service.

And of course we can't forget the importance of technology. Dialogue about emerging treatments for prostate cancer recently led to the procurement of a surgery robot. Evolving communication preferences of young mothers has prompted discussions about the development of a Web portal for OB/GYN patients at our clinics.

William Pollard may as well have been talking about health care when he said, "Without change there is no innovation, creativity, or incentive for improvement. Those who initiate change will have a better opportunity to manage the change that is inevitable."

We work hard to develop a culture that supports ideas to help us innovate and improve. This is what improves our patients' experiences. Having that culture itself though is ultimately what enhances our physicians' experiences.

About Trinity Regional Health System (2010 calendar year)
\# of beds: 584 licensed
\# of docs: 591 staff physicians
\# of staff: 3,117 employees

Campus locations:
Bettendorf and Muscatine, Iowa; Rock Island and Moline, Illinois

Specialty areas:
cardiology, cancer, surgery, behavioral health, wound care

Doctor/population ratio: 1:446

Community size:
Primary market consists of Scott and Muscatine Counties in Iowa and Rock Island County in Illinois. Primary market total population is 356,410 (2009 U.S. Census estimates). Secondary market also includes Clinton County in Iowa and Whiteside, Henry, and Mercer Counties in Illinois. Total population of primary and secondary markets is 529,895.

Major metro area and airport/transportation access: yes

Recreational environment:
Located on the banks of the Mississippi River, 2,200 acres of parks, live music festivals, professional sports teams, more than a dozen museums, a PGA golf tournament, a choice of theaters, and fine dining

Education environment:
Schools in this area are rated among the top ten in the nation. Four highly regarded colleges and universities also call the Quad-Cities home.

Moline • Rock Island • Bettendorf • Muscatine

www.trinityqc.com
www.trinitymuscatine.com

Your career starts here.

We are a patient-centered organization aimed at providing the best care for our patients, as well as a positive work environment for our staff. Our compensation model allows our physicians to be rewarded for their hard work and ability to meet performance benchmarks. Our culture delivers the strength and support of a large organization, while still promoting the physician leadership and individual initiatives also found in smaller groups.

OUR MISSION
As a Catholic healthcare ministry, we provide comprehensive and compassionate care that improves the health of the people we serve.

OUR VALUES
Patient-Centered - We place the patient at the center of every decision.
Teamwork - We work effectively together to create a unified culture.
Excellence - We strive to achieve the highest quality outcomes in all that we do.
Innovation - We seek creative solutions and embrace change as we grow.
Community - We give our time and resources to improve our region's health and well-being.
Accountability - We are responsible for our actions, decisions and effective use of resources.

We support almost 330,000 patients a year, in specialties including cardiology, endocrinology, family medicine, gastroenterology, general surgery, internal medicine, nephrology, neurology, obstetrics/gynecology, orthopaedics, pediatrics, pulmonology, and rheumatology. In addition to the aforementioned specialties, we have a particular need for physicians in internal medicine, family medicine and internal medicine—pediatrics.

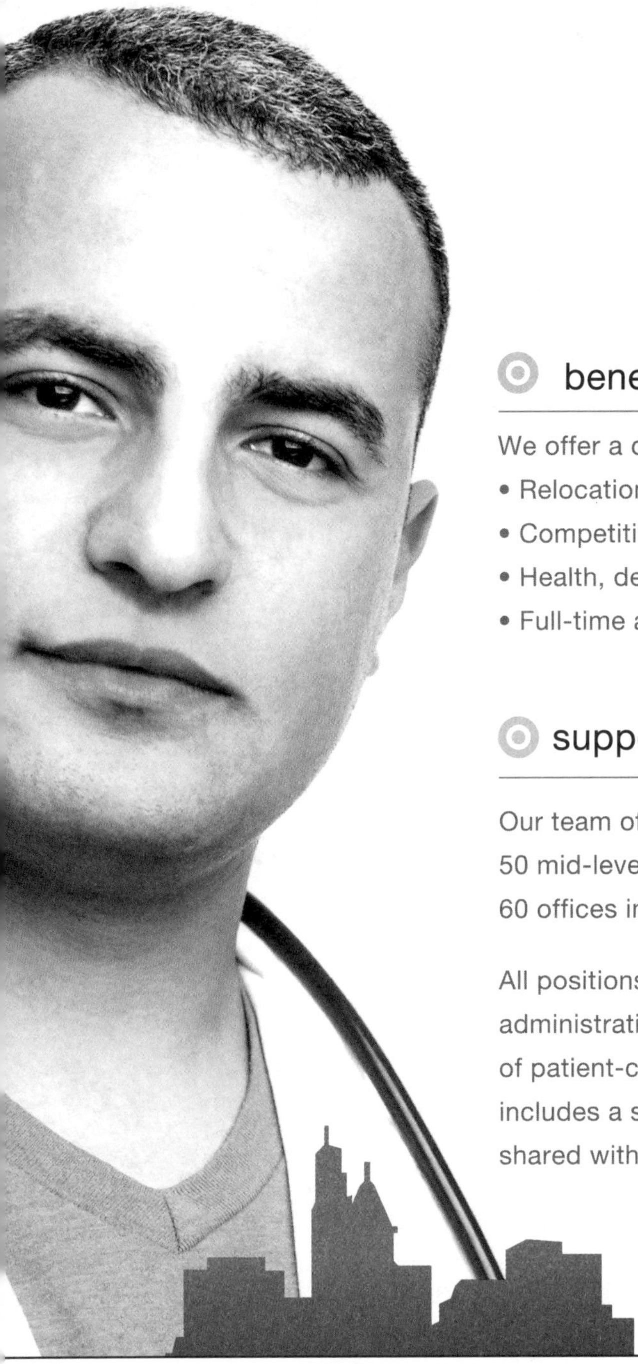

Defining Culture and Mission

An interview with **Bill Gorski, M.D.**, President and Chief Executive Officer SwedishAmerican Health System

Our Mission

"Through excellence in healthcare and compassionate service, we care for our community."

With over 5,000 hospitals in the U.S., what makes the SwedishAmerican culture unique? Our mission statement defines our culture. It is extremely important, and we live it every day. Our people make SwedishAmerican who we are. Let me explain how we view each of the three parts of our mission.

Through excellence in healthcare... Quality is our highest priority and it drives everything we do. That is why we've won so many national awards based on objective quality measures including Top 100 Hospital, Top 100 Quality Hospital, Top 100 Integrated Healthcare Network, Top 5% Excellence in Women's Health, Top 10% in Cardiac Surgery, and so on. Quality is a given at SwedishAmerican. Everyone who walks through our door expects it, and we do our best to live up to that expectation.

...and compassionate service... Every day, we are called upon to be our best when those we are privileged to serve are at their worst. Patients are gravely ill and afraid, but each member of the SwedishAmerican family, from the cardiac surgeon to housekeeper, is empowered to make a difference in someone's life, everyday. That is one reason we're rated highest in the region for patient preference and satisfaction.

...we care for our community. As the leading health system in northern Illinois, the third largest employer in Rockford, and a 100-year anchor of the Midtown District of Rockford, we have three definitions of community. I've already touched on how we care for the first, our patients and their families.

The second community we serve is that of our employees. We all face the challenge of balancing work and home, and that's why we provide unique benefits to help employees find balance. From on-site child care and sick-child care to college scholarships and free concierge services, we are compelled to improve the lives of our employees.

The third community we serve is, literally, our community. We are a community hospital and believe it's essential to be good corporate citizens. Our most visible contribution has been the ongoing renovation of the campus neighborhood. We have partnered with the City and Habitat for Humanity to purchase sub-standard properties in our neighborhood and replace them with over 30 new single-family homes.

Adventures in Medicine will help residents prepare to enter the real world of practice. What adventure would they find at SwedishAmerican?

Our greatest strength is **physician leadership** and every physician that joins us has the opportunity to share in that adventure. We've had a physician CEO for the last 35 years which is attractive to physicians. As a result, our medical group has grown to over 125 providers and is outstanding clinically.

With physician leadership, our physicians are heard and well represented throughout all layers of governance. Physicians love to be involved in the decision-making process, and they deserve to be involved because this is healthcare we're talking about, and doctors are ultimately responsible for that care.

"Physicians are the foundation of our culture at SwedishAmerican."

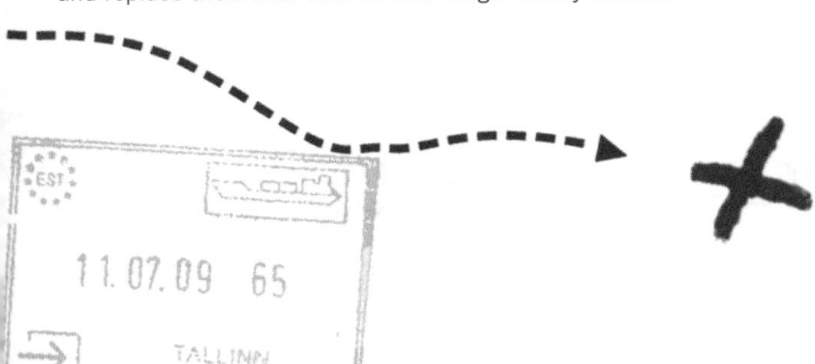

PLANT YOUR ROOTS IN OUR SAND.

Discover Beebe Medical Center, a progressive, not-for-profit community hospital located just six blocks from the Atlantic Coast in Lewes, Delaware. Here you can pursue an active, challenging medical career — and also enjoy an exceptional quality of life.

Our achievements mirror the skill and dedication of our physicians, clinical staff, Board and administration, support staff, and volunteers. We continue to be recognized with national awards that demonstrate our steadfast commitment to excellence. Beebe is financially solid, and we have clinical associations with Delaware's only tertiary care center and a major Philadelphia medical school.

You'll be captivated by our family-oriented beach resort communities that are rich in nature and history. We are in a recreational haven, where water sports, outdoor life, golf, and cycling thrive! Cultural amenities include beach life, jazz festival, film festival, visual and performing arts, and fine dining.

You'll also enjoy southern Delaware's unique benefits — a low crime rate, overall low taxes, and NO state sales tax. We're in close proximity to Washington, D.C., Baltimore, and Philadelphia, and just three hours from New York City.

Join us in our distinctive location, where you can pursue an active, challenging medical career and enjoy a great work–life balance at the beach. Beebe Medical Center — where we support our physicians' careers and where YOU can make a difference!

We look forward to hearing from you.

Marilyn Hill, Director of Physician Services
mhill@bbmc.org
302-645-3664, 1-800-69-BEEBE
www.beebemed.org

New York City
147 miles
Philadelphia
83 miles
Baltimore
87 miles
Cape May, N.J.
1 hour ferry ride from Lewes
Washington, D.C.
101 miles
DE
Lewes

A MESSAGE FROM THE PRESIDENT

Jeffrey M. Fried, FACHE, President and CEO

As a new physician, you are launching your career at a time of many healthcare challenges and unprecedented opportunities.

To those who want to build their own careers as they also build a better healthcare environment, we issue a special invitation for you to come to Beebe.

Here you'll find a staff dedicated to excellence and quality in patient care, outcomes, efficiency, and safety. We don't just say it. We prove it every year in independent performance reviews.

Here you'll also find a true community spirit, where outreach is more than a slogan, and where screenings, health fairs, and proactive involvement in underserved areas are important to all of us.

In return for your commitment and dedication to medical excellence, you'll be enriched by your many personal and professional experiences.

At Beebe Medical Center, we welcome and support you in your transition and throughout your professional career. We invite you to come visit us and see for yourself — that this is a great place to build your future!

Our community is growing, and if making a difference and striving for excellence in a progressive hospital and family-oriented environment fits your vision, then we look forward to hearing from you.

Beebe Medical Center

424 Savannah Road | Lewes, DE 19958
302-645-3664 | 1-800-69-Beebe
www.beebemed.org

Email cover letter and CV to:
Marilyn Hill,
Director of Physican Services
mhill@bbmc.org

Beebe Medical Center Fast Facts

210 beds

More than 300 providers

More than 1,400 staff members

120,000 year-round population and growing; nearly 500,000 in the summer

50,000+ Emergency visits yearly

Strong service lines: cardiovascular services, including cardiac surgery and interventional cardiology; orthopaedic services; OB/GYN and women's health; cancer care

Facilities include: free-standing surgery center; cancer center with medical, surgical, and radiation oncology; 256-slice CT scanner; 3.0T MRI; PET scan, imaging and lab centers; two outpatient health campuses with third planned; school of nursing

Strong community health program

Awards and Recognition

Premier Award for Quality (AFQ) awarded by Premier Healthcare Alliance — one of 21 hospitals and three health systems, and top 1% nationwide

2010-2011 HealthGrades® Distinguished Hospital Award for Clinical Excellence™ — top 5% of all hospitals in the nation for overall quality

Rated by HealthGrades as No. 1 in Delaware for Overall Orthopedics and Best on the Delmarva Peninsula for Overall Orthopedics

Five-star rating and No. 1 in Delaware for coronary interventional procedures by HealthGrades

Highest quality rating for Cardiac Surgery program from The Society of Thoracic Surgeons, part of a unique partnership with the Center for Heart & Vascular Health at Christiana Care Health System, which also received the top rating

Health Care: Where Compassion Meets Commitment

John Dawes, FACHE
President and CEO
Bothwell Regional Health Center

When I ask physicians finishing their residencies what's most important to them as they look for their first jobs, their answers invariably have a lot of similarities. They want to work at a good hospital where they can focus on quality patient care and perhaps become a physician leader. They want to live in a community that offers recreational opportunities, and they want to strike a satisfying balance between work and their personal lives.

Lifestyle Support

Bothwell offers employed first-year physicians a free, innovative program called Life Balance Coaching, which provides them access to a professional life coach. Here's what one of our new ob/gyn physicians had to say about the program: "(My coach) helped me focus on the big picture. It's easy to get caught up with the small things, especially transitioning into a new practice. She became my sounding board and helped me discover how to achieve the desired outcome."

Hospitalist Support

Our hospitalist program provides practice-based physicians with the support they need to ensure patients receive the very best possible care while they're in the hospital. Hospitalists allow other physicians to focus on the patients they're seeing in their offices and still be involved in coordination of care for their hospitalized patients. Both hospitalists and private practice physicians can provide ample mentoring for new physicians.

Facilities & Technology

Bothwell opened two new facilities in Summer 2011 – a free-standing, three-story medical office building for physician practices and a 15,000-square-foot cancer and cardiovascular addition to the main hospital. We have some of the latest technological advances, such as our new Elektra Synergy linear accelerator and high-field, open MRI. But just as important as this equipment is our heart. I have no doubt that our hospital is truly a place where physicians can provide patient-focused care as it was meant to be.

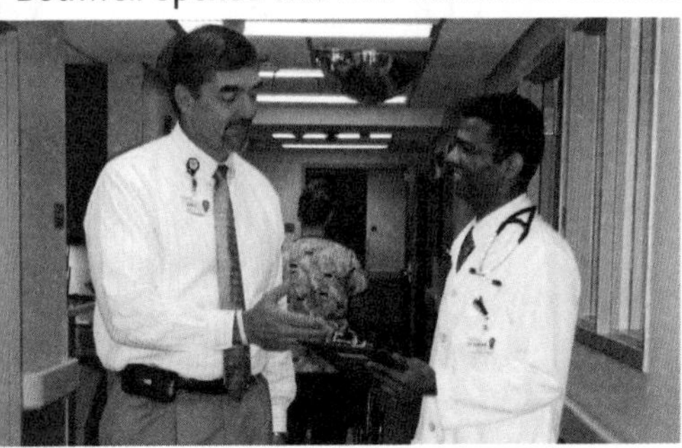

Local Leadership

The physicians and senior leaders of Bothwell Regional Health Center are not governed by policies ascribed by corporate owners. Our policies and procedures are developed locally with input from our physicians and leaders. We are led by an independent board of proven community leaders who have a vested interest in the success of this hospital. They know a strong hospital is an integral part of a strong community.

All of this combines to help make Bothwell Regional Health Center the best place for employees to work, the best place for patients to receive care, and the best place for physicians to practice medicine.

Bothwell Regional Health Center Fast Facts

- **140 beds**
- **Two primary care practices, free-standing diagnostic center, OB/GYN practice, two free-standing sleep centers, hospice, home health agency and medical equipment service**
- **50 physicians**
- **850+ staff members**
- **Specialty areas: cancer treatment, joint replacement, cardiovascular, ob/gyn, sleep medicine**
- **Community size of 30,000**
- **Micropolitan located in service area of 75,000**

New medical office complex provides physician office space

COMMUNITY

- **Within one hour of two major metro areas (Kansas City and Columbia)**
- **Recreational opportunities at the nearby Lake of the Ozarks and Truman Lake**
- **Excellent public and private schools, new public high school, community college with record enrollment**
- **Located half-hour east of a state university and one hour west of the University of Missouri-Columbia**

RECOGNITION

- **Joint Commission Accreditation**
- **America's Top 100 Most Wired Hospitals, 2009, 2010**
- **Center of Excellence, Oncology Nursing**
- **Patient Safety Organization designee**
- **American Academy of Sleep Medicine accreditation**

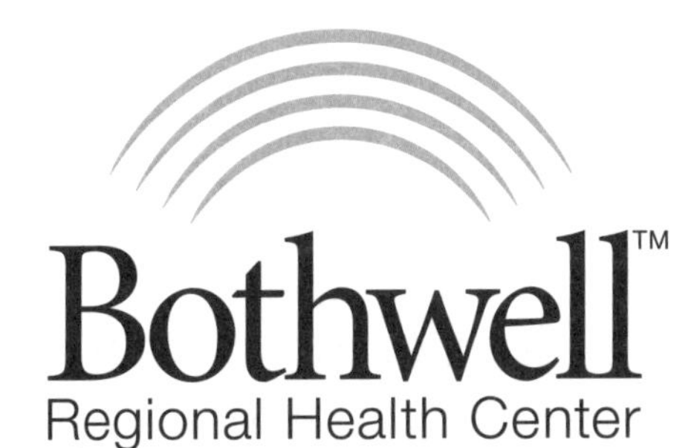

601 E. Fourteenth Street | Sedalia, Missouri
660-826-8833 | www.brhc.org

Exceptional Care, *close to home.*

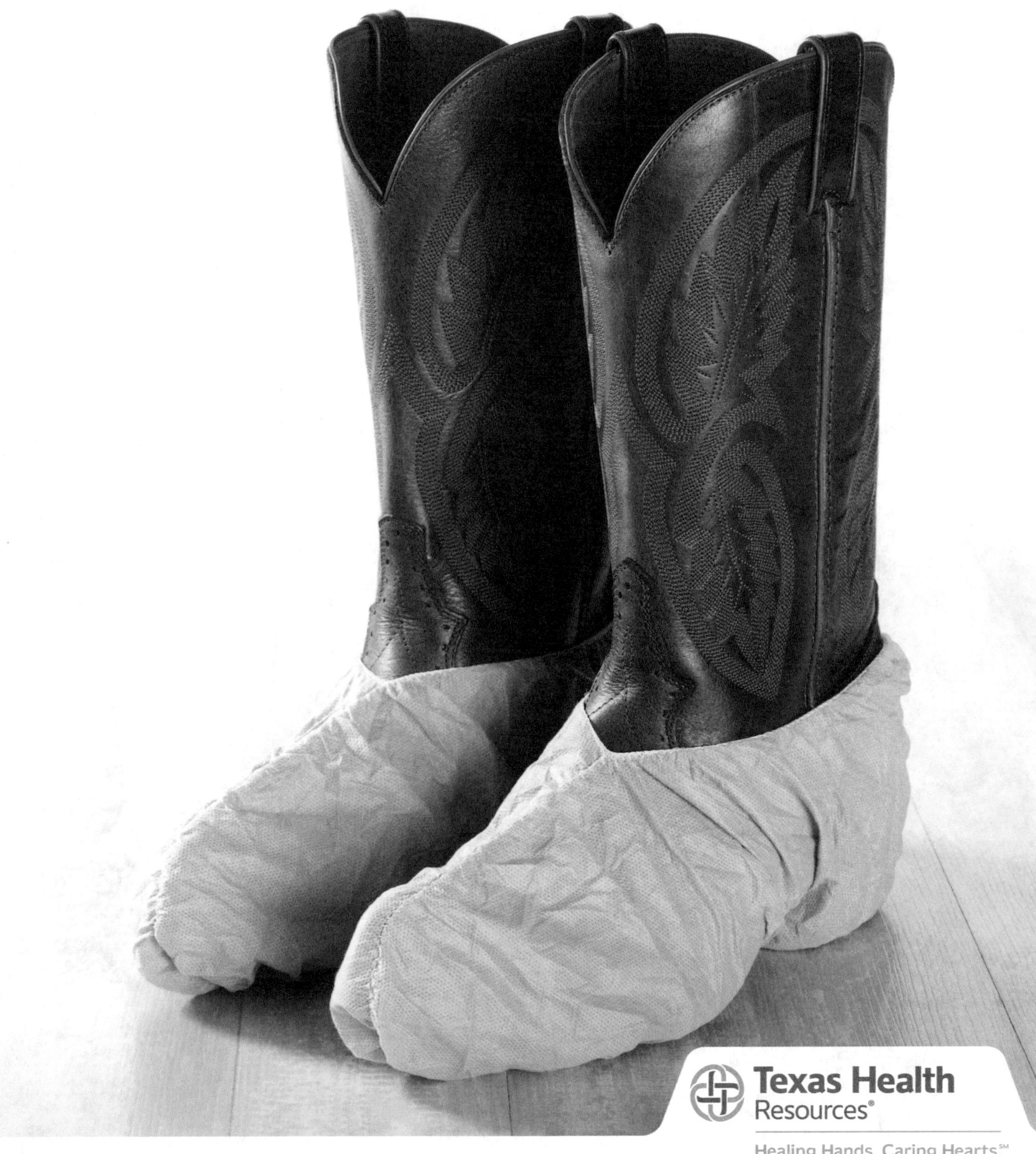
Texas Health
Resources®
Healing Hands. Caring Hearts.℠

Practice Type.
Everyone is Unique.
FIND THE RIGHT FIT.
Location and Lifestyle.
Different Needs.
Different Styles.

"Since the Sisters of Providence founded this ministry more than 150 years ago, the spirit of collaboration between Providence and its physicians has always been one of our greatest strengths. As a physician myself, I am particularly proud of our efforts to make Providence an attractive place to practice medicine. These efforts recognize that physicians are essential to living out our healing ministry. We offer opportunities for diverse clinical practices and leadership development, all guided by our Mission of service."

John Koster, M.D.
President and CEO
Providence Health & Services

Dr. Alice Nayak and Dr. Navin Nayak are Providence internal medicine physicians who are married and share work and parenting duties. As job-share partners at the Providence Medical Group clinic in Clackamas, Oregon, they each work half-time, covering each other's patients at the clinic and caring for their two children on off days. The freedom to job share was a major factor in their decision to join Providence. "There were lots of places where we applied that would not accommodate that," Dr. Navin Nayak says.

Alice Nayak, M.D. and Navin Nayak, M.D.
Internal Medicine Physicians and Job Share Partners
Providence Medical Group

The physician recruitment team at Providence really works together and always keeps the best interests of the physician and the hiring group in focus. We are passionate about finding the right fit for both parties. Our recruiters are salaried, employed People of Providence, so we know the culture of the organization intimately. We know our hiring partners (Providence and private practice), and we know the communities we serve. We offer a much different recruitment experience than commission-based agencies.

MaryBeth Cruz
Executive Director of Physician Recruitment
Providence Health & Services

- 5 states: Integrated system across Alaska, California, Montana, Oregon and Washington
- 27 hospitals
- 2 children's hospitals
- 200+ Providence Medical Group clinics
- 1,500+ employed Providence physicians
- 8,800+ physicians on medical staff
- 52,000+ employees ("People of Providence")
- $617 million annually in community benefits (2010)